It's another essential resource from CGP!

There's been a seismic shift in GCSE Geography — the latest
Grade 9-1 courses are tougher than ever. But fear not, help is at hand...

This fantastic CGP book covers everything you'll need for
the new OCR B course, with no-nonsense explanations,
easy-to-follow diagrams and cracking case studies.

There's also useful advice on fieldwork, geographical skills and the new
Geographical Exploration paper — so you'll be in peak condition for the exams.

CGP — still the best! ☺

Our sole aim here at CGP is to produce the highest quality books —
carefully written, immaculately presented and dangerously close to being funny.

Then we work our socks off to get them out to you
— at the cheapest possible prices.

Contents

Component 2: People and Society

Component 3: Geographical Exploration

Fieldwork

Geographical Skills

Published by CGP

Editors:
Claire Boulter, David Maliphant, Claire Plowman, Hannah Roscoe, David Ryan.

Contributor:
Paddy Gannon

Proofreading:
David Sefton, Karen Wells.

ISBN: 978 1 78294 618 2

With thanks to Ana Pungartnik for the copyright research.

Printed by Elanders Ltd, Newcastle upon Tyne.
Clipart from Corel®

Based on the classic CGP style created by Richard Parsons.

Structure of the Course

'Know thy enemy', 'forewarned is forearmed'... There are many boring quotes that just mean being prepared is a good thing. Don't stumble blindly into a GCSE course — find out what you're facing.

You'll have to do Three Exams

See pages 99-112 for more on geographical skills.

GCSE OCR B Geography is divided into three components — Our Natural World, People and Society and Geographical Exploration.

You'll have to do three exams — one on each of the three components. Geographical skills will be assessed in all three exams, but fieldwork (see p.97) will only be assessed in Papers 1 and 2. All your exams will take place at the end of the course.

Paper 1: Our Natural World

Paper 1 is divided into two sections (A and B).

Section A covers four topics:

- Global Hazards
- Changing Climate
- Distinctive Landscapes
- Sustaining Ecosystems

Section B covers Physical Geography Fieldwork.

You need to answer all the questions in this paper.

1 hour 15 minutes	70 marks in total	35% of your final mark

Paper 2: People and Society

Paper 2 is divided into two sections (A and B).

Section A covers four topics:

- Urban Futures
- Dynamic Development
- UK in the 21st Century
- Resource Reliance

Section B covers Human Geography Fieldwork.

You need to answer all the questions in this paper.

1 hour 15 minutes	70 marks in total	35% of your final mark

Paper 3: Geographical Exploration

1) There isn't any new content to learn for Paper 3, it's all about applying what you already know.

2) In the exam, you'll get a Resource Booklet with lots of information about a specific country.

3) You could be asked about anything from 'Our Natural World' or 'People and Society'.

4) The questions will ask you to combine ideas from the different topics.

5) There will also be a decision-making exercise, where you will have to use the sources you have been given to come to a conclusion about a particular issue.

You need to answer all the questions in this paper.

1 hour 30 minutes	60 marks in total	30% of your final mark

There's more information about this paper on page 96.

Each exam will have a separate Resource Booklet containing sources (e.g. photos, maps, graphs and diagrams) that you will be asked to use to answer some of the questions.

In each exam, there will be one question which has 3 extra marks available for spelling, punctuation and grammar (see p.99). These marks are included in the total marks given for each paper.

I'm all over those spelling marks.

May the course be with you...

I know... you just want to get started on some lovely Geography and you're dying to get out your freshly ironed map. Well, have no fear — it's non-stop Geography from here. But it's worthwhile knowing this stuff so you're not the person who doesn't realise there's a Section B in the exam — there's a fine line between being relaxed and sabotaging yourself...

Global Atmospheric Circulation

Let's kick things off with a load of <u>hot air</u>. Specifically, air that moves in <u>loops</u> around the <u>Earth</u>...

Air Circulates *between* High *and* Low Pressure Belts *as* Surface Winds

1) <u>Winds</u> are <u>large scale movements of air</u> caused by <u>differences in air pressure</u>.

2) Differences in air pressure are caused by <u>differences in temperature</u> between the <u>equator</u> and the <u>poles</u>. Winds move <u>**FROM**</u> the areas of <u>high</u> pressure <u>**TO**</u> the areas of <u>low pressure</u>.

3) Winds are part of <u>global atmospheric circulation</u> loops (called <u>cells</u>). These loops have <u>warm rising air</u> which creates a <u>low pressure belt</u>, and <u>cool falling air</u> which creates a <u>high pressure belt</u>.

4) There are <u>three loops</u> in each hemisphere. Here's how it all works:

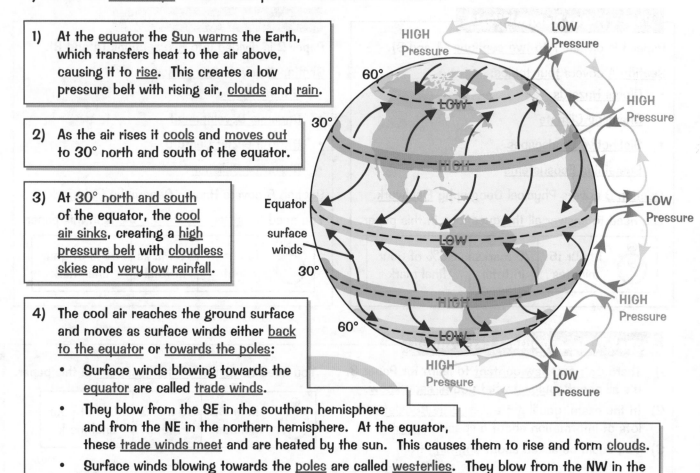

1) At the <u>equator</u> the <u>Sun warms</u> the Earth, which transfers heat to the air above, causing it to <u>rise</u>. This creates a low pressure belt with rising air, <u>clouds</u> and <u>rain</u>.

2) As the air rises it <u>cools</u> and <u>moves out</u> to 30° north and south of the equator.

3) At <u>30° north and south</u> of the equator, the <u>cool air sinks</u>, creating a <u>high pressure belt</u> with <u>cloudless skies</u> and <u>very low rainfall</u>.

4) The cool air reaches the ground surface and moves as surface winds either <u>back to the equator</u> or <u>towards the poles</u>:
    - Surface winds blowing towards the <u>equator</u> are called <u>trade winds</u>.
    - They blow from the **SE** in the southern hemisphere and from the **NE** in the northern hemisphere. At the equator, these <u>trade winds meet</u> and are heated by the sun. This causes them to rise and form <u>clouds</u>.
    - Surface winds blowing towards the <u>poles</u> are called <u>westerlies</u>. They blow from the **NW** in the southern hemisphere and from the **SW** in the northern hemisphere.

5) At <u>60° north and south of the equator</u>, the warmer surface winds meet colder air from the poles. The warmer air is less dense than the cold air so it <u>rises</u>, creating <u>low pressure</u>.

6) Some of the air <u>moves back</u> towards the equator, and the rest moves towards the <u>poles</u>.

7) At the <u>poles</u> the <u>cool air sinks</u>, creating <u>high pressure</u>. The high pressure air is drawn back towards the equator as <u>surface winds</u>.

And I thought baked beans were the main cause of wind patterns...

...sorry, that lowered the tone a bit. Best focus on three loops of air circulation between the equator and each pole. You need to know how these cause the pressure belts that give the world its climate. And go easy on the beans.

Global Atmospheric Circulation

Global atmospheric circulation affects the world's <u>weather</u> — and makes some of it really <u>rather extreme</u>...

There are **Different** Climate Zones **Around the** World

The <u>pressure belts</u> caused by <u>global atmospheric circulation</u> (see previous page) cause <u>variations</u> in <u>climate</u>.

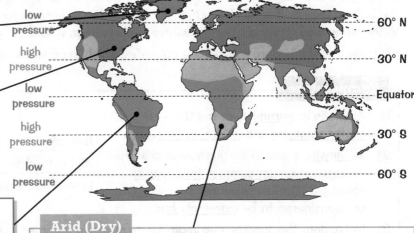

Polar

<u>Temperatures</u> are low <u>all year</u> round.

Temperate

<u>Moderate</u> summers and winters. A <u>low pressure</u> belt at about <u>60° N/S</u> caused by <u>rising air</u> from two cells meeting means <u>rainfall</u> is <u>frequent</u>.

Tropical

Temperatures are <u>hot</u> all the time and <u>rainfall</u> is <u>high</u>. Usually near the <u>equator</u>, where <u>rising air</u> from two cells meeting causes <u>low pressure</u> and lots of <u>rainfall</u>.

Arid (Dry)

<u>Rainfall</u> is <u>very low</u> all or most of the year. Temperatures are <u>hot</u> or <u>warm</u>. Usually near <u>30° N/S</u>, where <u>sinking air</u> from two cells meeting causes <u>high pressure</u> and <u>prevents rainfall</u>.

Global Atmospheric Circulation **leads to Extreme Weather** in Some Places

Wind

1) <u>Wind</u> is <u>air</u> moving from areas of <u>high to low</u> <u>pressure</u>. This means that atmospheric circulation <u>causes</u> winds, making some parts of the world <u>windier</u> than others.

2) Winds are <u>weak</u> in high and low <u>pressure belts</u>.

3) Winds are <u>strong</u> between <u>pressure belts</u>.

4) When the <u>difference in pressure</u> between high and low pressure areas is <u>large</u>, winds can be <u>extremely strong</u> — e.g. the north coast of Australia.

Temperature

1) The <u>equator</u> receives the <u>most</u> energy from the <u>Sun</u>. The <u>poles</u> receive the <u>least</u>.

2) <u>Heat</u> drives atmospheric circulation as <u>warm air</u> from the equator moves towards the <u>poles</u>.

3) Temperatures can be <u>very high</u> in high pressure areas around <u>30° N/S</u>. There are <u>few clouds</u> due to the <u>sinking air</u>, so there is little to <u>block</u> the Sun's <u>energy</u>.

4) In contrast, the temperatures in the polar regions of the <u>Arctic</u> and <u>Antarctic</u> are <u>very low</u>.

Precipitation

1) <u>Precipitation</u> (rain, snow, etc.) occurs when warm, wet air <u>rises</u> and <u>cools</u>, causing water vapour to <u>condense</u>.

2) Air <u>rises</u> in <u>low pressure belts</u>. This means that <u>precipitation</u> is <u>frequent</u> and <u>often intense</u> in these areas. <u>Rainforests</u> are usually in low pressure belts (e.g. the Amazon).

3) In high pressure belts where the <u>air sinks</u>, precipitation is <u>extremely low</u>. <u>Deserts</u> are normally near high pressure belts (e.g. the Sahara).

4) The <u>exact location</u> of high and low pressure belts <u>varies</u> slightly over time. Places that <u>normally</u> have <u>more moderate weather</u> can sometimes experience <u>extremely dry</u> or <u>wet weather</u> if they find themselves in a high or low pressure belt.

Global circulation — when your world map blows away...

The circulation pattern on the previous page affects the climate across the world. Have a go at this question:

1) Describe the distribution of tropical climates shown in the map above.   [2]

Extreme Weather

This page is a bit like the weather's greatest hits album — it's full of records. You'll need to be able to write about extreme weather in two contrasting countries for your exam, but it doesn't have to be these two.

Australia's Weather is More Extreme than the UK's

Extreme weather depends where you are — if a normal UK spring's amount of rain fell in the Sahara desert, it would be extremely wet for the Sahara desert.
In the same way, Iceland's normal winter temperatures would be extremely cold in the UK.

Australia and the UK are contrasting countries which experience different weather extremes:

Temperature

1) Australia is warmer than the UK — it has hotter summers and milder winters.

2) In Darwin, a city in northern Australia, the average maximum summer temperature about 33 °C. Temperatures over 40 °C are considered to be extremely hot.

3) In London, the average maximum temperature in summer is about 23 °C. Temperatures over 30 °C are considered extremely hot.

4) So Australian summers are about 10 °C warmer than UK summers. For both countries, extreme temperatures in summer are about 7 °C warmer than the average temperature.

	Australia	UK
Average summer high	33 °C	23 °C
Highest extreme	51 °C	38.5 °C
Lowest extreme	–23 °C	–27.2 °C

Precipitation

1) Australia has much lower precipitation (rain, snow etc.) than the UK. It is the world's driest inhabited continent.

2) The average annual rainfall in Australia is 465 mm. In the UK, average annual rainfall is over 1150 mm — more than twice as much rain as Australia gets.

3) Extremely wet years in Australia have over 550 mm of rain. In the UK, annual rainfall in extremely wet years is over 1210 mm.

4) Extremely dry years in Australia have less than 360 mm of rainfall. In the UK, extremely dry years have less than 950 mm of rain.

	Australia	UK
Average annual rainfall	465 mm	1154 mm
Annual rainfall in driest ever year	314 mm	835 mm
Annual rainfall in wettest ever year	760 mm	1337 mm

Wind

1) Australia has stronger extreme winds than the UK does.

2) Australia is affected by tropical cyclones (see next page). Tropical cyclones cause very strong winds of over 118 km/h.

3) In the UK, gales (winds of over 62 km/h) are rare — most places only have a few days of gales each year.

4) The strongest wind recorded in Australia is over 400 km/h, recorded on Barrow Island off Australia's north-west coast during tropical cyclone Olivia in 1996.

5) The UK's strongest ever sea-level wind was over 220 km/h, recorded in Fraserburgh in Scotland in 1989.

	Australia	UK
Strongest recorded wind	407 km/h	229 km/h

Not the sort of extremely hot Australians I was hoping for...

You might get an exam question on differences in extreme weather. A question a bit like this:

1) Describe how extreme weather varies in two contrasting countries. [6]

EXAM QUESTION

Tropical Storms

Tropical storms are <u>intense low pressure</u> weather systems with <u>heavy rain</u> and <u>strong winds</u> that spiral around the <u>centre</u>. They have a few names (<u>hurricanes</u>, <u>typhoons</u>, and <u>cyclones</u>), but they're all the <u>same thing</u>.

Tropical Storms Bring Extreme Weather Conditions

1) Tropical storms develop when the <u>sea temperature</u> is <u>27 °C or higher</u>. The warm ocean temperature means there is lots of <u>warm</u>, <u>moist</u> air to cause <u>extreme precipitation</u>.

2) <u>Condensation</u> when warm air rises and cools releases huge amounts of <u>energy</u>, which makes the storms <u>powerful</u>. The <u>rising air</u> creates an area of <u>low pressure</u>, which increases <u>surface winds</u>.

3) The Earth's <u>rotation</u> deflects the paths of the winds, which causes the storms to <u>spin</u>.

4) The storm <u>gets stronger</u> due to <u>energy</u> from the warm <u>water</u>, so <u>wind speeds increase</u>.

5) <u>Extreme weather</u> conditions are associated with tropical storms:

1 Extreme Winds

1) <u>Strong</u> winds in tropical storms are caused by an area of <u>very low pressure</u> at the <u>centre</u> of the storm that creates a big <u>pressure difference</u> to the surrounding area.

2) Tropical storms can have wind speeds of more than <u>250 kilometres per hour</u>.

3) These winds are strong enough to <u>damage</u> or <u>destroy buildings</u> and <u>plants</u>, and cause <u>loose objects</u> (e.g. bins) to be <u>picked up</u> and <u>transported</u>.

2 Extreme Rain

1) Extremely high amounts of <u>precipitation</u> can fall <u>rapidly</u> in tropical storms.

2) This is caused by <u>large amounts</u> of warm, moist air being sucked towards the <u>centre</u> of the storm due to the <u>difference in pressure</u>. As this happens, the air <u>rises</u>, <u>cools</u> and <u>condenses</u>, causing <u>rain</u>.

3) There can be enough rain to cause <u>flooding</u> and <u>mudslides</u>.

The Frequency of Tropical Storms Varies, but the Distribution Doesn't

Distribution

1) Most tropical storms occur between <u>5°</u> and <u>30°</u> north and south of the equator — any further from the equator and the water <u>isn't warm enough</u>.

2) The <u>majority</u> of storms occur in the <u>northern hemisphere</u> (especially over the <u>Pacific</u>), in <u>late summer</u> and <u>autumn</u>, when sea temperatures are <u>highest</u>.

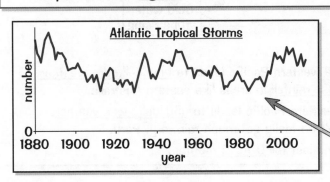

Equator

Tropic of Cancer (23.5° north)

Tropic of Capricorn (23.5° south)

→ path of tropical storm

sea surface temperature 27 °C or higher

Pacific

Atlantic Tropical Storms

number

0
1880 1900 1920 1940 1960 1980 2000
year

Frequency

1) The <u>number</u> of tropical storms <u>varies</u> each year.

2) In the <u>Atlantic</u>, the number of tropical storms has <u>increased</u> since <u>1984</u> — but there is <u>no overall trend</u> over the last <u>130 years</u>.

Forget warm water, you're in hot water when one of these turns up...

Make sure you know how tropical storms develop and the sorts of extreme weather they bring with them. In the UK, the closest you could get to a tropical storm is if they turn up in your exam — so you'd better get this page learnt.

El Niño and La Niña

Oh 'Elp, it's El Niño. Better pack your passport, it's time for a trip to the Pacific Ocean to see how El Niño can cause some quite worrisome weather conditions — when it bothers to turn up, that is...

El Niño *Events are when* Air *and Ocean Currents* Change

1) Air currents in the atmosphere and water currents in the ocean usually flow one way in the Pacific Ocean.

2) Every few years, they weaken or reverse — this is an El Niño event. Sometimes they get stronger — this is a La Niña event. Both cause changes in weather patterns in surrounding areas.

Normal Conditions

Normally, there's low pressure over the western Pacific and high pressure over the east:

La Niña

1) La Niña is when the NORMAL conditions become MORE EXTREME.

2) Trade winds blow to the west more strongly, and more cold water rises in the eastern Pacific.

3) It causes more heavy rainfall and floods in the west, and less rainfall and droughts in the east.

4) La Niña events occur every 2-7 years.

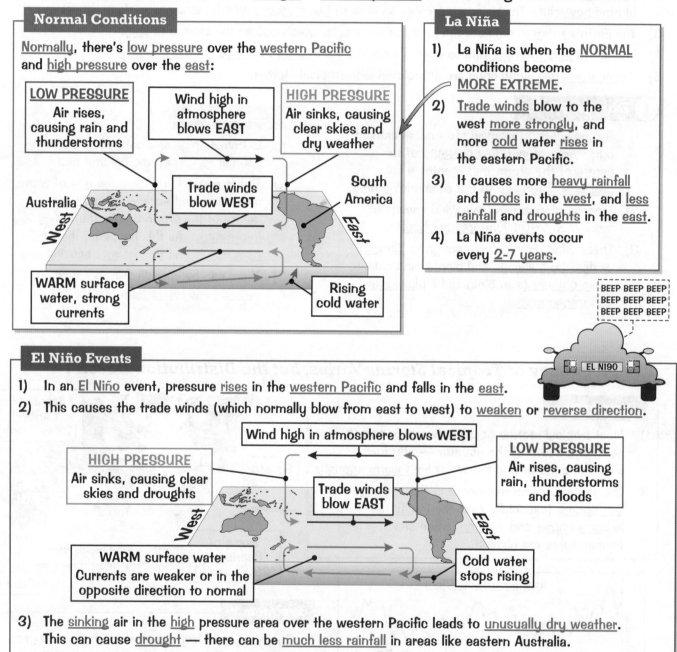

El Niño Events

1) In an El Niño event, pressure rises in the western Pacific and falls in the east.

2) This causes the trade winds (which normally blow from east to west) to weaken or reverse direction.

3) The sinking air in the high pressure area over the western Pacific leads to unusually dry weather. This can cause drought — there can be much less rainfall in areas like eastern Australia.

4) The rising air in the low pressure area over the eastern Pacific leads to unusually wet weather. This can cause serious floods in places that don't normally get much rain, e.g. Peru.

El Niño events occur every 3-4 years on average, and last for 9 to 12 months.

El Niño — worse than El Seveño, but not as bad as El Teño...

This whole El Niño thing can be tricky to get your head around, but it will help you understand some of the pages that are coming up. If you get the normal conditions in the Pacific sorted out, it's quite easy to remember that in an El Niño year, all the arrows are reversed. Then it's easy to work out why normally wet areas are drier, and dry areas are wetter.

Drought

You <u>already</u> know a couple of causes of drought from the previous page — time to go into a bit <u>more detail</u>...

Drought is when Conditions are Drier than Normal

1) A <u>drought</u> is a <u>long period</u> (weeks, months or years) when <u>rainfall</u> is <u>below average</u>.

2) <u>Water supplies</u>, e.g. lakes and rivers, become <u>depleted</u> during a drought because <u>people keep</u> <u>using them</u> but they <u>aren't replenished</u> by rainfall. Also, droughts are often accompanied by <u>high</u> <u>temperatures</u>, which <u>increase</u> the <u>rate of evaporation</u>, so water supplies are <u>depleted faster</u>.

3) The <u>length</u> of a drought is <u>different</u> in <u>different places</u>, e.g. the <u>worst drought</u> in <u>Britain</u> since records began lasted <u>16 months</u>, whilst droughts in <u>African countries</u> can last for <u>more than a decade</u>.

Causes of Drought

1) <u>Changes</u> in <u>atmospheric circulation</u>, such as El Niño or La Niña (see previous page), can mean it <u>doesn't rain much</u> in an area for <u>months</u> or <u>years</u>. For example, the drought in <u>Australia</u> (see p.11) in the 2000s was made <u>worse</u> by an <u>El Niño</u> event in <u>2002</u>.

2) Changes in atmospheric circulation can also make the <u>annual rains</u> <u>fail</u> (e.g. <u>monsoon rains don't come</u> when they normally do in places like <u>India</u>).

3) Droughts are also caused when <u>high pressure weather systems</u> (called <u>anticyclones</u>) <u>block depressions</u> (<u>weather systems</u> that <u>cause rain</u>), e.g. this can happen in the <u>UK</u>.

A drying riverbed during a period of drought.

The Frequency of Droughts Has Not Changed Much, but the Distribution Has

Distribution

1) The <u>map</u> on the right shows the <u>distribution</u> of <u>severe droughts</u> around the <u>world</u>.

2) Areas <u>most at risk</u> from drought are <u>central</u> and <u>southern Africa</u>, the <u>Middle East</u>, <u>Australia</u>, <u>eastern South America</u> and parts of <u>North America</u>.

3) The locations affected by drought <u>vary</u> over <u>time</u>.

4) Since 1950, there have been <u>more droughts</u> in <u>Africa</u>, <u>Asia</u> and the <u>Mediterranean</u> and <u>fewer droughts</u> in the <u>Americas</u> and <u>Russia</u>.

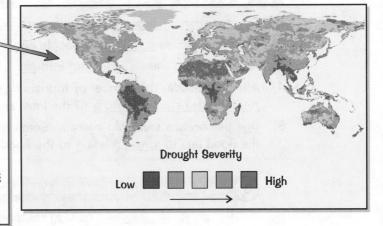

Drought Severity

Low ▮▮▮▮▮ High

Frequency

1) Globally, the <u>frequency</u> of droughts has <u>varied</u> from year to year but <u>overall</u> has <u>not changed</u> much since 1950.

2) Some scientists have <u>suggested</u> that droughts might become <u>more frequent</u> and <u>more severe</u> in future due to <u>climate change</u>.

Finally, a chance to show off my dry sense of humour...

Now you know what droughts are and how they happen. If not, then you've started in the wrong place — this book is most useful if you work your way down the pages, from top to bottom. So up to the top you go, and get learnin'.

Flash Flooding — Case Study

You need to learn __TWO__ extreme weather case studies: either <u>flash flooding</u> OR <u>tropical storms</u>, and either <u>heat waves</u> OR <u>droughts</u>. One of these case studies MUST be from the <u>UK</u>. Take your pick...

There was a *Flash Flood* in *Boscastle* in *August 2004*

1) A flash flood is when <u>lots</u> of water <u>suddenly</u> flows into a <u>river</u>, causing it to <u>overflow</u> its <u>banks</u>. They're often caused by a short period of <u>heavy rainfall</u>.

2) The village of <u>Boscastle</u> on the north coast of <u>Cornwall</u> was devastated by a <u>flash flood</u> on 16th August 2004.

1 Causes of the Boscastle Flash Flood

1) <u>75 mm</u> of rain (the amount that would <u>normally fall</u> in a <u>month</u>) fell in just <u>two hours</u>. A <u>low pressure</u> system brought <u>warm</u>, <u>moist</u> air from the Atlantic Ocean. This air mass <u>cooled</u> as it <u>rose</u> above the land, causing <u>thunderstorms</u> with <u>intense rainfall</u>.

2) Lots of rain over the <u>previous weeks</u> meant that the ground was <u>wetter than normal</u>, and could not <u>absorb</u> the water. So <u>much</u> of the rainfall simply <u>ran off</u> the land <u>surface</u>.

3) Boscastle is in a <u>steep-sided valley</u> close to the <u>confluence</u> of <u>three rivers</u>. The steep valley sides meant that <u>surface water</u> ran into the river channels very <u>quickly</u>, and the confluences meant that about <u>two billion litres</u> of water were <u>funnelled</u> down the river valleys into Boscastle.

4) The <u>old bridge</u> in the village had a <u>low arch</u> over a very <u>narrow river channel</u>. The flooding was <u>made worse</u> because trees and vehicles in the flood water became <u>trapped</u> under the bridge, forming a <u>dam</u>.

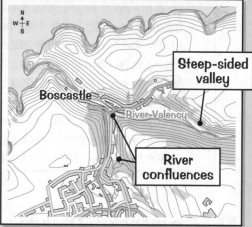

2 Consequences of the Boscastle Flash Flood

1) <u>58 properties</u>, <u>4 businesses</u>, <u>roads</u> and <u>bridges</u> were <u>destroyed</u> or <u>damaged</u>.

2) The flood was so <u>sudden</u> that people <u>couldn't evacuate</u> or move belongings to safer places.

3) About <u>50 cars</u> were <u>washed out</u> into <u>sea</u>. This caused some <u>environmental pollution</u>.

4) After the floods, the number of tourists <u>dropped</u> significantly. The village is a popular <u>tourist destination</u> and <u>90%</u> of the local economy <u>relies on tourism</u>.

5) <u>One</u> person was seriously injured. Some residents suffered <u>mental health problems</u> after the flood due to <u>stress</u> relating to the floods and <u>insurance claims</u>.

3 Responses to the Boscastle Flash Flood

1) <u>Emergency services</u> quickly responded to save people in Boscastle. Around <u>100 people</u> had to be <u>airlifted to safety</u> by <u>seven helicopters</u>.

2) Residents and tourists that were flooded out of their accommodation were looked after in <u>local accommodation</u> and the <u>village hall</u>.

3) Homes, businesses and roads were <u>eventually rebuilt</u>.

4) The <u>bridge</u> was <u>rebuilt</u> with a <u>higher arch</u>, so that <u>debris</u> is <u>less likely</u> to dam the river.

5) A £10 million new <u>flood defence scheme</u> was opened in <u>2008</u>, which included <u>widening</u> and <u>deepening</u> the river to improve its flow.

Flash flooding — like normal flooding, but with added bling...

Despite loads of people becoming trapped by flood water, somehow nobody died. As usual, you might have studied a different example of flash flooding. That's fine, just make sure you know the causes, consequences and responses.

Tropical Storm — Case Study

Remember — you need to learn a case study for flash flooding OR tropical storms, you don't have to do both.

Hurricane Katrina *struck Mississippi and Louisiana, USA, in August 2005*

Hurricane Katrina, a tropical storm, struck the south-east USA on 29th August 2005:

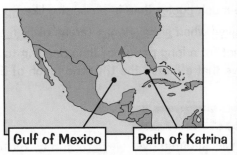

Gulf of Mexico | Path of Katrina

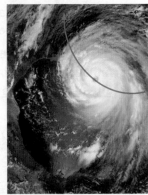

1 Causes of Hurricane Katrina

1) Louisiana and Mississippi are in the Gulf of Mexico, where sea temperatures are often 27 °C or warmer — this means tropical storms can form.

2) A storm formed 200 miles south-east of the Bahamas on the 23rd August. It moved north-west over the southern tip of Florida into the Gulf of Mexico.

3) As it travelled over the warm water of the Gulf of Mexico it became even stronger.

4) On the morning of the 29th it struck land, bringing winds of around 200 km/h and 200-250 mm rainfall in Louisiana and a storm surge of up to 8.5 m in Mississippi.

Tropical storms cause storm surges as strong winds push water towards the shore, causing the water level to rise. If the storm surge coincides with a high tide, flood defences can easily be breached.

2 Consequences of Hurricane Katrina

1) More than 1800 people were killed.

2) 300 000 houses were destroyed and hundreds of thousands of people were made homeless.

3) Large areas were flooded, including 80% of New Orleans.

4) 3 million people were left without electricity.

5) Roads were damaged and some bridges collapsed.

6) Coastal habitats were damaged.

7) 230 000 jobs were lost from damaged businesses.

8) Water supplies were polluted with sewage and chemicals.

9) The total cost of the damage was estimated at $150 billion.

10) Rescue and recovery efforts were hampered by disagreements between national, state and local officials.

3 Responses to Hurricane Katrina

1) 70-80% of New Orleans residents were evacuated before the hurricane reached land.

2) Mississippi and Louisiana declared states of emergency — they set up control centres and emergency shelters, and stockpiled supplies.

3) The coastguard, police, fire service and army rescued over 50 000 people.

4) Charities collected donations and provided aid, including millions of hot meals.

5) The US government provided over 16 billion dollars for the rebuilding of homes, and provided funds to repair other essential infrastructure.

6) The US Army recommended that buildings are rebuilt on stilts or not rebuilt at all in very low-lying areas.

7) Repaired and improved flood defences for New Orleans costing 14.5 billion dollars were completed in 2013.

The facts on Katrina make for grim reading, that's no joke.

Check you're clear on the causes, consequences and responses for your chosen tropical storm if you've studied one — try covering up the page and jotting down a list of points for each of the three boxes. No cheating...

Heat Wave — Case Study

You need to know a case study about EITHER a <u>heat wave</u> OR a <u>drought</u> (see next page)...

A Heat Wave is when Conditions are Hotter than Normal

1) A <u>heat wave</u> is a <u>long period</u> (days or weeks) during which the <u>temperature</u> is much <u>higher</u> than <u>normal</u>.

2) The <u>conditions</u> of a <u>heat wave</u> are <u>different</u> in <u>different places</u>, e.g. the conditions considered a heat wave in the <u>UK</u> would be much <u>cooler</u> than in a country like <u>Spain</u>, where higher temperatures are <u>expected</u>.

3) Heat waves are <u>caused</u> when <u>anticyclones</u> (areas of <u>high pressure</u>) stay in the <u>same place</u> for some time.

4) Anticyclones can last for a long period of time, leading to <u>heat waves</u>, like the <u>European Heat Wave</u> that affected the UK (and much of Europe) in <u>August 2003</u>.

1 Causes of the 2003 Heat Wave

1) An <u>anticyclone</u> was situated over <u>western Europe</u> for most of <u>August</u>.

2) Air moves <u>clockwise</u> around an anticyclone, so <u>hot</u>, <u>dry air</u> from the <u>centre of the continent</u> was brought to <u>western Europe</u>. This meant temperatures in the UK were <u>higher</u> than normal and rainfall was <u>lower</u> than normal.

3) The anticyclone <u>blocked low pressure systems</u> that would normally bring <u>cooler</u>, <u>rainier</u> conditions from the Atlantic Ocean.

2 UK Consequences of the 2003 Heat Wave

1) People suffered from <u>heat stroke</u>, <u>dehydration</u>, <u>sunburn</u> and <u>breathing problems</u> caused by <u>air pollution</u>. Some people <u>drowned</u> when cooling off in <u>rivers</u>, <u>lakes</u> and <u>pools</u>.

2) Around <u>2000</u> people <u>died</u> in the UK from causes linked to the heatwave.

3) <u>20 people</u> were <u>injured</u> when they were struck by <u>lightning</u> during thunderstorms caused by the heat wave.

4) <u>Water levels fell</u> in <u>reservoirs</u>, which threatened <u>water supplies</u> to houses and businesses.

5) <u>Livestock died</u> due to the heat, and <u>crop yields</u> were <u>lower</u> due to the lack of water.

6) <u>Trains</u> were disrupted by <u>rails buckling</u> in the heat and some <u>roads melted</u>, which caused <u>delays</u>.

Water levels in Haweswater reservoir dropped severely during the heatwave.

3 UK Responses to the 2003 Heat Wave

1) The <u>NHS</u> and the <u>media</u> gave <u>guidance</u> to the public on how to survive the heat wave — e.g. <u>drink</u> lots of <u>water</u>, have <u>cool baths</u> and <u>showers</u>, <u>block</u> out <u>sunlight</u> to keep rooms <u>cool</u>, etc.

2) <u>Limitations</u> were placed on water use, e.g. some parts of the UK had <u>hose pipe bans</u>.

3) A <u>speed limit</u> was imposed on <u>trains</u> because of the risk of <u>rails buckling</u>. Some rails were <u>painted white</u> to <u>reflect heat</u> and keep them <u>cooler</u>.

4) The UK created a '<u>heat wave plan</u>' to minimise the <u>consequences</u> of <u>future</u> heat waves.

I tried to surf the heat wave, but my board melted...

Turns out that hot, sunny weather isn't always great for everyone. While there are advantages to heat waves for a few people (think ice cream salesmen), for others it's a struggle to stay alive in the heat. CPR might have been useful in the heat wave, but for now you to need to concentrate on your CCR skills — that's Causes, Consequences and Responses.

Drought — Case Study

Grab a big bottle of water, it's time for a page on <u>drought</u>. If you did <u>heat waves</u>, you can <u>skip</u> this one.

There was a Drought in Australia in the Early 21st Century

1) <u>South-east Australia</u> suffered from a <u>severe</u>, <u>long-term drought</u> from roughly <u>2001 to 2009</u>, although scientists don't agree on exactly when it started and finished. It's known as the <u>Millennium Drought</u> or the "<u>Big Dry</u>".

2) The <u>worst-hit area</u> was the <u>Murray-Darling Basin</u>, an important <u>agricultural region</u>.

AUSTRALIA
Murray-Darling Basin
30° S

① Causes of the Millennium Drought in Australia

There were <u>several</u> factors that may have <u>contributed</u> to the Millennium Drought:

1) Australia has a <u>naturally low rainfall</u> due to <u>global atmospheric circulation</u> (see p.2). The 30° S <u>high pressure belt</u> passes through Australia, causing <u>low</u> precipitation.

2) <u>El Niño</u> events (see page 6) in 2002-2003, 2004-2005 and 2006-2007 led to <u>especially low</u> rainfall totals in south-east Australia.

3) Scientists think that <u>climate change</u> may be <u>increasing global temperatures</u> and <u>changing rainfall patterns</u>. So climate change may have <u>contributed</u> to the Millennium Drought:

- <u>Temperatures</u> in Australia were <u>higher</u> than normal during this period, resulting in <u>more water evaporating</u> than normal.

- <u>Weather fronts</u> that normally bring <u>rain</u> to south-east Australia <u>moved further south</u>, away from Australia, causing <u>annual rainfall totals</u> to be <u>lower</u>.

② Consequences of the Millennium Drought in Australia

1) <u>Water levels</u> in <u>lakes</u> and <u>rivers</u> (particularly the Murray and Darling) <u>fell</u>, so water supplies ran <u>low</u>.

2) The largest impacts were on <u>farming</u>:

- <u>Crop yields fell</u>, and crops that rely on <u>irrigation</u> (watering) were particularly badly affected, e.g. <u>rice production</u> fell to just <u>2%</u> of pre-drought totals. This <u>increased food prices</u>.

- Livestock <u>died</u> — the number of <u>sheep</u> in Australia <u>fell</u> by around <u>8 million</u> during 2002-2003.

- <u>Farmers' incomes</u> fell, and over <u>100 000</u> people employed in farming <u>lost their jobs</u>.

3) The drought caused <u>vegetation loss</u> and <u>soil erosion</u>, and rivers and lakes suffered from outbreaks of <u>toxic algae</u>.

4) <u>Dust storms</u> caused by the drought affected <u>inland Australia</u> and some <u>coastal cities</u>.

5) The drought conditions were perfect for <u>wildfires</u>. Over <u>30 000 km²</u> of land <u>burned</u>, and <u>hundreds</u> of <u>houses</u> were <u>destroyed</u>. <u>8 people</u> were <u>killed</u>.

③ Responses to the Millennium Drought in Australia

1) <u>Water conservation measures</u> were introduced. E.g. the <u>3 million people</u> who rely on the <u>River Murray</u> for their water supply had their allocation <u>reduced</u>.

2) Cities such as <u>Sydney</u> built <u>desalination plants</u> that can turn sea water into drinking water.

3) The Australian government provided more than <u>23 000</u> rural families and <u>1500</u> small businesses with <u>income support</u> to help them <u>survive</u>.

4) The government is also <u>investing</u> in <u>improving drought forecasts</u> so farmers can prepare better, <u>improving irrigation schemes</u> and developing <u>drought-resistant crops</u>.

Extreme temperatures — making Australia's rivers run dry...

After the Big Dry comes the Big Learn. If you chose to learn droughts, you'll need to learn the causes, consequences and responses for the Millennium Drought — unless you've got a different drought case study up your sleeve, that is.

Tectonic Plates

The <u>Earth's surface</u> is made of <u>huge floating plates</u> that are constantly moving... Rock on.

The Earth's Surface *is Separated into* Tectonic Plates

1) At the <u>centre</u> of the Earth is the <u>core</u> — it has an inner bit and an outer bit. The <u>inner</u> core is a ball of <u>solid iron and nickel</u>. The <u>outer</u> core is <u>liquid</u>.

2) Around the core is the <u>mantle</u>, which is <u>semi-molten rock</u> that <u>moves very slowly</u>.

3) The <u>outer layer</u> of the Earth is the <u>crust</u>. It's about <u>10-70 km</u> thick.

4) The crust is <u>divided</u> into slabs called <u>tectonic plates</u> that float on the mantle.

5) Plates are made of <u>two types</u> of crust — <u>continental</u> and <u>oceanic</u>:

> • <u>Continental crust</u> is <u>thicker</u> and <u>less dense</u>.
>
> • <u>Oceanic crust</u> is <u>thinner</u> and <u>more dense</u>.

Labels: Crust, Outer core, Inner core, Mantle

Tectonic Plates *Move* due to Convection Currents *in the Mantle*

1) The <u>lower</u> parts of the <u>mantle</u> are sometimes <u>hotter</u> than the <u>upper parts</u>. When these lower parts <u>heat up</u> they become <u>less dense</u> and slowly <u>rise</u>.

2) As they move towards the <u>top</u> of the mantle they <u>cool down</u>, become <u>more dense</u>, then slowly <u>sink</u>.

3) These <u>circular movements</u> are called <u>CONVECTION CURRENTS</u> — they cause tectonic plates to <u>move</u>.

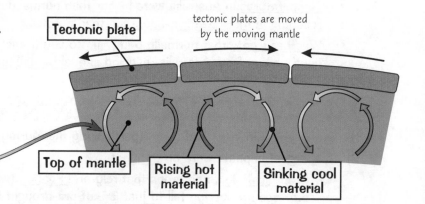

Labels: Tectonic plate; tectonic plates are moved by the moving mantle; Top of mantle; Rising hot material; Sinking cool material

Plate Boundaries *are where* Tectonic Plates *Meet*

The places where plates <u>meet</u> are called <u>plate boundaries</u> or <u>plate margins</u>:

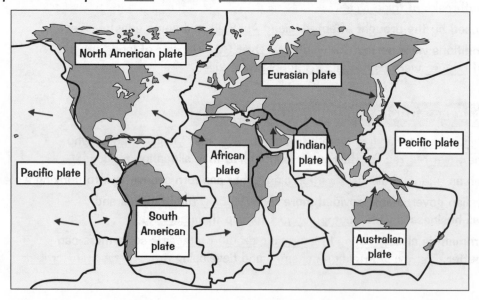

Map labels: North American plate, Eurasian plate, African plate, Indian plate, Pacific plate, South American plate, Australian plate

KEY
| Plate margin
→ Direction of plate movement

Wash tectonic plates by hand — they won't fit in the dishwasher...

Yes, I know this page isn't terribly exciting, but you need to understand the Earth's structure and what tectonic plates are or you'll really get your knickers in a twist later on in the section. Only carry on when your knickers are secure...

Plate Boundaries

Tectonic plate boundaries are places where plates meet. I like to think they have a cup of tea, a slice or two of cake and a natter about what's going on in the world. But in reality it's not so civilised...

There are *Four Types* of Plate Boundaries

1 Destructive Boundaries

- Destructive boundaries are where two plates are moving towards each other.

- Where an oceanic plate meets a continental plate, the denser oceanic plate is forced down into the mantle and destroyed. This often creates volcanoes and ocean trenches (very deep sections of the ocean floor where the oceanic plate goes down).

- EXAMPLE: the Pacific plate is being forced under the Eurasian plate along the east coast of Japan.

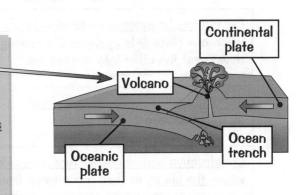

Continental plate
Volcano
Oceanic plate
Ocean trench

2 Collision Plate Boundaries

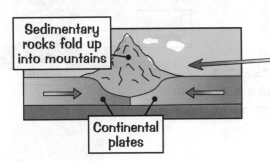

Sedimentary rocks fold up into mountains

Continental plates

- In collision plate boundaries, both plates are made from continental crust and move towards each other.

- Neither plate is forced down into the mantle — instead both plates are folded and forced upwards, creating fold mountains.

- EXAMPLE: the Eurasian and Indian plates are colliding to form the Himalayas.

3 Constructive Boundaries

- Constructive boundaries are where two plates are moving away from each other.

- Magma (molten rock) rises from the mantle to fill the gap and cools, creating new crust.

- EXAMPLE: the Eurasian plate and the North American plate are moving apart at the Mid-Atlantic Ridge.

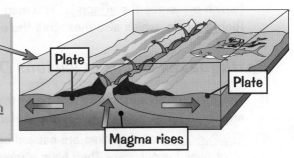

Plate
Plate
Magma rises

4 Conservative Boundaries

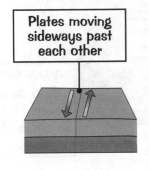

Plates moving sideways past each other

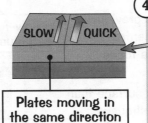

SLOW QUICK

Plates moving in the same direction at different speeds

- Conservative boundaries are where two plates are moving sideways past each other, or are moving in the same direction but at different speeds.

- Crust isn't created or destroyed.

- EXAMPLE: the Pacific plate is moving past the North American plate on the west coast of the USA, e.g. at the San Andreas fault.

Giant plates whacking into each other — smashing stuff...

Make sure you know the diagrams on this page well — they could come in handy in the exam.

1) Describe what a collision boundary is. [2]

EXAM QUESTION

Earthquakes

Where plates meet, earthquakes can occur. If only the waiter would carry them more carefully.

Earthquakes Occur at All Four Types of Plate Boundaries

1) Earthquakes are caused by the tension that builds up at all four types of plate boundaries:

> Destructive boundaries — tension builds up when one plate gets stuck as it's moving down past the other into the mantle.

> Collision boundaries — tension builds as the plates are pushed together.

> Constructive boundaries — tension builds along cracks within the plates as they move away from each other.

> Conservative boundaries — tension builds up when plates that are grinding past each other get stuck.

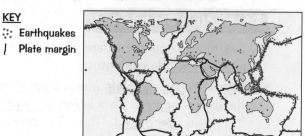

KEY
- :: Earthquakes
- | Plate margin

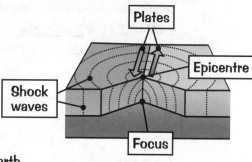

2) The plates eventually jerk past each other, sending out shock waves (vibrations). These vibrations are the earthquake.

3) The shock waves spread out from the focus — the point in the Earth where the earthquake starts. Near the focus the waves are stronger and cause more damage.

4) The epicentre is the point on the Earth's surface straight above the focus.

5) Earthquakes are measured using the moment magnitude scale (which measures the energy released by an earthquake) or the Mercalli scale (which measures the effects). You may still see some references to the Richter scale, which also measures the energy released but is no longer used.

Damage after the magnitude 7.8 earthquake in Nepal in 2015

Earthquakes Occur at Various Depths

1) The focus of an earthquake can be at the Earth's surface, or anywhere up to 700 km below the surface.

2) Shallow-focus earthquakes are caused by tectonic plates moving at or near the surface. They have a focus between 0 km and 70 km below the Earth's surface.

3) Deep-focus earthquakes are caused by crust that has previously been subducted into the mantle moving towards the centre of the Earth, heating up or decomposing. They have a focus between 70 km and 700km below the Earth's surface.

4) In general, deeper earthquakes do less damage at the surface than shallower earthquakes. Shock waves from deeper earthquakes have to travel through more rock to reach the surface, which reduces their power (and the amount of shaking) when they reach the surface.

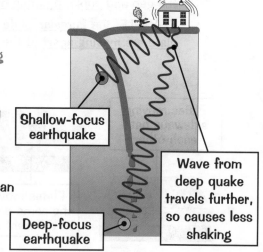

Tension, jerks, major damage — sounds like my dance moves...

I'd better say this now... don't be put off by maps like the one at the top of the page — you won't ever have to draw them. But you might need to use one you're given in the exam to answer a question...

1) Using the map above, describe the global distribution of earthquakes. [2]

Volcanoes

Volcanoes usually look like mountains... until they explode and throw molten rock everywhere. Honestly, they've got such a temper, though I'd probably be in a bad mood if I was sitting on a load of magma.

Volcanoes are Found at Destructive and Constructive Plate Margins

1) At destructive plate margins the oceanic plate goes under the continental plate because it's more dense.

- The oceanic plate moves down into the mantle, where it's melted and destroyed.
- A pool of magma forms. The magma rises through cracks in the crust called vents.
- The magma erupts onto the surface (where it's called lava) forming a volcano.

2) At constructive margins the magma rises up into the gap created by the plates moving apart, forming a volcano.

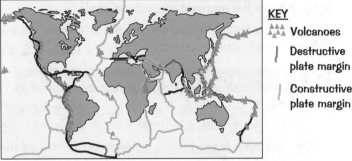

KEY
▲▲▲ Volcanoes
| Destructive plate margin
| Constructive plate margin

3) When a volcano erupts, it emits lava and gases. Some volcanoes emit lots of ash, which can cover land, block out the sun and form pyroclastic flows (super-heated currents of gas, ash and rock).

Hotspots are Found Away From Plate Boundaries

Most volcanic activity occurs at plate boundaries, but there are some areas of intense volcanic activity that aren't at any plate boundaries. These areas are called hotspots:

1) A hotspot is a bit of the Earth's crust that is hotter than normal. They occur where a plume of hot magma from the mantle moves towards the surface, causing an unusually large flow of heat from the mantle to the crust.

2) Sometimes the magma can break through the crust and reach the surface. When this happens, there is an eruption and a volcano forms.

3) Hotspots can be found in oceanic or continental crust, and can be near or far from plate boundaries.

4) Hotspots remain stationary over time, but the crust moves above them. This can create chains of volcanic islands, e.g. Hawaii is a chain of volcanic islands in the middle of the Pacific plate.

There are Different Types of Volcano

1) Composite volcanoes (E.g. Mount Fuji in Japan)

- Occur at destructive plate boundaries (see p.13).
- Subducted oceanic crust contains lots of water. The water can cause the subducted crust to erupt.
- The eruptions start with ashy explosions that deposit a layer of ash, then erupt a layer of thick, sticky lava that can't flow far. This forms a steep-sided cone.

Steep-sided volcano
Vent
Layer of lava
Layer of ash

2) Shield volcanoes (E.g. Mauna Loa on the Hawaiian islands)

- Occur at hotspots or constructive plate boundaries.
- They are not very explosive and are made up of only lava.
- The lava is runny. It flows quickly and spreads over a wide area, forming a low, gentle-sided volcano.

Runny lava
Layers of lava
Low, flat volcano

Studying volcanoes — what a blast...

There are different types of volcano, but they've all got one thing in common — throwing up lava without bothering to rush to the toilet. You need to know how moving tectonic plates cause both shield and composite volcanoes.

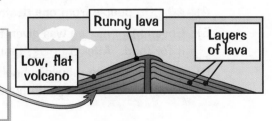

Tectonic Hazards — Case Study

Don't think you could get away without learning a <u>real-world example</u> of a tectonic event...

There was a Deadly Earthquake in Pakistan in 2005

<u>Place</u>: Kashmir, Pakistan

<u>Date</u>: 8th October, 2005

<u>Size</u>: 7.6 on the moment magnitude scale

Although the epicentre and most serious effects were in <u>Pakistan</u>, it also affected neighbouring countries including <u>India</u>, <u>Afghanistan</u> and <u>China</u>.

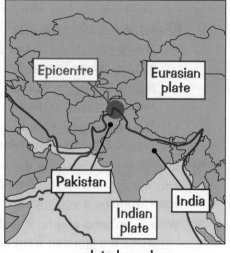

~ plate boundary

1 Causes of the 2005 Pakistan Earthquake

1) The <u>Eurasian plate</u> and the <u>Indian plate</u> meet at a <u>collision plate boundary</u> (see p.13) that runs through the <u>middle</u> of <u>Pakistan</u>.

2) The area is <u>very prone</u> to seismic activity as the plates meet and fold, forming the <u>Himalayan fold mountain range</u>.

3) On <u>8 October 2005</u>, strain that had built up along the fault was <u>suddenly released</u> in a powerful earthquake.

2 Consequences of the 2005 Pakistan Earthquake

1) Around <u>80 000 deaths</u>, mostly from <u>collapsed buildings</u>.

2) <u>Tens of thousands</u> of people were <u>injured</u>.

3) <u>Hundreds of thousands</u> of <u>buildings</u> were <u>damaged or destroyed</u>, including whole villages.

4) Around <u>3 million people</u> were made <u>homeless</u>.

5) <u>Water pipelines</u> and <u>electricity lines</u> were <u>broken</u>, cutting off supply.

6) <u>Landslides</u> buried <u>buildings</u> and <u>people</u>. They also <u>blocked access roads</u> and <u>cut off water supplies</u>, <u>electricity supplies</u> and <u>telephone lines</u>.

7) <u>Diarrhoea</u> and <u>other diseases</u> spread due to little <u>clean water</u>.

8) <u>Freezing winter conditions</u> shortly after the earthquake caused <u>more casualties</u> and meant <u>rescue</u> and <u>rebuilding</u> operations were <u>difficult</u>.

9) Children's <u>education</u> was affected as schools were <u>destroyed</u> and <u>not rebuilt quickly</u>.

3 Responses to the 2005 Pakistan Earthquake

1) <u>International aid</u> and <u>equipment</u> such as <u>helicopters</u> and <u>rescue dogs</u> were brought in, as well as teams of people from <u>other countries</u>.

2) Despite this, help <u>didn't reach</u> many areas for <u>days</u> or <u>weeks</u>, and many people had to be rescued <u>by hand</u> without any <u>equipment</u> or help from <u>emergency services</u>.

3) <u>Tents</u>, <u>blankets</u> and <u>medical supplies</u> were distributed, although it took up to a <u>month</u> for them to reach most areas.

4) <u>40 000</u> people from one destroyed town were relocated to a <u>new settlement</u>.

5) <u>Government money</u> was given to people to <u>rebuild their homes</u>, but many had to use it for food. After <u>3 years</u>, thousands of people were still living in <u>temporary tents</u>.

6) <u>Aid</u> was given to rebuild schools, but some schools were <u>still</u> not rebuilt <u>10 years</u> after the earthquake, with pupils being taught <u>outside</u>.

80 000 dead, 3 million homeless. There's nothing funny to say.

To put that in context, it's roughly the same as if every single person in Wales lost their home. You might have studied a different tectonic hazard event — either way, make sure you know the causes, consequences and responses.

Managing the Impacts of Tectonic Hazards

<u>Plenty of people</u> live in areas affected by tectonic hazards, so they need ways to <u>reduce</u> the <u>impact</u> of them...

Technology **can** *Reduce* **the Impact** *of Tectonic Hazards*

Although tectonic hazards can't be <u>prevented</u>, modern technology and knowledge can help to <u>reduce</u> the <u>threat</u> from earthquakes and volcanoes. There are several ways to reduce the <u>number</u> of people <u>killed</u> and <u>injured</u>, and the <u>amount of damage</u> done, when tectonic hazards occur:

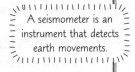

Early Warning Systems for Earthquakes

1) Earthquakes <u>cannot</u> be reliably <u>predicted</u> in advance, but <u>networks</u> of <u>seismometers</u> and <u>lasers</u> can be used to monitor <u>earth movements</u> in areas <u>at risk</u> of earthquakes. These can give a <u>small</u> (i.e. a few seconds or minutes) but vital amount of <u>warning</u> before a large earthquake occurs.

A seismometer is an instrument that detects earth movements.

2) <u>Early warning systems</u> mean that warnings can be communicated <u>quickly</u> and <u>automatically</u> to <u>people</u> and <u>control systems</u> when shaking is detected, using the <u>internet</u>, <u>SMS</u> networks and <u>sirens</u>.

3) The warning is useful because:
   - People can get <u>under cover</u> (e.g. under tables) <u>before</u> the shaking starts.
   - People doing <u>delicate</u> or <u>dangerous jobs</u> can <u>stop</u> what they're doing and make the situation <u>safe</u>, e.g. surgeons can stop delicate procedures and cooks can turn off stoves.
   - <u>Utilities</u> like <u>gas</u> can be <u>shut off</u>, preventing <u>leaks</u> and <u>fires</u>.
   - <u>Trains</u> can start <u>slowing down</u>, making <u>derailments</u> due to damaged track <u>less likely</u>.

Predicting and Monitoring Volcanoes

1) Volcanic eruptions can be predicted if the volcano is <u>well-monitored</u>. Predicting when a volcano is going to erupt <u>gives people time</u> to <u>evacuate</u> — this <u>reduces</u> the number of <u>injuries</u> and <u>deaths</u>.

2) Scientists can <u>monitor</u> the tell-tale <u>signs</u> that come <u>before</u> a <u>volcanic eruption</u>. Remotely operated <u>seismometers</u>, <u>lasers</u> and other sensors can detect <u>indications</u> that an eruption is likely, such as <u>tiny earthquakes</u>, <u>escaping gas</u> and <u>changes</u> in the <u>shape</u> of the volcano (e.g. <u>bulges</u> in the land where <u>magma</u> has <u>built up</u> under it).

3) Volcanoes are also monitored <u>during eruptions</u>, which helps authorities <u>respond</u> appropriately, for example:
   - Evacuation zones can be <u>extended</u> if the eruption becomes <u>more violent</u>.
   - <u>Ash clouds</u> that can damage aircraft can be <u>tracked</u> — this means that flights can be <u>diverted</u> or <u>cancelled</u>, so passengers aren't put at risk.
   - If <u>ash</u> and <u>poisonous gases</u> spread, authorities can warn people to put on <u>gas masks</u>.

Building Design

Modern building technologies can be used to design buildings that don't <u>collapse</u> in <u>earthquakes</u> or when <u>covered in volcanic ash</u>. This <u>reduces deaths</u> and <u>injuries</u> from falling masonry and reduces the cost of <u>repairs</u> and <u>rebuilding</u> afterwards too.

1) <u>Buildings</u> can be <u>designed</u> to <u>withstand earthquakes</u>, e.g. by using <u>materials</u> like <u>reinforced concrete</u> or building <u>special foundations</u> that <u>absorb</u> an <u>earthquake's energy</u>.

2) Existing buildings and bridges can be <u>strengthened</u> (e.g. by wrapping pillars in steel frames).

3) <u>Pipelines</u> (e.g. for gas and water) can be designed to <u>flex</u> and <u>not break</u> during earthquakes. This helps to <u>prevent deaths</u> and <u>damage</u> to property caused by <u>flooding</u> and <u>fires</u>.

Scientists are still working on a cork big enough for a volcano...

That's your lot for tectonics and this section — but there's just time for a practice question before the end...

1) To what extent can modern technology mitigate the impacts of volcanic eruptions or earthquakes? [6]

Revision Summary

Well, you just survived a very hazardous section. It may be all about disasters, but get a load of these questions down you and there won't be any kind of disaster in the exam. I know it looks like there's a lot of stuff here, but you'll be surprised how much you just learned. Try them out a few at a time, then check the answers on the pages. Once you can answer them all standing on your head and juggling five balls, move on to the next section. It's got some lovely graphs...

Global Atmospheric Circulation (p.2-3) ☑

1) How does global atmospheric circulation lead to high and low pressure belts?
2) How do high and low pressure belts create climatic zones?
3) How does global atmospheric circulation cause extremes of precipitation in some parts of the world?

Extreme Weather (p.4-11) ☑

4) Compare extreme temperatures in two different countries.
5) What conditions are required for a tropical storm to develop?
6) What causes tropical storms to rotate?
7) What are the extreme weather conditions caused by tropical storms?
8) How has the distribution of tropical storms varied over time?
9) How has the frequency of tropical storms varied over time?
10) What is El Niño?
11) How does an El Niño event cause dry weather in some places?
12) What is La Niña?
13) What is a drought?
14) How has the distribution of droughts varied over time?
15) How has the frequency of droughts varied over time?
16) What were the consequences of a flash flood or tropical storm that you have studied?
17) What were the responses to a flash flood or tropical storm that you have studied?
18) What were the causes of a heat wave or drought that you have studied?

Tectonic Plates (p.12-13) ☑

19) Describe the Earth's structure.
20) What is the mantle?
21) What are the places where tectonic plates meet called?
22) Why do tectonic plates move?
23) Name the type of plate boundary where two plates of continental crust are moving towards each other.
24) Name the type of plate boundary where two plates are moving sideways against each other.

Tectonic Hazards (p.14-17) ☑

25) What causes earthquakes?
26) What is a shallow-focus earthquake?
27) How do volcanoes form at destructive plate boundaries?
28) What is a hotspot?
29) What is a composite volcano?
30) For a tectonic hazard event you have studied:
    a) Describe the causes of the hazard event.
    b) Give three consequences of the hazard event.
    c) What were the responses to the hazard event?
31) How can early warning systems reduce the impact of tectonic hazards?
32) How can building design reduce the impact of tectonic hazards?

Evidence for Climate Change

We British like to talk about the weather, so global climate change should give us plenty to go on...

The Earth is Getting Warmer

Climate change is any significant change in the Earth's climate over a long period. The climate constantly changes, it always has, and it always will.

1) The Quaternary period is the most recent geological time period, spanning from about 2.6 million years ago to the present day.

2) In the period before the Quaternary, the Earth's climate was warmer and quite stable. Then things changed a lot.

The Quaternary period includes the whole of human history.

3) During the Quaternary, global temperature has shifted between cold glacial periods that last for around 100 000 years, and warmer interglacial periods that last for around 10 000 years.

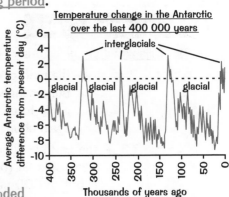

Temperature change in the Antarctic over the last 400 000 years

This graph shows the last 400 000 years but the glacial-interglacial cycles have been repeating throughout the Quaternary period — there have been at least 20.

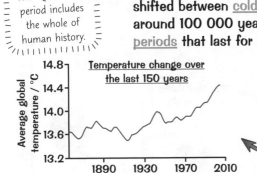

Temperature change over the last 150 years

4) The last glacial period ended around 15 000 years ago. Since then the climate has been warming.

5) Global warming is the term used to describe the sharp rise in global temperatures over the last century. It's a type of climate change.

Evidence for Climate Change Comes from Many Sources

Scientists can work out how the climate has changed over time using a range of methods. For example:

Ice Cores

1) Ice sheets are made up of layers of ice — one layer is formed each year.

2) Scientists drill into ice sheets to get long cores of ice.

3) By analysing the gases trapped in the layers of ice, they can tell what the temperature was each year.

4) One ice core from Antarctica shows the temperature changes over the last 400 000 years (see graph above).

5) Data collected from ice cores is very detailed and reliable.

Sea Ice Positions

1) Sea ice forms around the poles in winter when ocean temperatures fall below -1.8 °C and melts during the summer when it's warmer.

2) By observing the maximum and minimum extent of sea ice each year, scientists can tell how ocean temperatures are changing.

3) The data is very reliable, but accurate records don't go very far back.

Diaries and Paintings

1) Historical diaries can show what the climate was like in the past, e.g. by giving the number of days of rain or snow and the dates of harvests (e.g. an early harvest suggests warm weather).

2) Paintings of fairs and markets on frozen rivers show that winters in Europe were regularly much colder 500 years ago than they are now.

3) However, diaries and paintings aren't very reliable, as they just give one person's viewpoint.

Temperature Data

1) Since the 1850s, global temperatures have been measured accurately using thermometers. This gives a reliable but short-term record of temperature change.

2) However, weather stations are not evenly distributed across the world — data from some areas is patchy.

Glacial cycles — as used by the polar bears in the Tour de Greenland...

There were no thermometers 2.6 million years ago but scientists can reconstruct climates using these clever methods. Climate change is a hot topic (sorry), so make sure you learn this stuff inside out and sideways before your exam.

Causes of Climate Change

Climate change <u>isn't</u> a new phenomenon — it's been happening for <u>millions of years</u>. This page is all about the <u>natural causes</u> of climate change, from the Earth's <u>wobble</u> to the Sun's <u>complexion</u>...

Some Natural Factors are Possible Causes of Climate Change

① Milankovitch Cycles

1) <u>Milankovitch cycles</u> are <u>variations</u> in the <u>way</u> the <u>Earth</u> moves round the <u>Sun</u>.

   • <u>Stretch</u> — the path of the Earth's <u>orbit</u> around the Sun changes from an almost perfect <u>circle</u> to an <u>ellipse</u> (an oval) and back again about every 96 000 years.

   • <u>Tilt</u> — the Earth is <u>tilted</u> at an <u>angle</u> as it orbits the Sun. This tilt (or <u>axis</u>) changes over a cycle of about 41 000 years.

   • <u>Wobble</u> — the <u>axis</u> of the Earth wobbles like a <u>spinning top</u> on a cycle of about 22 000 years.

2) These cycles affect <u>how far</u> the Earth is from the Sun, and the <u>angle</u> that the Sun's rays <u>hit</u> the Earth. This changes the amount of <u>solar radiation</u> (how much of the Sun's <u>energy</u>) the Earth receives. If the Earth receives <u>more energy</u>, it gets <u>warmer</u>.

3) Tilt and wobble also affect how much solar radiation is received at <u>different latitudes</u> at <u>different times of year</u>.

4) Orbital changes may have caused the <u>glacial</u> and <u>interglacial cycles</u> of the <u>Quaternary period</u>.

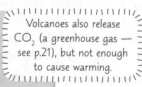

② Sunspots

1) <u>Sunspots</u> are <u>cooler areas</u> of the Sun's surface that are visible as <u>dark patches</u>. They <u>increase</u> the Sun's <u>output</u> of <u>energy</u>.

2) Sunspots come and go in cycles of about <u>11 years</u>. There may also be <u>longer sunspot cycles</u> of several <u>hundreds</u> or <u>thousands</u> of years.

3) Periods when there are <u>very few</u> sunspots and solar output is <u>reduced</u> may cause the Earth's climate to become <u>cooler</u> in <u>some areas</u>.

4) Most <u>scientists</u> think that changes in solar output <u>don't have</u> a <u>major effect</u> on global <u>climate change</u>.

③ Volcanic Activity

1) Major <u>volcanic eruptions</u> eject large quantities of material into the atmosphere.

2) Some of these particles <u>reflect</u> the <u>Sun's rays</u> back out to space, so the Earth's surface <u>cools</u>.

3) Volcanic activity may cause <u>short-term changes</u> in climate, e.g. the <u>cooling</u> that followed the eruption of <u>Mount Pinatubo</u> in 1991.

Volcanoes also release CO_2 (a greenhouse gas — see p.21), but not enough to cause warming.

That's right, even the Sun gets acne from time to time...

These ideas can seem a bit confusing, but don't panic — take your time and go through each one carefully. Basically, the more energy the Earth receives, or gets trapped here, the hotter it gets (and vice versa).

1) Outline two natural factors that can cause climate change   [4]

Causes of Climate Change

Climate may have been changing long before humans roamed the Earth, but in the last 150 years or so human activities have begun to change it too. It's pretty bad, but what's worse is that you have to know all about it.

The Natural Greenhouse Effect is Essential for Keeping Our Planet Warm

1) The temperature of the Earth is a balance between the heat it gets from the Sun and the heat it loses to space.

2) Gases in the atmosphere naturally act like an insulating layer — they trap outgoing heat, helping to keep the Earth at the right temperature.

3) This is called the greenhouse effect ('cos it's a bit like a greenhouse trapping heat).

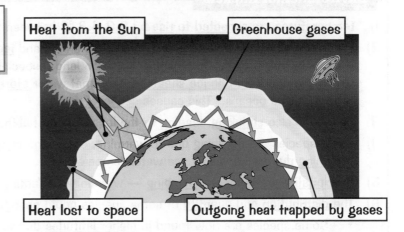

Heat from the Sun

Greenhouse gases

Heat lost to space

Outgoing heat trapped by gases

4) Gases that trap heat are called greenhouse gases — they include carbon dioxide (CO_2) and methane (CH_4).

Human Activities are Contributing to the Greenhouse Effect

1) The rate of the recent rise in global temperature (global warming) is unheard of.

2) There's a scientific consensus (general agreement) that human activities are causing global warming by making the greenhouse effect stronger. This is called the enhanced greenhouse effect.

3) Too much greenhouse gas in the atmosphere means too much energy is trapped and the planet warms up.

4) Humans are increasing the concentration of greenhouse gases by:

Farming

How very dare you!

1) Farming of livestock produces a lot of methane — cows love to fart...

2) Rice paddies contribute to global warming, because flooded fields emit methane.

Cement Production

Cement is made from limestone, which contains carbon. When cement is produced, lots of CO_2 is released into the atmosphere.

Burning Fossil Fuels

CO_2 is released into the atmosphere when fossil fuels like coal, oil, natural gas and petrol are burnt, e.g. in thermal power stations or in cars.

Deforestation

1) Plants remove CO_2 from the atmosphere and convert it into organic matter using photosynthesis.

2) When trees and plants are chopped down, they stop taking in CO_2.

3) CO_2 is also released into the atmosphere when trees are burnt as fuel or to make way for agriculture.

The greenhouse effect — an irresistible urge to throw stones...

Global warming isn't as confusing as you first think — it's just like humans are adding an extra-snuggly duvet around the world. The only thing is, the Earth was happy enough with just one duvet and now it's getting a bit sweaty. Eugh.

Global Effects of Climate Change

Whether <u>human</u> or <u>natural</u> factors are to blame, scientists are <u>pretty sure</u> climate change is having an <u>impact</u>...

Climate Change has Environmental, Economic and Social Impacts

Environmental Impacts

1) Temperatures are <u>expected</u> to <u>rise</u> by <u>0.3-4.8 °C</u> between <u>2005</u> and <u>2100</u>.

2) <u>Warmer</u> temperatures are causing <u>glaciers</u> to <u>shrink</u> and <u>ice sheets</u> like Greenland to <u>melt</u>. The <u>melting</u> of ice on <u>land</u>, especially from the <u>Greenland</u> and <u>Antarctic ice sheets</u>, means that water <u>stored on land</u> as ice <u>returns</u> to the <u>oceans</u>. This causes <u>sea level rise</u>.

3) <u>Sea ice</u> is also <u>shrinking</u>, leading to the loss of polar habitats.

4) Other species are <u>declining</u> due to warming, e.g. some <u>coral reefs</u> are suffering from <u>bleaching</u> due to increasing sea water temperatures.

5) <u>Precipitation patterns</u> are <u>changing</u> — warming is affecting <u>how much rain</u> areas get.

6) The <u>distribution</u> and <u>quantity</u> of some species could change and <u>biodiversity</u> could <u>decrease</u>:
   - Some species are now found in <u>higher latitudes</u> due to warming temperatures.
   - Some <u>habitats</u> are being <u>damaged</u> or <u>destroyed</u> due to climate change — species that are specially <u>adapted</u> to these areas may become <u>extinct</u>.

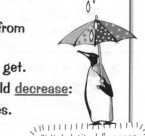
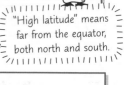

"High latitude" means far from the equator, both north and south.

Economic Impacts

1) Climate change means the <u>weather</u> is getting <u>more extreme</u>. This means <u>more money</u> has to be <u>spent</u> on <u>predicting</u> extreme weather events (e.g. floods, droughts and tropical storms), <u>reducing their impacts</u> and <u>rebuilding after</u> them.

2) Rising temperatures are causing areas of <u>permafrost</u> (see p.48) to melt — this can lead to the <u>collapse</u> of <u>buildings</u>, pipelines etc. built on it. However, it's easier to extract <u>natural resources</u> from <u>unfrozen</u> ground.

3) Climate change is affecting <u>farming</u> in <u>different ways</u> around the <u>world</u>:
   - <u>Globally</u>, some crops have <u>suffered</u> from climate change (e.g. <u>maize crops</u> have got <u>smaller</u> due to <u>warming</u> in recent years).
   - But some farmers in <u>high-latitude countries</u> are finding that crops <u>benefit</u> from warmer conditions.

4) <u>Water shortages</u> might affect our ability to generate <u>power</u> — <u>hydroelectric</u> power and <u>thermal</u> power stations require <u>lots</u> of water.

Social Impacts

1) In some places, reduced rainfall means there's an increased <u>threat</u> from <u>wildfires</u>. These can <u>damage homes</u> and also put people's lives <u>at risk</u>.

2) Some areas could become so <u>hot and dry</u> that they're <u>difficult</u> or <u>impossible</u> to inhabit. <u>Low-lying coastal areas</u> could be <u>lost</u> to the <u>sea</u> or <u>flood</u> so often that they also become <u>impossible</u> to inhabit. This could lead to <u>migration</u> and <u>overcrowding</u> in other areas.

3) Some areas are <u>struggling</u> to supply <u>enough</u> water for their residents due to <u>problems</u> with <u>water availability</u> caused by changing rainfall patterns. This can lead to <u>political tensions</u>, especially where rivers <u>cross borders</u>.

4) <u>Lower crop yields</u> could <u>increase malnutrition</u>, <u>ill health</u> and <u>death</u> from starvation, particularly in lower latitudes.

The effects of not learning this page include declining mark availability...

Well, that was a cheerful read — a whole load of ways that climate change can affect people, the economy and the environment. But these are exactly the sort of things that might turn up in your exam, so you'd better get learning them.

Effects of Climate Change on the UK

Now, don't you go thinking that the <u>effects</u> of <u>climate change</u> are all happening in a faraway land — the impacts can be felt in the <u>UK</u> too. Grab your <u>sunscreen</u> and an <u>umbrella</u>, and I'll tell you how.

Climate Change *in the UK Causes Environmental Impacts...*

Climate

1) <u>Temperature</u> will <u>increase</u>. The increase is expected to be greatest in southern England, where the average summer temperature is projected to increase by 3.9 °C by 2080.

2) <u>Winter rainfall</u> is expected to <u>increase</u> by 16% in parts of the western side of the UK.

3) <u>Summer rainfall</u> is expected to <u>decrease</u> by 23% in parts of southern England.

Extreme Events

1) Droughts are expected to be more <u>frequent</u> and <u>intense</u>, especially in <u>southern England</u>.

2) <u>Flooding</u> will become <u>more common</u> due to increased <u>rainfall</u> and <u>sea level rise</u>.

Sea Level Rise

1) Sea level is expected to rise by <u>12-76 cm</u> by 2095.

2) This will lead to the loss of <u>habitats</u>, e.g. <u>saltmarsh</u>.

Wildlife

Climate change will change the UK's habitats. Some species have already left their original habitats and moved <u>north</u> to areas with <u>lower temperatures</u> (e.g. the comma butterfly). This can upset the balance of natural <u>ecosystems</u> (see p.40) and lead to <u>species extinction</u>.

...Economic Impacts...

Tourism

1) Warmer weather in the UK could <u>boost</u> the tourist industry if more people decide to holiday <u>at home</u>.

2) However, in some areas, it could also lead to a <u>decline</u>, e.g. <u>skiing</u> in the <u>Cairngorms</u>.

Agriculture

1) <u>Temperature increase</u> and a <u>longer growing season</u> may increase <u>productivity of some crops</u>, e.g. asparagus, onions, courgettes, peas and beans.

2) New <u>crops adapted</u> to <u>warmer climates</u> could be grown in <u>southern England</u> (e.g. soya and grapes), but <u>reduced rainfall</u> and <u>droughts</u> would increase the need for irrigation and water storage schemes.

Fishing

1) The <u>UK fishing industry</u> could also be affected — more <u>extreme</u> UK weather conditions could put <u>fishing infrastructure</u> (e.g. ports, boats) at risk from storm damage.

2) Fishermen's <u>livelihoods</u> could be affected by changing <u>fish populations</u> and <u>species</u> found in UK waters.

...and Social Impacts

Health

Deaths from <u>cold-related</u> illnesses may decrease, but health services may have to treat more <u>heat-related</u> illnesses, e.g. <u>heat exhaustion</u>.

Water Shortages

<u>Drier summers</u> will affect water availability, particularly in areas of south east England where <u>population density</u> is <u>increasing</u>.

Floods

Flooding from increased rainfall and sea level rise might damage <u>homes</u> and <u>businesses</u>, especially those on <u>estuaries</u> (e.g. in cities such as Hull, Cardiff, Portsmouth and London) and <u>low lying areas near the coast</u> (e.g. large areas of Norfolk).

All this talk of climate change has got me hot and bothered...

...and there's nothing I like more than cooling off with some exam practice.

1) Describe two potential impacts of global warming in the UK.   [4]

Revision Summary

This section may be short, but there's nothing sweet about it. Never mind rising temperatures, just reading about the effects of climate change has made me break into a sweat. Still, at least you can avoid a disaster in the exam by learning this topic really well. Have a go at these questions a few at a time and check you can answer them all confidently.

Evidence for Climate Change (p.19) ☑

1) What is the Quaternary period?
2) Describe how climate has changed from the beginning of the Quaternary period to the present day.
3) Why are ice cores a useful source of information about past climate?
4) How do sea ice positions provide evidence for climate change?
5) Describe how diary entries and paintings can give evidence of climate change.
6) Why might data provided by weather stations be unreliable as a record of global climate?

Causes of Climate Change (p.20-21) ☑

7) a) What are Milankovitch cycles?
   b) How do they affect the Earth's climate?
8) How might sunspots affect the Earth's climate?
9) Describe how volcanic activity might cause climate change.
10) What is the natural greenhouse effect?
11) Name two greenhouse gases.
12) What is the enhanced greenhouse effect?
13) Give four ways that human activities increase the concentration of greenhouse gases in the atmosphere.

Global Effects of Climate Change (p.22) ☑

14) What effect might increasing temperatures have on polar habitats?
15) How might species distribution be affected by climate change?
16) Outline the possible global economic impacts of extreme weather.
17) Describe one possible economic impact of climate change on areas of permafrost.
18) Give one possible social impact of sea level rise.
19) Give one way that climate change might have an impact on health.

Effects of Climate Change on the UK (p.23) ☑

20) Give two ways that extreme weather events in the UK might be affected by climate change.
21) Give one possible environmental impact of sea level rise in the UK.
22) How might climate change affect tourism in the UK?
23) Outline the possible economic impacts of climate change on agriculture in the UK.
24) How might the UK fishing industry be affected by climate change?
25) Describe one social impact of climate change in the UK.

The UK Landscape

Ah, the UK landscape. Majestic <u>mountains</u>, luscious <u>lowlands</u> and rugged <u>rocks</u> — I could go on all day...

A *Landscape* is *Characterised* by *Specific Geographic Features*

1) <u>Landscapes</u> are made up of all the <u>visible features</u> of an area of land.
2) A landscape with more <u>physical</u> features, such as mountains or forest, is described as a <u>natural landscape</u>.
3) If a landscape has more visible <u>human</u> features, like a town or a city, it's described as a <u>built landscape</u>.

Natural landscape

Built landscape

The UK's *Upland* and *Lowland* Areas Have Distinctive *Characteristics*

1) The UK's natural landscape can be split into <u>upland</u>, <u>lowland</u> and <u>glaciated</u> landscapes.
2) The <u>geology</u>, <u>climate</u> and <u>land uses</u> in these landscapes give them <u>distinctive characteristics</u>.

Upland Areas

* These are mostly found in the <u>north</u> and <u>west</u> of the UK.
* They are generally formed of <u>harder</u> rocks which <u>resist erosion</u>, e.g. slate, granite and some limestones.
* Many are <u>glaciated</u> landscapes, e.g. Snowdonia.
* The <u>gradient</u> of the land is often <u>steep</u>.
* The climate tends to be <u>cooler</u> and <u>wetter</u>.
* The <u>harsh climate</u> and <u>thin soils</u> allow rough vegetation to thrive, and some upland areas are used for <u>forestry</u>.
* Land uses include <u>sheep farming</u>, <u>quarrying</u> and <u>tourism</u>.

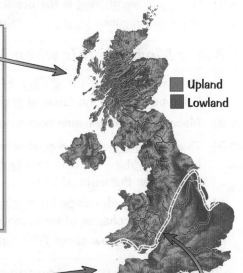

Upland
Lowland

Lowland Areas

* These are mostly found in the <u>south</u> and <u>east</u>.
* They are generally formed from <u>softer</u> rocks, e.g. chalk, clay and some sandstones.
* The landscape is <u>flatter</u> with gently rolling hills.
* The climate tends to be <u>warmer</u> and <u>drier</u>.
* Vegetation grows easily in the more <u>fertile soils</u> and includes <u>grassy meadows</u> and <u>deciduous forests</u> (see page 43).
* Land uses include <u>quarrying</u> and <u>tourism</u>, as well as <u>dairy</u> and <u>arable</u> farming (growing crops).
* Most <u>urban areas</u> and <u>industries</u> (e.g. factories) are located in lowland areas.

Glaciated Landscapes

* During the last <u>glacial period</u> (p.19), <u>ice</u> covered the UK roughly as far <u>south</u> as this line, so <u>glaciated landscapes</u> are mostly found in <u>upland areas</u> in the <u>north-west</u> of the UK.
* Ice is very <u>powerful</u>, so it was able to <u>erode</u> the landscape, carving out <u>valleys</u>. It also <u>deposited</u> lots of material as it <u>melted</u>.
* Landscapes formed by <u>glacial meltwater</u> and <u>deposits</u> extend <u>south</u> of this line.

I think you'll find the UK portrait is much easier to fit on a page...

This is a nice little introduction to the distinctive landscapes section. You can actually revise it by looking through your holiday snaps. Or by gazing at a lovely map... Though you should really read this page too.

Weathering and Erosion

Weathering and erosion are examples of geomorphic processes. Geomorphic is a big ol' word, but these are just processes which change the shape of a landscape and create landforms.

Rock is Broken Down by Mechanical and Chemical Weathering

1) Mechanical weathering is the breakdown of rock without changing its chemical composition. The main type of mechanical weathering that affects landscapes in the UK is freeze-thaw weathering:

> 1) It happens when the temperature alternates above and below 0 °C (the freezing point of water).
> 2) Water gets into rock that has cracks, e.g. granite. When the water freezes it expands, which puts pressure on the rock. When the water thaws it contracts, which releases the pressure on the rock.
> 3) Repeated freezing and thawing widens the cracks and causes the rock to break up.

Salt weathering is a similar process caused by the build-up of salt crystals deposited in cracks by waves.

2) Chemical weathering is the breakdown of rock by changing its chemical composition. Carbonation weathering is a type of chemical weathering that happens in warm and wet conditions:

> 1) Rainwater has carbon dioxide dissolved in it, which makes it a weak carbonic acid.
> 2) Carbonic acid reacts with rock that contains calcium carbonate, e.g. carboniferous limestone, so the rocks are dissolved by the rainwater.

3) Biological weathering is the breakdown of rocks by living things, e.g. plant roots break down rocks by growing into cracks on their surfaces and pushing them apart.

Mass Movement is when Material Falls Down a Slope

1) Mass movement is the shifting of rocks and loose material down a slope, e.g. a cliff or valley side. It happens when the force of gravity acting on a slope is greater than the force supporting it.

2) Mass movements cause coasts to retreat rapidly.

3) They're more likely to happen when the material is full of water — it acts as a lubricant, and makes the material heavier.

4) Undercutting of a slope by erosion will increase the chance of mass movement.

5) You need to know about TWO types of mass movement.

Slides: Material shifts in a straight line

Slumps: Material shifts with a rotation

There are Four Processes of Erosion

The same four processes of erosion occur along coasts and in river channels:

1) Hydraulic action — along coasts waves crash against rock and compress the air in the cracks. This puts pressure on the rock. Repeated compression widens the cracks and makes bits of rock break off. In rivers, the force of the water breaks rock particles away from the river channel.

2) Abrasion — eroded particles in the water scrape and rub against rock in the sea bed, cliffs or river channel, removing small pieces and wearing them away. Most erosion in rivers happens by abrasion.

3) Attrition — eroded particles in the water smash into each other and break into smaller fragments. Their edges also get rounded off as they rub together. The further material travels, the more eroded it gets. E.g. attrition causes particle size to decrease between a river's source and its mouth.

4) Solution — dissolved carbon dioxide makes river and sea water slightly acidic. The acid reacts chemically with some rocks e.g. chalk and limestone, dissolving them.

If you find yourself slumping — have a little break from revision...

This page is packed full of information, but it's really only about how coasts and river channels are worn away and rocks are broken down into smaller pieces. Smash revision to bits by learning these processes one at a time.

Transportation and Deposition

Material that has been <u>eroded</u> gets <u>pushed around</u> and <u>moved</u> from place to place before finally being <u>dumped</u> somewhere. It's a hard life being a <u>rock</u>, I tell you. There's just no respect.

Transportation is the Movement of Eroded Material

<u>Eroded</u> material is moved by <u>rivers</u> and the <u>sea</u>. There are <u>four processes</u> of transportation:

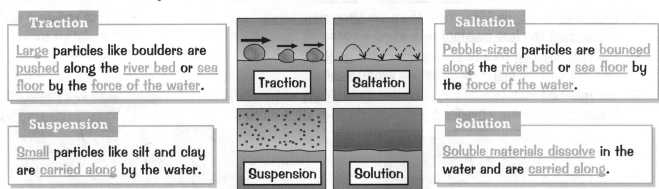

Traction
<u>Large</u> particles like boulders are <u>pushed</u> along the <u>river bed</u> or <u>sea floor</u> by the <u>force of the water</u>.

Saltation
<u>Pebble-sized</u> particles are <u>bounced along</u> the <u>river bed</u> or <u>sea floor</u> by the <u>force of the water</u>.

Suspension
<u>Small</u> particles like silt and clay are <u>carried along</u> by the water.

Solution
<u>Soluble materials dissolve</u> in the water and are <u>carried along</u>.

Deposition is the Dropping of Material

Deposition is when <u>material</u> being <u>carried</u> by sea water or a river is <u>dropped</u>. It occurs when water carrying sediment <u>loses velocity</u> (<u>slows down</u>) so that it isn't moving <u>fast enough</u> to carry so much sediment.

1 Coastal Deposition

1) Waves that <u>deposit more material</u> than they <u>erode</u> are called <u>constructive waves</u>.
   - Constructive waves have a <u>low frequency</u> (6-8 waves per minute).
   - They're <u>low</u> and <u>long</u>.
   - The <u>swash</u> (the movement of water <u>up the beach</u>) is <u>powerful</u> and it <u>carries material up the coast</u>.
   - The <u>backwash</u> (the movement of water <u>down the beach</u>) is <u>weaker</u> and it <u>doesn't</u> take a lot of material <u>back down the coast</u>. This means there's <u>lots of deposition</u> and <u>very little erosion</u>.

> Low, long wave
> Backwash
> Swash

2) The <u>amount of material</u> that's <u>deposited</u> on an area of coast is <u>increased</u> when:
   - There's <u>lots</u> of <u>erosion</u> elsewhere on the coast, so there's <u>lots of material available</u>.
   - There's <u>lots</u> of <u>transportation</u> of material <u>into</u> the area.

2 River Deposition

There are a <u>few reasons</u> why rivers slow down and deposit material. Deposition in rivers occurs when:
- The <u>volume</u> of <u>water</u> in the river <u>falls</u>.
- The <u>amount</u> of <u>eroded material</u> in the water <u>increases</u>.
- The water is <u>shallower</u>, e.g. on the <u>inside of a bend</u>.
- The river <u>reaches</u> the sea or a lake at its mouth.

Oi!

I can't bear the suspension — just go ahead and dump me...

There are lots of similar names to remember here — try not to confuse saltation, solution and suspension. And yes, confusingly, solution is both a process of erosion and transportation. Now try this question...

1) Describe the process of traction. [2]

EXAM QUESTION

Coastal Landforms

Erosion by waves forms many coastal landforms over long periods of time. But don't worry, you don't have to sit around for thousands of years to see what happens, it can all be explained with a few simple diagrams.

Headlands and Bays Form Where Erosion Resistance is Different

1) Some types of rocks are more resistant to erosion than others.

2) Headlands and bays form where there are alternating bands of resistant and less resistant rock along a coast.

3) The less resistant rock (e.g. clay) is eroded quickly and this forms a bay — bays have a gentle slope.

4) The resistant rock (e.g. chalk) is eroded more slowly and it's left jutting out, forming a headland — headlands have steep sides.

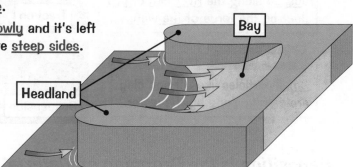

■ = Less resistant rock
■ = Resistant rock
⇀ = Erosion

Cardigan Bay, Wales

Headlands are Eroded to form Caves, Arches and Stacks

1) Headlands are usually made of resistant rocks that have weaknesses like cracks.

2) Waves crash into the headlands and enlarge the cracks — mainly by hydraulic power and abrasion.

3) Repeated erosion and enlargement of the cracks causes a cave to form.

4) Continued erosion deepens the cave until it breaks through the headland — forming an arch, e.g. Durdle Door in Dorset.

5) Erosion continues to wear away the rock supporting the arch, until it eventually collapses.

6) This forms a stack — an isolated rock that's separate from the headland, e.g. Old Harry in Dorset.

Durdle Door, Dorset

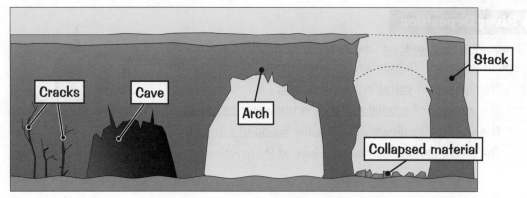

Cracks | Cave | Arch | Stack | Collapsed material

Erosion and gravity — they've always been arch enemies...

Some lovely coastal features here, formed as a result of erosion. Learning the diagrams will give you a helping hand in the exam to explain how each feature is formed. But make sure you can explain it clearly using words too.

Coastal Landforms

Here are some more exciting <u>landforms</u> for you to learn about. This time it's all about <u>deposition</u>. Unfortunately you're going to be slightly disappointed — sandcastles won't be in the exam.

Beaches *are formed by Deposition*

1) Beaches are found on coasts <u>between</u> the <u>high water mark</u> (the <u>highest point on the land</u> the <u>sea level</u> gets to) and the <u>low water mark</u> (the <u>lowest point</u> on the land the <u>sea level</u> gets to).

2) They're formed by <u>constructive waves</u> (see p. 27) depositing material like <u>sand</u> and <u>shingle</u>.

3) <u>Sand</u> and <u>shingle beaches</u> have different <u>characteristics</u>:

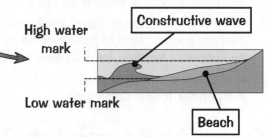

- <u>Sand</u> beaches are <u>flat</u> and <u>wide</u> — sand particles are <u>small</u> and the weak backwash <u>can</u> move them <u>back down</u> the beach, creating a <u>long</u>, <u>gentle slope</u>.
- <u>Shingle</u> beaches are <u>steep</u> and <u>narrow</u> — shingle particles are <u>large</u> and the weak backwash <u>can't</u> move them back down the beach. The shingle particles <u>build up</u> and create a <u>steep slope</u>.

Longshore Drift **can form** *Spits* **at Bends** *in the Coastline*

1) <u>Spits</u> are just <u>beaches</u> that <u>stick out</u> into the sea — they're <u>joined</u> to the coast at <u>one end</u>. Spits form at <u>sharp bends</u> in the coastline, e.g. at a <u>river mouth</u>.

2) Spits are formed by <u>longshore drift</u> — a process that moves material <u>along coasts</u>:

1) <u>Waves</u> follow the <u>direction</u> of the <u>prevailing</u> (most common) <u>wind</u>.

2) They usually hit the coast at an <u>oblique angle</u> (any angle that <u>isn't a right angle</u>).

3) The <u>swash</u> carries material <u>up the beach</u>, in the <u>same direction as the waves</u>.

4) The <u>backwash</u> then carries material <u>down the beach</u> at <u>right angles</u>, back towards the sea.

5) Over time, material <u>zigzags</u> along the coast.

3) <u>Longshore drift</u> transports sand and shingle <u>past</u> the bend and <u>deposits</u> it in the sea.

4) Strong winds and waves can <u>curve</u> the end of the spit (forming a <u>recurved end</u>).

5) The <u>sheltered area</u> behind the spit is <u>protected from waves</u> — lots of material <u>accumulates</u> in this area, which means <u>plants</u> can grow there.

6) <u>Over time</u>, the sheltered area can become a <u>mud flat</u> or a <u>salt marsh</u>.

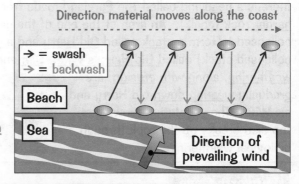

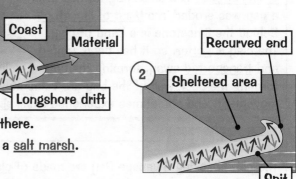

Depositing material on a beach? Sounds like littering to me.

Spits in geography have a very specific meaning. Don't get the wrong one and make a mess of your book.

1) Explain how spits are formed. You may include a diagram in your answer. [2]

UK Coastal Landscape — Case Study

If coastal landforms are your thing (and let's face it, how could they not be), then the Dorset coast is paradise on Earth. It's got the lot — headlands, bays, arches, stacks, coves, lagoons...

The Dorset Coast is a Popular Tourist Destination in Southern England

1) The Dorset coast is located on the south coast of England.

2) It is called the Jurassic Coast because it has lots of fossils dating from the Jurassic period. Lots of people come to the area to hunt for fossils, and it's an important location for scientists studying geology.

3) It also has a variety of coastal landforms, including sandy beaches, making it a popular tourist destination.

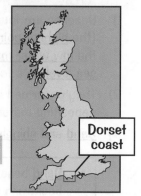

Dorset coast

Geomorphic Processes have Created a Variety of Landforms

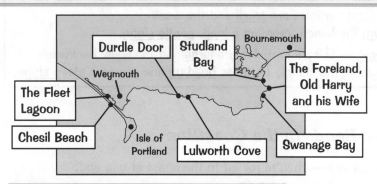

Durdle Door • Studland Bay • Bournemouth • The Foreland, Old Harry and his Wife • Weymouth • The Fleet Lagoon • Chesil Beach • Isle of Portland • Lulworth Cove • Swanage Bay

Durdle Door

Durdle Door is a great example of an arch (see page 28). It formed on a hard limestone headland. Erosion by waves opened up a crack in the headland, which became a cave and then developed into an arch. The arch is being gradually broken down by mechanical, chemical and biological weathering.

The Foreland, Old Harry and his Wife

In between two areas of softer rock that have formed bays, there is a headland called The Foreland made from a band of harder rock (chalk). An arch at the end of the headland has collapsed to form a stack called Old Harry and a stump (a collapsed stack) called Old Harry's Wife. Salt and carbonation weathering, along with erosion, are gradually wearing down old Harry and his Wife. The vegetation growing on top also breaks up the rock through biological weathering.

Chesil Beach

Chesil Beach is a tombolo (a type of spit that extends out to an island). It joins the Isle of Portland to the mainland. It has been formed by longshore drift. Behind Chesil Beach is a shallow lagoon called The Fleet Lagoon.

Lulworth Cove

Lulworth Cove is a small bay formed after a gap was eroded in a band of limestone. Behind the limestone is a band of clay. The clay is softer, so it has been eroded and transported away, forming the bay. The limestone cliffs forming the back wall of the bay are vulnerable to mass movement, and sometimes experience small slides and slumps.

Swanage Bay

The cliffs backing Swanage Bay are made of clay, which is a soft rock. Towards the northern end of the bay, the cliffs are covered in vegetation, stabilising them and protecting them from weathering. Elsewhere, the cliffs are not stabilised by vegetation, so wet weather weakens them and can cause slumps. Longshore drift carries material (mainly gravel) from the south to the north of the beach in the bay. Overall, erosion is the dominant process in the bay — the beach has been losing material for decades.

UK Coastal Landscape — Case Study

Climate *and* Weather *influence* Geomorphic Processes *on the Dorset Coast...*

There are several <u>climate</u> and <u>weather</u> factors that affect how <u>weathering</u> and <u>erosion</u> shape the Dorset coast:

Temperature

1) The Dorset coast has <u>warm</u>, <u>dry</u> summers (around 21 °C in July) and <u>mild</u> and <u>wet</u> winters (average minimum temperature in January is about 3 °C).

2) <u>Salt weathering</u> is the dominant form of <u>mechanical</u> weathering, particularly in summer. The warm temperatures cause sea water to evaporate from rocks <u>quickly</u>, leaving a <u>build-up</u> of salt crystals in tiny <u>cracks</u> in the rock.

3) The <u>mild</u> winters mean that <u>freeze-thaw weathering</u> is <u>less common</u> because it's usually <u>not cold enough</u> for ice to form.

Wind

1) The Dorset coast's <u>location</u> means that it's <u>exposed</u> to <u>prevailing winds</u> from the <u>south-west</u>.

2) These prevailing winds can bring <u>storms</u> to the UK from the <u>Atlantic Ocean</u>. Storms bring <u>high energy</u>, <u>destructive</u> waves which <u>increase erosion</u> of the cliffs.

3) <u>Hydraulic action</u> and <u>abrasion</u> both increase during a storm and <u>erode</u> the <u>base</u> of the cliffs. This makes the cliffs <u>unstable</u>, making <u>mass movement</u> more likely to happen.

Rainfall

1) The Dorset coast receives relatively <u>low amounts</u> of rainfall <u>annually</u>, but can experience <u>very wet winters</u>, with rainfall <u>heaviest</u> during <u>storm periods</u>.

2) Soils and rocks become <u>heavier</u> when they're <u>saturated</u>, which can make them more prone to <u>mass movement</u>.

3) In <u>January 2016</u>, <u>intense</u> rainfall combined with <u>high-energy</u> waves during Storm Frank to cause the collapse of cliffs between <u>Burton Bradstock</u> and <u>West Bay</u>.

...and so does Geology

1) The coastline is made from bands of <u>hard rock</u> and <u>soft rock</u>. The rocks have been <u>eroded at different rates</u>, which has created the area's coastal landforms, e.g. <u>Lulworth Cove</u>.

2) <u>Soft rock</u> like sandstone and clay are <u>easily eroded</u> by hydraulic action and abrasion.

Soft **Kimmeridge**
Hard
Soft
Soft **Hard**
Lulworth Cove
Swanage Bay

Key
☐ Clay and sandstone
◻ Chalk
■ Limestone
▨ Clay

3) The harder <u>chalk</u> and <u>limestone</u> cliffs are <u>weathered</u> and <u>eroded</u> more <u>slowly</u>, meaning that they stick out into the sea as exposed <u>headlands</u>. <u>Chalk</u> and <u>limestone</u> are vulnerable to erosion by <u>solution</u>, where the sea water <u>chemically reacts</u> with the rock, causing it to <u>dissolve</u>.

4) Weathering tends to happen <u>gradually</u> and cause <u>small changes</u>. Erosion can happen more <u>suddenly</u> on a <u>much larger</u> scale. A single storm can cause <u>large amounts</u> of erosion along a big stretch of the coast.

Geology, Climate *and* Weather *can also* Interact

1) It's often a <u>combination</u> of <u>climatic</u> and <u>geological</u> factors that affect how erosion and weathering <u>shape</u> the landscape.

2) Lots of <u>rain</u> makes <u>chalk</u> and <u>limestone</u> vulnerable to <u>carbonation weathering</u> because the rain water is <u>slightly acidic</u>.

3) <u>Prolonged heavy rain</u> causes clay to become heavier, <u>softer</u> and more <u>slippery</u>, making <u>mass movement</u> more <u>likely</u>. During the winter, when there is more <u>rainfall</u>, there are often <u>slides</u> and <u>slumps</u> on the clay cliffs.

Mudslides and rock falls near Kimmeridge

Topic 3 — Distinctive Landscapes

UK Coastal Landscape — Case Study

Coastal Management Strategies are Protecting the Coastline

1) Areas of the Dorset coast are being eroded, putting properties and infrastructure at risk. There is also danger to people from landslides and rockfalls.

2) Coastal management strategies have been used to protect the coastline for roughly the last 150 years.

3) These management strategies have helped prevent erosion in some areas, but they have impacted the landscape and caused changes to the natural environment.

Groynes

1) Groynes are wooden or stone fences that are built at right angles to the coast.

2) They trap material transported by longshore drift. This creates wider beaches which slow the waves, giving greater protection from erosion.

3) New timber groynes were put in place along Swanage beach in 2005-6. They've helped to stop the loss of beach material.

4) However, by stopping beach material from moving along the coast, they've starved areas further down the coast of sediment, making them narrower. Narrow beaches don't protect the coast as well, so there may be more erosion.

Sea Walls

1) There are concrete sea walls in place along most of Swanage beach.

2) Sea walls reflect waves back out to sea, preventing the erosion of the coast.

3) But they can create a strong backwash, which removes sediment from the beach and can erode under the wall.

4) They also prevent the cliffs from being eroded, so there's no new material to replenish the beach. This will gradually lower the level of the beach.

Beach Replenishment

1) In winter 2005/2006, sand and shingle dredged from the sea bed at Poole Harbour was added to the upper parts of Swanage beach.

2) This has created wider beaches, which slow the waves and help protect cliffs and coastal properties from erosion.

3) However, it cost £5 million to replenish the beach and it will need to be repeated roughly every 20 years.

Industry and Tourism are also Shaping the Landscape

1) A lot of quarrying has taken place along the coast because limestone is a valuable building stone. There are a number of quarries on the Isle of Portland and to the west of Chesil Beach. Quarries expose large areas of rock, making them vulnerable to chemical weathering and erosion.

2) Up until the 1960s, gravel was removed from Chesil Beach for use in the construction industry. Material was removed from the beach much more quickly than the sea could replenish it, so this began to damage the landform.

3) The Dorset coast attracts large numbers of tourists every year. Coastal footpaths run along the cliff tops, and are gradually worn down as people repeatedly walk on them. Vegetation along the cliff top may be trampled and worn away by repeated use of the footpaths. This can expose the underlying soil and rock to weathering and erosion by wind and rain.

I heard Chesil Beach was actually formed by some bored sculptors...

Old Harry's actually on to his second wife. His first wife collapsed into the sea in 1896. It was sad, but she would've wanted him to move on. You don't have to learn about Dorset if you've studied a different example in class. But before you go on, make sure you know the ins and outs of the landforms, physical processes and human impacts in your chosen area.

Topic 3 — Distinctive Landscapes

River Landforms

Weathering, erosion, transport and deposition combine to produce the characteristic landforms of rivers. But before we float away to visit those lovely landforms, here's some basic river terminology...

A River Basin is an Area of Land Drained by a River

1) A river basin is the area of land surrounding a river, where any rain falling on the land eventually makes its way into that river. This area is also called the river's catchment.

2) River basins are separated by a boundary called a watershed. They're ridges of high land — water falling either side of these ridges will go into different river basins.

3) Here are a few of the key features of a river basin:

> • A tributary is a smaller river (e.g. a stream) that joins a main river.
> • The source is where a river starts, usually in an upland area (e.g. mountains).
> • The mouth is where a river flows into the sea or a lake.

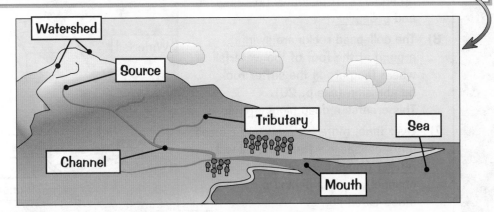

4) The path of a river as it flows downhill is called its course.

5) Rivers have an upper course (closest to the source of the river), a middle course and a lower course (closest to the mouth of the river).

6) Rivers form channels and valleys as they flow downhill.

7) They erode the landscape — wear it down, then transport the material to somewhere else where it's deposited.

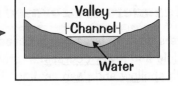

8) The shape of the valley and channel changes along the river depending on whether erosion or deposition is the dominant process.

V-Shaped Valleys are Formed by Vertical Erosion in the Upper Course

1) In the upper course of a river, fast-flowing water following heavy rain and high turbulence causes loose rough particles and boulders to be transported by the river and scraped along the river bed.

2) This causes downwards erosion of the river channel by the process of abrasion.

3) The valley sides are exposed to weathering (e.g. by freeze-thaw). The weathered material that falls down the valley sides into the river channel causes further erosion by abrasion.

4) The river doesn't have enough energy to erode sideways (laterally), so vertical erosion of the river bed is dominant, which deepens the river valley, creating a steep-sided V-shape.

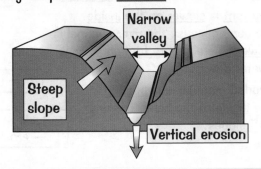

The river channel — every geographer's TV choice...

Well that was a splendid introduction to the watery world of rivers. Some of it may seem like basic stuff, but there are more landforms and river basins coming up, so a good understanding of river terminology will really help.

River Landforms

If you don't know anything about <u>waterfalls</u> then you haven't been watching enough <u>shampoo adverts</u>. Now's your chance to find out all about them as well as some beautifully bendy <u>meanders</u>.

Waterfalls and Gorges are Found in the Upper Course of a River

1) <u>Waterfalls</u> form where a river flows over an area of <u>hard rock</u> followed by an area of <u>softer rock</u>.

2) The <u>softer rock</u> is <u>eroded</u> (by <u>hydraulic action</u> and <u>abrasion</u>) <u>more</u> than the <u>hard rock</u>, creating a '<u>step</u>' in the river.

3) As water goes over the step it <u>erodes more and more</u> of the softer rock.

4) A <u>steep drop</u> is eventually created, which is called a <u>waterfall</u>.

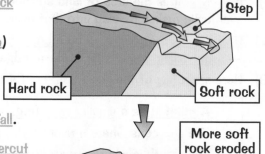

5) The <u>hard rock</u> is eventually <u>undercut</u> by erosion. It becomes <u>unsupported</u> and <u>collapses</u>.

6) The collapsed rocks are <u>swirled around</u> at the foot of the waterfall where they <u>erode</u> the softer rock by <u>abrasion</u> (see p. 26). This creates a deep <u>plunge pool</u>.

7) Over time, <u>more undercutting</u> causes <u>more collapses</u>. The waterfall will <u>retreat</u> (move back up the channel), leaving behind a steep-sided <u>gorge</u>.

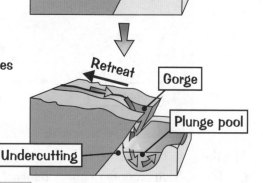

Meanders are Formed by Erosion and Deposition

Rivers develop <u>large bends</u> called <u>meanders</u> in their <u>middle</u> and <u>lower courses</u>, in areas where there are both <u>shallow</u> and <u>deep</u> sections in the channel:

1) The <u>current</u> (the flow of the water) is <u>faster</u> on the <u>outside</u> of the bend because the river channel is <u>deeper</u> (there's <u>less friction</u> to <u>slow</u> the water down).

2) So more <u>erosion</u> takes place on the <u>outside</u> of the bend, forming <u>river cliffs</u>.

3) The <u>current</u> is <u>slower</u> on the <u>inside</u> of the bend because the river channel is <u>shallower</u> (there's <u>more friction</u> to <u>slow</u> the water down).

4) So eroded material is <u>deposited</u> on the <u>inside</u> of the bend, forming <u>slip-off slopes</u>.

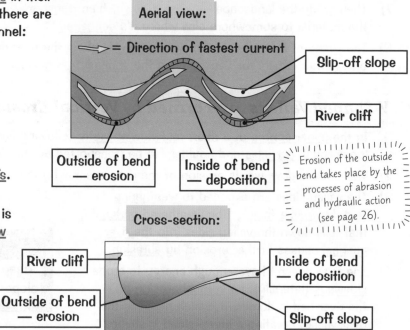

Erosion of the outside bend takes place by the processes of abrasion and hydraulic action (see page 26).

Some river landforms are beautiful — others are gorge-ous...

Step over the hard rock and plunge into the pool — that's how I remember how waterfalls are formed. Geography examiners love river landforms (they're a bit weird like that) so make sure you learn how they form.

River Landforms

When <u>rivers dump material</u> they don't do it by text message — they make attractive <u>landforms</u> instead. But before we get to that, a little bit more on what can happen to <u>meanders</u>...

Ox-Bow Lakes *are Formed from* Meanders

Meanders get <u>larger</u> over time — they can eventually turn into an <u>ox-bow lake</u>:

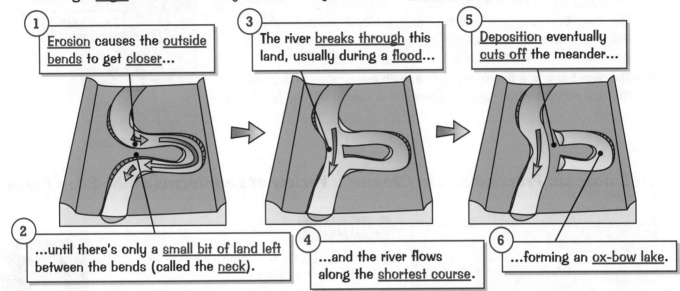

1 <u>Erosion</u> causes the <u>outside</u> <u>bends</u> to get <u>closer</u>...

2 ...until there's only a <u>small bit of land left</u> between the bends (called the <u>neck</u>).

3 The river <u>breaks through</u> this land, usually during a <u>flood</u>...

4 ...and the river flows along the <u>shortest course</u>.

5 <u>Deposition</u> eventually <u>cuts off</u> the meander...

6 ...forming an <u>ox-bow lake</u>.

Floodplains *are Flat Areas* of Land that Flood

1) The <u>floodplain</u> is the <u>wide valley floor</u> on either side of a river which occasionally <u>gets flooded</u>.

2) When a river <u>floods</u> onto the floodplain, the water <u>slows down</u> and <u>deposits</u> the <u>eroded material</u> that it's <u>transporting</u>. This <u>builds up</u> the floodplain (makes it <u>higher</u>).

3) <u>Meanders migrate</u> (move) <u>across</u> the floodplain, making it <u>wider</u>.

4) Meanders also migrate <u>downstream</u>, <u>flattening</u> out the valley floor.

5) The <u>deposition</u> that happens on the <u>slip-off slopes</u> of meanders also <u>builds up</u> the floodplain.

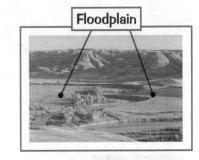
Floodplain

Floodplains and levees are found in the lower course of a river.

Levees *are Natural Embankments*

1) Levees are <u>natural embankments</u> (raised bits) along the <u>edges</u> of a <u>river channel</u>.

2) During a flood, <u>eroded material</u> is <u>deposited</u> over the whole floodplain.

3) The <u>heaviest material</u> is <u>deposited closest</u> to the river channel, because it gets <u>dropped first</u> when the river <u>slows down</u>.

4) <u>Over time</u>, the <u>deposited material builds up</u>, creating <u>levees</u> along the edges of the channel, e.g. along the Yellow River (Huang He River) in China.

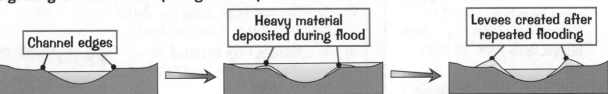

Channel edges

Heavy material deposited during flood

Levees created after repeated flooding

Oh, I just love a levee — it must be my cheery deposition...

EXAM QUESTION

OK, last few river landforms to learn. Cover the page and scribble down the steps in their formation.

1) Describe the process of formation of river levees. [3]

UK River Basin — Case Study

Grab a <u>paddle</u> and hold on to your <u>hat</u> — it's time for a <u>voyage</u> along some <u>northern rivers</u>.

The Eden Basin is in North-West England

1) The <u>Eden basin</u> is in <u>north-west England</u>, between the <u>mountains</u> of the <u>Lake District</u> and the <u>Pennines</u>.

2) The River Eden's <u>source</u> is in the Pennine hills in south Cumbria. It flows north-west through <u>Appleby-in-Westmorland</u> and <u>Carlisle</u>. Its mouth is in the <u>Solway Firth</u> at the <u>Scottish border</u>.

3) The river basin is a largely <u>rural</u> area, with many <u>scenic</u> landscapes that are popular with <u>tourists</u>. There are a variety of <u>river landforms</u>.

Eden basin

Geomorphic Processes have Created a Variety of Landforms in the Eden Basin

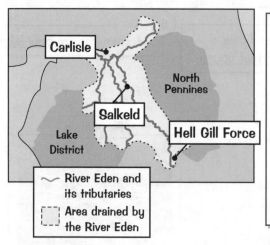

Carlisle

North Pennines

Salkeld

Lake District

Hell Gill Force

~ River Eden and its tributaries

[ ] Area drained by the River Eden

Waterfalls

1) <u>Hell Gill Force</u> is a waterfall near the <u>source</u> of the River Eden.

2) It has formed where there is a <u>change</u> in the <u>rock type</u> from <u>hard limestone</u> to <u>softer sandstone</u>.

3) The water has <u>eroded</u> the <u>soft rock</u>, forming a <u>step</u> in the river channel.

4) <u>Below</u> the waterfall there is a <u>steep-sided gorge</u>, left behind as the waterfall has <u>retreated</u> up the valley.

V-shaped Valleys

1) Many streams flow down the <u>steep slopes</u> of the hillsides at the <u>edge</u> of the basin from about <u>600 m</u> above sea level.

2) <u>Weathering</u> (by freeze-thaw), <u>transportation</u> (traction) and <u>erosion</u> (by abrasion) have carved out steep-sided <u>V-shaped valleys</u>, e.g. in the north-east <u>Lake District</u>.

Meanders

1) As more <u>tributaries</u> join the River Eden, the river gets <u>bigger</u>. This gives it more power to <u>erode</u> the river channel <u>sideways</u>.

2) In the lower course, the river valley becomes <u>wider</u> and <u>flatter</u>, and <u>meanders</u> form on the valley floor, e.g. near <u>Salkeld</u>.

3) As these meanders have <u>grown</u>, some have been <u>cut off</u> to form ox-bow lakes, e.g. where <u>Briggle Beck</u> joins the Eden near Salkeld.

Floodplains

1) <u>Carlisle</u> is built on the <u>floodplain</u> of the River Eden.

2) Here the land is <u>low-lying</u> and <u>flatter</u> (less than 100 m above sea level).

3) As <u>meanders</u> have <u>migrated</u> across the valley floor, the <u>floodplain</u> has become <u>wider</u>.

4) <u>Sediment</u> has also been <u>deposited</u> when the river has <u>flooded</u>, <u>building up</u> the floodplain.

UK River Basin — Case Study

Climate *and* Weather *Influence Geomorphic Processes* in the Eden Basin...

1) Cumbria is on the <u>west coast</u> of the UK, facing the prevailing <u>south-westerly</u> winds.
As a result, Cumbria's <u>climate</u> is <u>mild</u> and <u>wet</u>. The area generally has <u>cool summers</u> and <u>mild winters</u>.

2) Cumbria is one of the <u>wettest</u> parts of the UK*, often experiencing periods of <u>intense rainfall</u>.
Many of the UK's <u>highest rainfall records</u> were recorded in Cumbria.

Temperature

1) Despite the generally <u>mild winters</u>, temperatures can be <u>much colder</u> on <u>higher ground</u>, such as the land around the <u>source</u> of the River Eden. In winter, this higher ground can <u>regularly freeze</u>.

2) During these cold periods, <u>freeze-thaw weathering</u> can slowly break up the <u>exposed rock</u> of the <u>valley sides</u> in the upper course of the river. If the valley sides are <u>weakened</u>, sudden <u>mass movement</u>, such as <u>landslides</u>, becomes more likely.

3) <u>Material</u> from landslides is added to the river's <u>load</u> (the rocks, stones and sediment transported by the river), <u>increasing</u> the <u>erosive power</u> of the river through <u>abrasion</u>.

Rainfall

1) During periods of <u>intense rainfall</u>, the ground becomes <u>saturated</u>. This makes it <u>heavier</u> and <u>less stable</u>. This can cause the <u>river banks</u> to slide or <u>slump</u> into the river channel.

2) Heavy rain can <u>flow quickly</u> over the surface and into the river Eden and its tributaries. This can cause the <u>volume</u> of water in the river to <u>rapidly increase</u>.

3) The high volume of water can <u>increase transportation</u> of material by the river, which can cause <u>more erosion</u> by <u>abrasion</u> — particularly in the <u>upper course</u> of the river.

A landslide near Appleby.

...and so does the Geology of the Area

1) The <u>harder rocks</u> around the edge of the Eden basin have remained as <u>high ground</u> as they are more <u>resistant</u> to <u>erosion</u>. However, exposed <u>limestone</u> is vulnerable to slow <u>carbonation weathering</u> (p. 26).

2) <u>Igneous</u> rocks, such as those found in the west of the Eden basin, tend to be <u>impermeable</u> (i.e. water <u>won't soak</u> into the rock). Because water can't soak into the ground, high rainfall causes lots of <u>surface streams</u> to form, which have a lot of power to erode <u>vertically</u>, creating <u>steep-sided</u> V-shaped valleys.

3) Through the <u>middle</u> and <u>lower courses</u> of the Eden, the river <u>valley</u> is made up of sandstone (a <u>softer</u> rock). The river's increasing volume and <u>energy</u> in its lower course mean that there's lots of <u>lateral</u> (sideways) <u>erosion</u> of the sandstone. This <u>widens</u> the river channel and forms <u>meanders</u> and steep <u>river cliffs</u>.

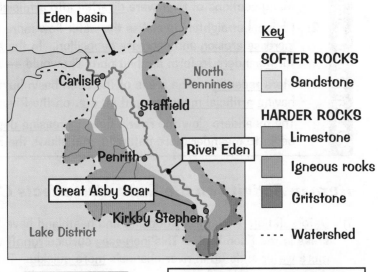

Eden basin

Carlisle

North Pennines

Staffield

River Eden

Penrith

Great Asby Scar

Kirkby Stephen

Lake District

Key

SOFTER ROCKS
☐ Sandstone

HARDER ROCKS
■ Limestone
■ Igneous rocks
■ Gritstone

---- Watershed

Sandstone cliffs near Staffield.

Carbonation weathering of limestone at Great Asby Scar.

*Trust me, I live there.

UK River Basin — Case Study

The River Landscape has been Altered by Management Schemes

The rivers in the Eden basin have been <u>managed</u> to meet the <u>needs</u> of people in the area. <u>Management strategies</u> have affected the geomorphic processes in the <u>river basin</u>.

Flood Walls & Embankments

1) 10 km of <u>raised flood defences</u> (flood walls and embankments) have been built along the Rivers Eden and Caldew in Carlisle.

2) These are designed to <u>contain</u> the water <u>within</u> the river channel, so that the <u>floodplain</u> can be <u>built on</u>.

3) They <u>interrupt</u> the <u>natural processes</u> of the river and can <u>prevent</u> the <u>natural formation</u> of meanders and the <u>deposition</u> of <u>sediment</u> on the <u>floodplain</u>.

Reservoirs

1) <u>Castle Carrock beck</u> (to the south-east of Carlisle) has been <u>dammed</u> to create a <u>reservoir</u>.

2) Reservoirs limit the <u>natural flow</u> of water downstream. Material carried by the river is <u>deposited</u> in the reservoir and not along the river's <u>natural course</u>. This can increase erosion <u>downstream</u>, and <u>reduce</u> the <u>natural buildup</u> of the floodplain in the lower course of the river.

Planting Trees

1) Near Dalston (south of Carlisle), the landscape has been changed by the planting of <u>1000 trees</u> to <u>reduce flooding</u> and also to <u>reduce erosion</u> by stabilising the soil.

2) Trees <u>intercept rainfall</u> and reduce <u>surface runoff</u>. This <u>prevents</u> rapid <u>increases</u> in the <u>volume</u> of water in the river because it takes <u>longer</u> for water to reach the river channel.

3) As a result, the river will have <u>less energy</u>, reducing <u>lateral</u> and <u>vertical</u> <u>erosion</u>, meaning that <u>meanders</u> may take longer to form.

Channel Management

1) In the past, the river landscape in the Eden basin was changed by <u>channel straightening</u>. Many sections of river were <u>diverted</u> into <u>artificial channels</u> to try to <u>reduce</u> flooding.

2) Channel straightening makes the water flow more <u>quickly</u> than it naturally would, which can <u>increase erosion</u> and <u>decrease deposition</u>. In the <u>artificial channel</u>, conditions <u>aren't right</u> for <u>meanders</u> to form as they normally would — so the <u>natural</u> river landscape is changed.

3) More <u>recently</u>, some areas of the Eden basin have been <u>restored</u> to their original state by having <u>artificial meanders</u> put <u>in</u>, e.g. on the River Lyvennet to the south-west of Appleby.

4) The meanders <u>slow</u> the river's flow, <u>increasing deposition</u>. This <u>encourages</u> the river to begin to <u>meander</u> more naturally, and allows the natural build-up of the <u>floodplain</u>.

Human Activity on the Land also affects Geomorphic Processes

1) <u>Deforestation</u> — <u>Natural woodland</u> and <u>heathland</u> have been <u>cleared</u> from many upland areas in the Eden basin. This <u>increases</u> surface <u>runoff</u> when it rains, and means that <u>more water</u> ends up in river channels <u>more quickly</u>. This increase in volume gives rivers more <u>energy</u> for <u>erosion</u>, and can cause <u>sliding</u> and <u>slumping</u> of the river banks.

2) <u>Farming</u> — Some upland areas have been <u>drained</u> of moisture to make them more suitable for farming. This reduces the <u>stability</u> of the soil, meaning that <u>more soil</u> is washed into the river channel by rain. The <u>increased load</u> of the river increases <u>deposition downstream</u>, changing the <u>floodplain landscape</u> from its natural state.

The Eden Basin — a physical geographer's paradise...

Whether you choose this river basin or a different one you've studied, make sure you know the landforms in that basin, and understand how geology, climate and human activity influence the processes that impact the landscape.

Revision Summary

Wat-er load of fun that was. Now it's time to see how much information your brain has soaked up. I think you'll be surprised — I reckon about 16 litres of knowledge has been taken in. Have a go at the questions below and then go back over the topic to check your answers. If something's not quite right, pore over the page again. Once you can answer everything correctly you're ready to sail away, sail away, sail away... to the next topic.

The UK Landscape (p. 25) ☐

1) a) What is a natural landscape?
   b) What is a built landscape?

2) Give three characteristics of upland areas in the UK.

3) Give three characteristics of lowland areas in the UK.

4) Describe the distribution of glaciated landscapes in the UK.

Geomorphic Processes (p. 26-27) ☐

5) How does freeze-thaw weathering break up rock?

6) Describe the process of chemical weathering.

7) What is biological weathering?

8) What are the two types of mass movement?

9) What's the difference between abrasion and attrition?

10) Name two processes of transportation.

11) When does deposition occur in rivers?

Coastal Landforms (p. 28-32) ☑

12) Are headlands made of more or less resistant rock?

13) Describe how erosion can turn a crack in a cliff into a cave.

14) What is a stack?

15) a) Which type of wave allows deposition to occur?
    b) What can increase the amount of material that is deposited?

16) What are the characteristics of shingle beaches?

17) How does longshore drift transport sediment along a coast?

18) Where do spits form?

19) a) For a named coastline, describe the climate of the region.
    b) Explain how geology and climate have affected one of the landforms found there.
    c) Describe one negative impact that human activity has had on the landscape.

River Landforms (p. 33-38) ☐

20) Describe how V-shaped valleys are formed.

21) Where do waterfalls form?

22) How is a gorge formed?

23) a) Where is the current fastest on a meander?
    b) What feature of a meander is formed where the flow is fastest?

24) Name the landform created when a meander is cut off by deposition.

25) Describe the formation of a floodplain.

26) What is a levee?

27) a) For a named river basin, describe how the geology has influenced the landscape.
    b) Describe two landforms that can be found there.
    c) Explain two ways in which human activity has changed the landscape.

Ecosystems

Welcome to a lovely new topic. Take your coat off, sit down and make yourself at home.
Do have a slice of cake — I made it myself. Just relax and I'll tell you all the gossip about ecosystems.

An Ecosystem Includes all the Living and Non-Living Parts in an Area

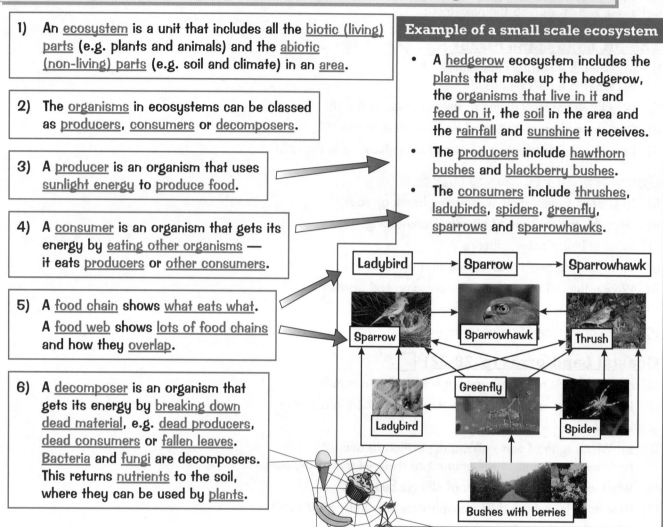

1) An ecosystem is a unit that includes all the biotic (living) parts (e.g. plants and animals) and the abiotic (non-living) parts (e.g. soil and climate) in an area.

2) The organisms in ecosystems can be classed as producers, consumers or decomposers.

3) A producer is an organism that uses sunlight energy to produce food.

4) A consumer is an organism that gets its energy by eating other organisms — it eats producers or other consumers.

5) A food chain shows what eats what. A food web shows lots of food chains and how they overlap.

6) A decomposer is an organism that gets its energy by breaking down dead material, e.g. dead producers, dead consumers or fallen leaves. Bacteria and fungi are decomposers. This returns nutrients to the soil, where they can be used by plants.

Example of a small scale ecosystem

- A hedgerow ecosystem includes the plants that make up the hedgerow, the organisms that live in it and feed on it, the soil in the area and the rainfall and sunshine it receives.

- The producers include hawthorn bushes and blackberry bushes.

- The consumers include thrushes, ladybirds, spiders, greenfly, sparrows and sparrowhawks.

Ladybird → Sparrow → Sparrowhawk

Sparrow | Sparrowhawk | Thrush

Greenfly

Ladybird | Spider

Bushes with berries

The Different Parts of Ecosystems are Interdependent

Some parts of an ecosystem depend on the others, e.g. consumers depend on producers for a source of food and some depend on them for a habitat (a place to live). So, if one part changes it affects all the other parts that depend on it. Here are two hedgerow examples:

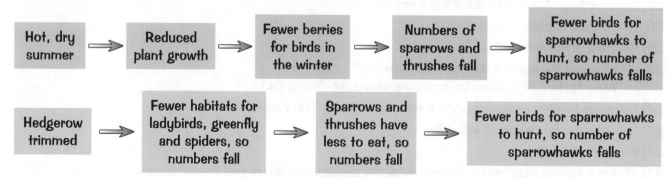

Hot, dry summer ⇒ Reduced plant growth ⇒ Fewer berries for birds in the winter ⇒ Numbers of sparrows and thrushes fall ⇒ Fewer birds for sparrowhawks to hunt, so number of sparrowhawks falls

Hedgerow trimmed ⇒ Fewer habitats for ladybirds, greenfly and spiders, so numbers fall ⇒ Sparrows and thrushes have less to eat, so numbers fall ⇒ Fewer birds for sparrowhawks to hunt, so number of sparrowhawks falls

Food webs — used by spiders everywhere...

Time to see if you really know this page as well as (deep down inside) you know you should:

1) Describe how an increase in rainfall might affect the plants and animals in a hedgerow ecosystem.   [2]

Global Ecosystems

Time for a whistle-stop tour of the world's ecosystems. All aboard...

You Need to Know the Global Distribution of Six Ecosystems

1) The climate in an area determines what type of ecosystem forms. So different parts of the world have different ecosystems because they have different climates.

2) The map shows the global distribution of six types of ecosystem — there are a lot more, but these are some of the major ones.

Coral Reefs
Mostly found between 30° north and south of the equator, a few miles off the coast.

Grassland
There are two types of grassland. Tropical savannah grasslands are found between the tropics. Temperate grasslands are found at mid-latitudes.

Temperate Forest
Found mainly in the mid-latitudes, between the tropics and the polar regions.

Tropic of Cancer, 23.5° N

Equator

Tropic of Capricorn, 23.5° S

Tropical Rainforest
Found around the equator, between the tropics.

Hot Desert
Found between 15° and 35° north and south of the equator.

Polar
Found around the north and south poles.

Plants are sometimes called flora and animals are sometimes called fauna. (I remember it because flora is like floral, meaning flowery.)

Polar Ecosystems are Cold and Dry

Climate

1) Polar areas are very cold. Temperatures are usually less than 10 °C. Winters are normally below −40 °C and can reach almost −90 °C.

2) Rainfall (and snowfall) is low — no more than 500 mm a year (mainly in the summer).

3) There are clearly defined seasons — cold summers and even colder winters.

Animals

1) There are relatively few different species of animals compared with other ecosystems.

2) Polar bears, penguins and marine mammals like whales, seals, and walruses are examples of animals found in polar regions.

Plants

1) There are very few plants — some lichens and mosses are found on rocks, and there are a few grasses and flowering plants on the coast where it's warmer.

2) Plants grow slowly and don't grow very tall — grasses are the most common plants. Closer to the poles, only mosses and lichens can survive.

3) Some small, short trees and shrubs grow in warmer, sheltered areas.

Topic 4 — Sustaining Ecosystems

Global Ecosystems

Hot Deserts **Have Low Rainfall**

Climate

1) There's very little rainfall — less than 250 mm per year. When it rains varies a lot — it might only rain once every two or three years.

2) Temperatures are extreme — they range from very hot in the day (e.g. 45 °C) to cold at night (below 0 °C).

Plants

1) Plant growth is sparse due to the lack of rainfall. Plants that do grow include cacti and thornbushes.

2) Plant roots are often very long to reach deep water supplies, or spread out wide near the surface to catch as much water as possible when it rains. Some plants (e.g. cacti) have fleshy stems and thick, waxy skin to cope with the dry climate.

Animals

1) Hot deserts are home to lizards, snakes, insects and scorpions. Mammals tend to be small, e.g. kangaroo rats. Many birds leave during the hottest weather.

2) Animals are adapted to cope with the harsh climate. Many animals are nocturnal, so they can stay in burrows or in the shade during the day. Some bigger animals have evolved to lose very little water and to tolerate dehydration, e.g. camels.

There are Two Types **of Grassland**

Climate

1) Savannah grasslands have quite low rainfall (800-900 mm per year) and distinct wet and dry seasons. Temperatures are highest (around 35 °C) just before the wet season and lowest (about 15 °C) just after it.

2) Temperate grasslands have hot summers (up to 40 °C) and cold winters (down to −40 °C). They receive 250-500 mm precipitation each year, mostly in the late spring and early summer.

Plants

1) Savannah grasslands consist mostly of grass, scrub and small plants, with a few scattered trees, e.g. acacia tree. Plants are adapted to cope with low levels of rainfall — many have long roots to reach deep water or small, waxy leaves to reduce water loss.

2) Temperate grasslands are also dominated by grasses and small plants. They have very few trees. Grasses often have roots that spread out wide to absorb as much water as possible.

Animals

1) Savannah grasslands are home to lots of insects, including many species of grasshoppers, beetles and termites. Larger animals include lions, elephants, giraffes, zebras and antelope.

2) Temperate grasslands are home to fewer animal species than savannah grasslands. Mammals include bison and wild horses, and rodents such as mole rats.

3) In both types of grassland, grazing animals (e.g. antelope) travel long distances in search of food and water, while other animals (e.g. mole rats) dig burrows to escape the harsh climate.

Coral Reefs Support a Large Number of Animals

Climate

1) Coral reefs are most common in warm areas that receive lots of sunlight.

2) They grow best in shallow, clear, salty water.

Plants

1) Coral reefs form underwater, so few plants grow there.

2) Tiny algae (plant-like organisms) live inside the tissue of corals. The algae and the coral depend on each other for nutrients.

Animals

1) Coral itself is an animal — it's a bit like a sea anemone, but some species create a hard outer coating for protection.

2) Around 25% of all marine species live in coral reefs, including fish, molluscs, sea snakes, turtles and shrimps. Many fish have flat bodies so they can easily swim through and hide in small gaps in the coral.

Global Ecosystems

Temperate Forests Have a Mild, Wet Climate

Climate

1) Temperate forests have <u>four</u> distinct <u>seasons</u> — spring, summer, autumn and winter. The <u>summers</u> are <u>warm</u> and the <u>winters</u> are <u>cool</u>.

2) <u>Rainfall</u> is very <u>high</u> (up to 1500 mm per year) and there's <u>rain all year</u> round.

3) The forests that receive the <u>highest amount of rainfall</u> are sometimes called <u>temperate rainforests</u>.

Animals

1) Temperate forests support lots of different species of <u>mammals</u> (e.g. foxes, squirrels), <u>birds</u> (e.g. woodpeckers, cuckoos) and <u>insects</u> (e.g. beetles, moths).

2) <u>Streams</u> and <u>ponds</u> are <u>habitats</u> for insects (e.g. <u>mosquitoes</u>) to breed. Insects provide food for <u>fish</u>, including trout and salmon.

Plants

Temperate forests have lots of <u>trees</u>. The type of vegetation depends on the <u>type of forest</u>:

- <u>Deciduous forests</u> have <u>broad-leaved trees</u> that <u>drop their leaves</u> in autumn (e.g. oak), <u>shrubs</u> (e.g. brambles) and <u>undergrowth</u> (e.g. ferns). <u>Forest-floor plants</u> (e.g. bluebells) often flower in <u>spring</u> before the trees grow leaves and <u>block out</u> the light.

- <u>Coniferous forests</u> have <u>evergreen trees</u> (e.g. pine, fir) and an <u>understory</u> of grasses and low-growing plants. Trees are evergreen so they can make use of available <u>sunlight</u> <u>all year</u> round.

Tropical Rainforests Have a Hot, Wet Climate

See pages 44-47 for more on rainforests.

Climate

1) The climate is <u>the same all year</u> round — there are <u>no definite seasons</u>.

2) It's <u>hot</u> (the temperature is generally between <u>20-28 °C</u> and only varies by a few degrees over the year). This is because near the <u>equator</u>, the <u>Sun</u> is <u>overhead</u> all year round.

3) <u>Rainfall</u> is very <u>high</u>, around 2000 mm per year. It <u>rains every day</u>, usually in the <u>afternoon</u>.

Animals

1) Rainforests are believed to contain <u>more animal species</u> than any other ecosystem. Gorillas, jaguars, anacondas, tree frogs and sloths are all <u>examples</u> of rainforest animals. There are also loads of species of <u>insects</u> and <u>birds</u>.

2) Many animals are <u>camouflaged</u>, e.g. leaf-tailed geckos look like leaves so they can <u>hide</u> from <u>predators</u>. Other animals are <u>nocturnal</u> (active at <u>night</u>), e.g. sloths. They <u>sleep</u> through the day and <u>feed</u> at night when it's <u>cooler</u> — this helps them to <u>save energy</u>.

Plants

1) Most trees are <u>evergreen</u> (they don't <u>drop</u> their <u>leaves</u> in a particular <u>season</u>) to take advantage of the <u>continual growing season</u>.

2) Vegetation cover is <u>dense</u>, so very <u>little light</u> reaches the forest floor. There are lots of <u>epiphytes</u> (plants that grow on other living plants and take <u>nutrients</u> and <u>moisture</u> from the air), e.g. orchids and ferns.

3) The rainforest has <u>four distinct layers</u> of plants with different adaptations. For example, trees in the highest layer (<u>emergents</u>) are <u>very tall</u>, have big roots (called <u>buttress roots</u>) to support their trunks and <u>only</u> have branches at their <u>crown</u> (where <u>most light</u> reaches them). Plants lower down in the <u>undercanopy</u> have <u>large leaves</u> to absorb as <u>much light</u> as possible.

Global echo-systems — they go round and round and round...

Aah, wasn't that lovely. Don't just gaze at the pretty pictures though — you need to know where these ecosystems are found and what they're like. And you'll be pleased to know there's more on some of them coming up next. Hurrah.

Tropical Rainforests

It's time to venture <u>deep</u> into the heart of the <u>rainforest</u> and find out just how they <u>function</u>.
First up is the <u>water cycle</u>, which kind of explains why rainforests are so blimmin' <u>wet</u>...

The Water Cycle Shows How Water Moves in Tropical Rainforests

1) The water cycle has <u>different parts</u> — bodies of <u>water</u> (e.g. rivers and lakes), the <u>land</u> and the <u>atmosphere</u>.

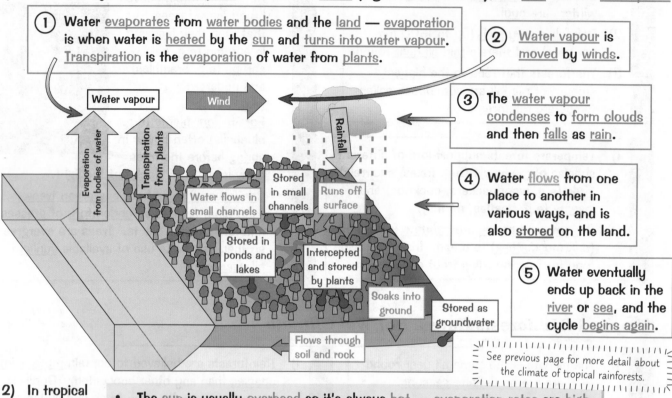

① Water <u>evaporates</u> from <u>water bodies</u> and the <u>land</u> — <u>evaporation</u> is when water is <u>heated</u> by the <u>sun</u> and <u>turns into water vapour</u>. <u>Transpiration</u> is the <u>evaporation</u> of water from <u>plants</u>.

② <u>Water vapour</u> is <u>moved</u> by <u>winds</u>.

③ The <u>water vapour</u> <u>condenses</u> to <u>form clouds</u> and then <u>falls</u> as <u>rain</u>.

④ Water <u>flows</u> from one place to another in various ways, and is also <u>stored</u> on the land.

⑤ Water eventually ends up back in the <u>river</u> or <u>sea</u>, and the cycle <u>begins again</u>.

See previous page for more detail about the climate of tropical rainforests.

2) In tropical rainforests:
- The <u>sun</u> is usually <u>overhead</u> so it's always <u>hot</u> — <u>evaporation rates</u> are <u>high</u>.
- High evaporation rates mean there's <u>lots of water vapour</u>, so <u>rainfall</u> is <u>high</u>.
- <u>Vegetation</u> is <u>dense</u>, so lots of water is <u>intercepted</u> and <u>stored</u> by plants.

Nutrients are Cycled Quickly in Tropical Rainforests

1) The <u>nutrient cycle</u> is the way that nutrients move through an ecosystem.

2) In tropical rainforests:

- Trees are <u>evergreen</u>, so dead leaves and other material fall <u>all year round</u>.
- The <u>warm</u>, <u>moist climate</u> means that fungi and bacteria <u>decompose</u> the dead organic matter <u>quickly</u>, releasing <u>nutrients</u> into the soil.
- <u>Rainwater</u> soaks into the <u>soil</u> and the <u>nutrients</u> are <u>dissolved</u> in the water.
- <u>Dense vegetation</u> and <u>rapid plant growth</u> mean that the nutrient-rich water is <u>rapidly taken up</u> by plants' roots.

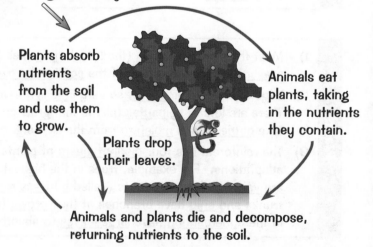

Plants absorb nutrients from the soil and use them to grow.

Animals eat plants, taking in the nutrients they contain.

Plants drop their leaves.

Animals and plants die and decompose, returning nutrients to the soil.

Riding your bike through a puddle — a different kind of water cycle...

You need to know the characteristics of the water and nutrient cycles in tropical rainforests, so have another read through this lot. Once you've got your head round it all, head on over to the next page for some more rainforest fun.

Tropical Rainforests

The warm, moist conditions combined with the nutrient cycle give rainforest soils distinct characteristics. Fascinating, I know. If that's not your cup of tea, there's some thrilling stuff on interdependence here too.

Rainforest *Soils* are *Low in Nutrients*

Soils in tropical rainforests are often very deep but they only have a very thin fertile layer and are generally nutrient poor. This is a result of the combination of high temperatures and high rainfall:

1) The hot, wet climate means that chemical weathering is rapid. This means there is usually a deep layer of soil — the bedrock can be up to 30 m below the surface.

2) The trees drop their leaves all year round, so there is a constant supply of dead leaves and twigs falling onto the soil surface, forming a thick leaf layer.

3) This is quickly broken down (see previous page) to form humus, which then gets mixed with the soil.

4) The layer of humus is thin because the high density, fast-growing plants quickly absorb the nutrients.

5) Nutrients are also leached (washed downwards) through the soil by the heavy rainfall, making the soil nutrient poor.

6) Trees and other vegetation have roots close to the surface, where the nutrients are — there are lots of roots in the humus layer.

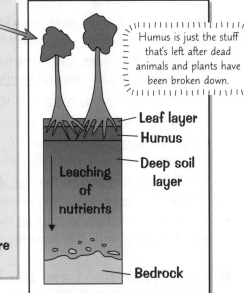

Humus is just the stuff that's left after dead animals and plants have been broken down.

Leaf layer
Humus
Deep soil layer
Leaching of nutrients
Bedrock

Rainforests are *Interdependent Ecosystems*

All the parts of the rainforest (climate, soils, water, plants, animals and people) are dependent on one another — if any one of them changes, everything else is affected. For example:

1) The warm and wet climate means that plants grow quickly — the dense leaf cover protects the forest floor from wind and heavy rainfall, while root systems hold the soil together — this stops it being eroded.

2) The lack of wind near the forest floor means that many plants there have to rely on bees, butterflies, or other animals for pollination. Symbiotic relationships between plants and animals (where they each depend on the other for survival) are very common in tropical rainforests. For example:

Agouti (a rodent) are one of the only animals who can crack open the hard seed pod of the Brazil nut to eat the nut inside. Sometimes, the agouti bury the nuts — these can sprout into new seedlings. If the agouti became extinct, the Brazil nut trees would decline and so could all the other animals who live in or feed on the Brazil nut trees. People who sell Brazil nuts to make a living may also be affected.

3) There are lots of epiphytes (plants that grow on other plants) in rainforests. They get access to light by growing high up on other plants, but they don't have access to the nutrients in the soil — they are dependent on rainfall to provide water and nutrients.

4) Changes to the rainforest ecosystem can have knock-on effects on the whole ecosystem. For example, deforestation reduces the amount of CO_2 being absorbed from the atmosphere, which adds to the greenhouse effect and changes the climate (see p. 21).

My humus is leaching through my bread — eugh, soggy sandwich...

Make sure you know the characteristics of rainforest soils and how the plants, animals and so on are all interdependent. Cover the page and scribble down what you know to check you've got it all. Now drip on over to the next page for...

Tropical Rainforests — Human Impacts

If we didn't have <u>rainforests</u>, I might not be having <u>chocolate</u> brownies for tea. However, human activity is having all kinds of impacts on these giant <u>providers</u> — some <u>good</u>, some <u>bad</u> and some downright <u>ugly</u>.

Tropical Rainforests *Provide Lots* of Goods *and* Services

<u>High biodiversity</u> (the range of <u>plants</u> and <u>animals</u> found there) means rainforests are a <u>rich source</u> of <u>goods</u>:

* Many <u>products</u>, including <u>rubber</u>, <u>coffee</u>, <u>chocolate</u> and <u>medicines</u>, are sourced from the rainforest. Undiscovered species might give us <u>new medicines</u> and other <u>new products</u>.
* <u>Hardwoods</u>, e.g. mahogany, are widely used for furniture and building. <u>Logging</u> of hardwoods can contribute a huge amount to a country's <u>economy</u>.
* Rainforests provide opportunities for <u>farming</u> and <u>mining</u> if the vegetation is cleared. This provides lots of <u>jobs</u> and <u>income</u> in many rainforest areas.

I worked in a mine for a while. Now I'm in de-mole-ition...

Rainforests also provide <u>services</u> through their impact on the <u>global climate</u> and <u>local environment</u>:

* They are home to the <u>highest diversity</u> of animal and plant species on the planet.
* Rainforest <u>plants</u> absorb around <u>0.7 billion tonnes of carbon dioxide</u> (CO_2) from the atmosphere each year, which helps to <u>reduce</u> climate change (see p.21).
* Rainfall is <u>intercepted</u> by the <u>high density</u> of <u>vegetation</u> — this <u>reduces</u> the risk of local <u>flooding</u> because the movement of water to rivers is <u>slowed down</u>.
* Rainforests also help to <u>regulate</u> the <u>global water cycle</u> by storing water and releasing it into the atmosphere slowly. This can reduce the <u>risk</u> of <u>drought</u> and <u>flooding</u> in areas a long way away.

Rainforests also directly provide services for people, e.g. tourists visit to see the plants and animals.

Human Activities *have Big Impacts on the* Rainforest

Although human activities can bring <u>jobs</u> and <u>wealth</u>, they also have lots of <u>negative impacts</u>:

Logging

* With <u>no trees</u> to <u>hold</u> the <u>soil together</u>, heavy rain <u>washes away the soil</u> (<u>soil erosion</u>). Eroded soil can enter <u>rivers</u>, silting up habitats that <u>fish</u> use for breeding.
* The removal of trees <u>interrupts</u> the <u>water cycle</u> — this can lead to some areas becoming very <u>dry</u> with an <u>increased</u> risk of <u>wildfires</u>, while other areas become more likely to <u>flood</u>.
* Logging requires the building of <u>new roads</u>, which opens up the rainforest to <u>further development</u>.

Clearing trees can also make an area less appealing to tourists, so income from tourism decreases.

Agriculture

* Land is often cleared using <u>slash-and-burn</u> techniques. <u>Burning</u> vegetation <u>produces CO_2</u>, which adds to the <u>greenhouse effect</u>.
* Without <u>trees</u> to <u>intercept rainfall</u>, <u>more water reaches</u> the <u>soil</u>. <u>Nutrients</u> are <u>washed away</u>, so <u>soil fertility</u> is <u>reduced</u> — rainforest soils usually lose their fertility in <u>3-5 years</u>.
* Artificial <u>fertilisers</u> added to improve soil fertility are washed into <u>streams</u>, <u>threatening wildlife</u>.

Mineral Extraction

* <u>Mining</u> of precious metals, e.g. gold, often requires <u>heavy machinery</u> and the <u>removal</u> of <u>trees</u>.
* <u>Toxic chemicals</u> used to extract and purify the metals are <u>washed</u> into streams and rivers, <u>killing wildlife</u> and <u>polluting</u> people's drinking water.
* There can also be <u>conflict</u> with local people over <u>rights</u> to the land.

Tourism

* Tourists may <u>scare wildlife</u>, e.g. causing nesting birds to abandon their young.
* They may also <u>damage vegetation</u> and leave behind lots of <u>litter</u>.
* If tourism is unregulated, a <u>lack</u> of <u>infrastructure</u>, e.g. sewers, can lead to <u>pollution</u> of <u>waterways</u>. In order to <u>build</u> infrastructure (e.g. roads and airports), vegetation must be <u>cleared</u>.

Rainforest service — monkeys delivered straight to your door...

Practising exam questions about impacts could have a big impact on your exam results. So try this one:

1) Outline the impacts of logging in tropical rainforests. [4]

EXAM QUESTION

Topic 4 — Sustaining Ecosystems

Tropical Rainforests — Case Study

Cor blimey, rainforests do face a lot of threats. It's not all doom and gloom for them though. In fact, this page is all about ways people are trying to manage the biggest rainforest of them all — the mighty Amazon.

People are Trying to Use and Manage the Amazon Sustainably

1) The Amazon rainforest is the north of South America and covers an area of around 8 million km², including parts of Brazil, Peru, Colombia, Venezuela, Ecuador, Bolivia, Guyana, Suriname and French Guiana.

2) Some management strategies aim to use the Amazon rainforest in a way that's sustainable — that is, allowing people today to get the things that they need, without stopping people in the future getting what they need. Here are some of the ways they're doing it:

Sustainable Forestry

1) Sustainable forestry balances the removal of trees to sell with the conservation of the forest as a whole. It can involve selective logging, where only some trees are felled so that the forest is able to regenerate or planting new trees to replace the ones that were cut down.

2) International agreements try to reduce illegal logging, and promote wood from sustainably managed forests. For example, the Forest Stewardship Council® (FSC) is an organisation that marks sustainably sourced timber products with its logo so that consumers can choose sustainable products.

3) Precious Woods Amazon is a logging company operating in Brazil. They place limits on the number of trees that can be cut down, to make sure the forest can regenerate. They also use a variety of species, so that no species is over-exploited. They are FSC®-certified.

Community Programmes

1) Natütama is an organisation in Puerto Nariño in Colombia that is working with the local community to protect river species, e.g. the Amazon river dolphin.

2) It employs local people to teach other people in the community how they can protect endangered river animals and their habitats.

3) Local fishermen collect information about the number and distribution of species, and report any illegal hunting or fishing that is taking place.

4) The team also organise clean-up days to remove litter from the local rivers.

Ecotourism

Ecotourism is tourism that minimises damage to the environment and benefits the local people.

1) Yachana Lodge is an ecotourism project in Ecuador, in a remote area of the Amazon rainforest where local people rely on subsistence farming to provide a living.

2) It employs local people, giving them a more reliable income and a better quality of life.

3) It also encourages the conservation of the rainforest so that visitors continue to want to visit.

4) Tourists visit in small groups so that harm to the environment is minimised, and take part in activities to raise awareness of conservation issues.

5) Tourists have to pay entrance fees — this brings in more money for rainforest conservation. Profits are invested in education projects to promote conservation in the local community.

Biosphere Reserves

A biosphere reserve is an internationally recognised protected area that aims to combine conservation and sustainable use.

1) The Central Amazon Conservation Complex (CACC) in Brazil is the largest protected area in the rainforest, covering around 60 000 km². It's home to loads of different species of plants and animals, e.g. black caimans and river dolphins.

2) Access to the CACC is restricted, and there are strict limits on hunting, logging and fishing.

3) Scientific research projects and environmental education activities are encouraged to make people more aware of conservation issues.

If only we could order a few billion trees with next day delivery...

And that's about it for rainforests. Make sure you understand the different ways of managing rainforests sustainably and learn plenty of case study facts — you'll need them in the exam. Now make like a tree and get out of here...

Polar Environments

Woolly hats at the ready — it's time for a foray into the ice cold world of polar environments...

Antarctica and the Arctic have Distinctive Characteristics

Antarctica and the Arctic are both polar ecosystems but they are slightly different. The Arctic is usually defined as the region north of the Arctic Circle (about 66° N).

Some people define the Arctic as anywhere north of the tree line or where average summer temperatures are less than 10 °C.

	The Arctic	Antarctica
Climate	Average summer temperatures are less than 10 °C and winter temperatures are about -20 °C to -40 °C. Annual precipitation is usually less than 500 mm.	Antarctica is colder than the Arctic. Summer temperatures are usually -20 °C to -5 °C and winter temperatures can reach almost -90 °C. Annual precipitation is also lower (only 50 mm inland and 200 mm at the coast).
Features of the land and sea	The majority of the Arctic is made up of ocean, which has lots of drifting pack ice and icebergs. The sea ice extends further in winter. On land there are mountainous regions, areas that are permanently covered with snow and ice, and areas of treeless tundra (where only a surface layer of the soil thaws each summer).	Antarctica is a land mass which is 99% covered with an ice sheet. A few mountains poke up out of the ice, e.g. the Transantarctic Mountains, which run across the continent. The sea freezes in the winter, nearly doubling the size of the continent.
Flora (plants)	Low-growing shrubs, lichen, moss, some flowering plants, e.g. Arctic poppies.	Much less vegetation — mainly moss and lichen. The sea contains lots of phytoplankton.
Fauna (animals)	E.g. whales, seals, fish, wolves, polar bears, reindeer, caribou and lots of birds. Most animals are adapted to the specific conditions of the Arctic. Caribou	E.g. whales, seals, penguins, sea-birds. All the animals in Antarctica rely on the sea, e.g. for food or to provide a habitat for breeding. Penguins

Cold Environments are Fragile, Interdependent Ecosystems

The biotic (living) components of cold environments (plants, animals and people) and the abiotic (non-living) components (climate, soils, water) are closely related — if one of them changes, the others are affected.

1) The cold, dry climate means that biodiversity is low in the Arctic and Antarctica.

2) Ocean currents and winds open up gaps in the sea ice. This increases light levels in the water, meaning algae and other producers can produce more food. This causes populations of fish, e.g. cod, to increase, supporting consumers such as seals, penguins and polar bears.

3) If temperatures increase (e.g. due to climate change caused by human activities) more sea ice melts in the summer — animals such as seals and polar bears rely on sea ice for breeding and hunting, so if sea ice cover decreases, these animals are threatened.

4) In the Arctic tundra, the cold climate causes plants to grow slowly and decompose slowly. This means that the soil is low in nutrients, further reducing growth rates. In summer, the surface layer of soil thaws and plant cover increases. Plants absorb heat from the Sun, and prevent the permanently frozen ground below (permafrost) from thawing. Slow melting of the upper layer of permafrost provides water for plants.

5) In the Antarctic there are very few plants — phytoplankton in the sea are the most important producers. These form the basis of all the food chains, e.g. they are eaten by krill, which are eaten by fish, which are eaten by penguins or sea-birds. Phytoplankton depend on nutrient-rich currents of seawater rising to the surface from deep underwater — if these were reduced, the whole ecosystem would be threatened.

Carry-boo — the piggyback version of hide and seek...

Brrr, I'm shivering just thinking about this. Once your hands have warmed up enough to handle a pen, cover the page and jot down the characteristics of one of these environments and how the components in the ecosystem are related. You only need to learn about interdependence in one polar ecosystem, so take your pick — North or South.

Polar Environments — Human Impacts

No surprises here — you've learnt about the <u>characteristics</u> of polar environments, so now it's time to hear about all the <u>terrible things</u> people are doing to them (and a few of the <u>good</u> things too)...

Human *Activities* Impact *Polar Ecosystems*

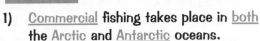

Tourism

1) <u>Tourism</u> occurs in <u>both</u> the <u>Arctic</u> and <u>Antarctica</u>.

2) It <u>increases shipping</u> and <u>air travel</u>, leading to <u>water</u> and <u>air</u> pollution. There is also a <u>risk</u> of <u>boats grounding</u>, which can cause <u>oil spills</u>.

3) Tourists can <u>disturb breeding colonies</u> of <u>birds</u> and <u>seals</u>. <u>Trampling</u> damages fragile <u>vegetation</u> and <u>erodes</u> the landscape, leaving paths.

4) <u>Litter</u> and <u>waste disposal</u> damages <u>habitats</u> and can <u>harm wildlife</u>, especially because <u>decomposition rates</u> in the cold environments are so <u>slow</u>.

5) In Antarctica, there is concern over the introduction of <u>non-native species</u>, which could alter <u>food webs</u>, changing the ecosystem <u>irreversibly</u>.

Indigenous People

1) There are <u>no permanent inhabitants</u> in <u>Antarctica</u> and the <u>Arctic</u> only has a population of about <u>4 million</u>, including the <u>Inuit</u> of Greenland and Canada.

2) Traditional indigenous people rely on <u>reindeer herding</u>, or <u>fishing</u> and <u>hunting</u> to support themselves — but they only take what they <u>need</u> and don't upset the <u>balance</u> of the <u>ecosystem</u>.

3) Many indigenous people now live in <u>modern towns</u> and <u>cities</u>, e.g. Anchorage in Alaska — this impacts the environment through <u>waste disposal</u>, <u>air</u> and <u>noise pollution from vehicles</u>, and <u>heat</u> from buildings, which can <u>melt permafrost</u>.

Mineral Extraction

1) The <u>Arctic</u> has large <u>gas</u> and <u>oil reserves</u>, e.g. at Prudhoe Bay in Alaska, as well as other <u>mineral deposits</u>, e.g. uranium and phosphate are mined in Arctic Russia.

2) <u>Drilling</u> for gas and oil is <u>risky</u> — oil spills are <u>difficult</u> to <u>clean up</u> and can <u>harm habitats</u> and <u>kill wildlife</u>.

3) <u>Pipelines</u> also have to be built to <u>transport</u> the oil and gas — these can <u>melt</u> the <u>permafrost</u> below and <u>interrupt</u> the <u>migration routes</u> of caribou herds.

4) The <u>extraction</u> of <u>metals</u> from mined rocks produces lots of <u>pollution</u>, damaging <u>ecosystems</u> in the surrounding area.

There are mineral reserves in Antarctica too but they're not allowed to be extracted (see next page).

Fishing

1) <u>Commercial</u> fishing takes place in <u>both</u> the <u>Arctic</u> and <u>Antarctic</u> oceans.

2) <u>Over-fishing threatens</u> many species, e.g. in Antartica the <u>Patagonian Toothfish</u> has been fished to near <u>extinction</u>.

3) <u>Reduced fish populations</u> have <u>knock-on effects</u> on other species in the <u>food chain</u>, e.g. the <u>larger fish</u> and <u>birds</u> that <u>eat</u> them.

4) Other species can also be affected, e.g. <u>albatrosses</u> and <u>petrels</u> get <u>caught</u> in the fishing lines and <u>drown</u>.

Scientific Research

1) <u>Scientists</u> use polar environments for important <u>research</u>, e.g. on global climate change. This has a <u>positive</u> impact on <u>global environmental management</u>, and on management of <u>polar ecosystems</u>.

2) In the past, some scientists working in Antarctica <u>dumped rubbish</u> in the sea and <u>abandoned</u> broken equipment. This polluted the <u>land</u> and <u>sea</u>, damaging habitats and posing a <u>risk</u> to <u>wildlife</u>.

3) <u>Research stations</u> and <u>ships</u> produce <u>chemical</u> and <u>sewage pollution</u>. However, research organisations try to <u>limit</u> this.

Whaling

1) <u>Whaling</u> was a <u>big industry</u> in <u>both</u> the <u>Arctic</u> and <u>Antarctic</u> during the last <u>two centuries</u>.

2) Many species of whale were hunted to <u>near extinction</u>, e.g. Blue, Fin and Minke whales.

3) Whales are very <u>slow breeders</u>, so it takes a <u>long time</u> for their populations to <u>recover</u>.

4) Whaling has mostly <u>stopped</u> in polar areas. Numbers of some whale species are <u>recovering</u>.

Whale meat again — don't know where, don't know when...

I'll admit this isn't the cheeriest of pages, but it's gotta be learnt. So what are you waiting for... Get to it.

1) Outline the impacts of human activities on either the Arctic or Antarctic ecosystem. [4]

Polar Environments — Case Studies

Almost time to leave these <u>frozen lands</u>. But first, button up your duvet jacket and look out for <u>polar bears</u> (only for the first half of the page though) and I'll tell you all about how <u>people</u> are trying to make things <u>better</u>...

Tourism *is Being* Managed Sustainably *on Svalbard*

1) <u>Svalbard</u> is a group of islands in the <u>Arctic Circle</u>, north of Norway, that is <u>promoting sustainable tourism</u>.

2) Over <u>60%</u> of Svalbard is <u>protected</u>. For example, there are <u>strict limits</u> on the use of off-road <u>motorised vehicles</u>, and tour operators and visitors have to get <u>permission</u> to <u>visit</u> the <u>nature reserves</u>.

3) Different zones have <u>different levels</u> of <u>protection</u> — <u>nature reserves</u> allow <u>very little access</u>, while <u>tourism areas</u> have <u>fewer regulations</u>.

4) Here's an <u>example</u> of how tourism is being managed <u>sustainably</u> in one part of Svalbard:

Ny-Ålesund

<u>Ny-Ålesund</u> is the most <u>northerly</u> settlement in the world and is run by a company called <u>Kings Bay AS</u>. The population is mostly made up of <u>scientific researchers</u>. The company and researchers have taken actions to <u>limit</u> the <u>impact</u> of tourism on the area. For example:

- <u>Cruise ships</u> are required to <u>tell passengers</u> about the <u>rules</u> visitors have to follow, e.g. not <u>disturbing nesting birds</u> or leaving <u>litter</u>.

- Visitors have to stick to the <u>1.5 km path</u> around the settlement and there are lots of <u>boards</u> with <u>environmental information</u>, to make tourists <u>aware</u> of the issues.

- The ships are only allowed to <u>remain anchored</u> for a <u>few hours</u> — this reduces the amount of <u>pollution</u> from e.g. diesel fumes entering the <u>local environment</u>.

5) More recently there has been a <u>ban</u> on the <u>most polluting fuels</u> used by cruise ships — this means that the bigger cruise ships are now <u>unable</u> to visit <u>Ny-Ålesund</u>, as well as some other areas around Svalbard.

The Antarctic Treaty *is an* Example *of* Global Sustainable Management

1) The <u>Antarctic Treaty</u> is an <u>agreement</u> made by <u>twelve countries</u> in 1959 about how to <u>sustainably manage</u> Antarctica's ecosystems.

2) The <u>environmental protocol</u> (which came into force in 1998) sets out <u>6 basic principles</u> for <u>human activity</u>:
- no <u>mineral exploitation</u> is allowed
- <u>plants</u> and <u>animals</u> must be <u>conserved</u>
- <u>areas</u> of the <u>environment</u> must be <u>protected</u>
- there are <u>rules</u> for <u>waste disposal</u> and <u>waste</u> must be <u>minimised</u>
- there are <u>regulations</u> for the <u>discharge</u> of <u>sewage</u> from vessels
- <u>activities</u> must have an <u>Environmental Impact Assessment</u> before they are able to go ahead

3) There are <u>strict rules</u> about the introduction of <u>non-native species</u> so that ecosystems aren't <u>disturbed</u>, e.g. visitors have to wear <u>disinfected overboots</u> when they land and there are restrictions on <u>eating</u>, <u>drinking</u> and <u>weeing</u> whilst ashore.

4) There are also globally agreed <u>rules</u> amongst <u>tour operators</u> — only <u>100 visitors</u> are allowed to land at any one time and <u>cruise ships</u> of over <u>500 passengers</u> are <u>prevented</u> from stopping.

5) There have been <u>no major problems</u> with the <u>treaty</u> and some people think it should be <u>extended</u> to cover the <u>ocean</u> surrounding Antarctica so that there is <u>more protection</u> for <u>marine life</u>, e.g. whales and fish.

Ice cream sundae — that's my kind of Antarctic treat-y...

Congratulations on sustaining your revision to the end of the section. Sustainable management is one of those topics that examiners love asking about, so make sure you've got a couple of case studies up your sleeve for the exam.

Revision Summary

What a world — I feel pretty alive right now, let me tell you. Now's the time to check you've got everything you need to know about sustaining ecosystems learnt, and I've got just the thing to help you — a page of summary questions. If you get stuck, all the answers are in this section — so go back and learn that bit again.

Global Ecosystems (p.40-43) ☑

1) What is an ecosystem?
2) Give two abiotic features of ecosystems.
3) What is a producer?
4) Describe the role of decomposers in ecosystems.
5) Where are temperate forests found?
6) What type of ecosystem is mostly found between the Tropics of Cancer and Capricorn?
7) What kinds of plants grow in hot deserts?
8) Describe the climate in savannah grasslands.
9) What sorts of animals are found in coral reef ecosystems?
10) Describe the vegetation in temperate forest ecosystems.
11) Describe the climate of tropical rainforests.

Tropical Rainforests (p.44-47) ☑

12) Outline the main features of the water cycle in tropical rainforests.
13) Why is there rapid nutrient cycling in tropical rainforests?
14) Why is the humus layer thin in rainforest soils?
15) Why are tree roots usually close to the soil surface in tropical rainforests?
16) Give an example of interdependence in the tropical rainforest ecosystem.
17) Why is it important to protect tropical rainforests?
18) What are two environmental services that tropical rainforests perform for the planet?
19) What effects can agriculture have on tropical rainforests?
20) What are the effects of mineral extraction on tropical rainforests?
21) Give one example of how ecotourism is being used to manage rainforests sustainably.
22) What is a biosphere reserve?

Polar Environments (p.48-50) ☐

23) How does the climate differ between the Arctic and Antarctica?
24) What are the main features of the land and sea in the Arctic?
25) Describe the animals found in Antarctica.
26) Give one example of interdependence in either the Arctic or Antarctic ecosystem.
27) What are the impacts of fishing on polar ecosystems?
28) What are the impacts of mineral extraction on the Arctic ecosystem?
29) Describe a small-scale example of sustainable management in either the Arctic or Antarctica.
30) How is either the Arctic or Antarctica being managed sustainably on a global scale?

Urban Growth

Urban areas (towns and cities) are <u>popular places</u> to be and are getting <u>ever more so</u>...

Urbanisation is Happening Fastest in Poorer Countries

1) <u>Urbanisation</u> is the <u>growth</u> in the <u>proportion</u> of a country's population living in <u>urban areas</u>.

2) It's happening in countries <u>all over the world</u> — more than <u>50%</u> of the world's population currently live in <u>urban areas</u> (<u>3.9 billion</u> people) and this is <u>increasing</u> every day.

3) The <u>rate</u> of urbanisation <u>differs</u> between countries that are <u>richer</u> and those that are <u>poorer</u>.

4) <u>Advanced countries (ACs)</u> are <u>more</u> economically developed, e.g. UK, Japan and Germany. Urbanisation happened <u>earlier</u> in ACs than in less developed countries, e.g. during the <u>Industrial Revolution</u>, and <u>most</u> of the population now <u>already live</u> in <u>urban areas</u>.

5) ACs have very <u>slow rates</u> of urban growth, and many people desiring a <u>better quality of life</u> are moving <u>away</u> from overcrowded cities to rural areas. Good <u>transport</u> and <u>communication networks</u> mean that people in ACs can <u>live</u> in <u>rural areas</u> and <u>commute</u> to cities, or <u>work from home</u>.

   See p.63 for more on ACs, LIDCs and EDCs.

6) <u>Low-income developing countries (LIDCs)</u> are <u>less</u> economically developed, e.g. Ethiopia, Nepal and Afghanistan. <u>Not many</u> of the population in LIDCs <u>currently live</u> in urban areas. In general, the <u>fastest rates</u> of urbanisation in the world are in LIDCs.

7) <u>Emerging and developing countries (EDCs)</u> are those where economic development is <u>increasing</u>, sometimes <u>rapidly</u>, e.g. Brazil, China, Russia, India. The percentage of the population living in urban areas <u>varies</u>. Some EDCs, such as <u>Thailand</u>, <u>Mexico</u> and <u>China</u>, are experiencing <u>rapid urban growth</u>.

The World's Biggest Cities are Now Found in Poorer Countries

1) There are <u>two</u> types of city that you need to know about:

   - <u>Megacity</u> — an urban area with <u>over 10 million people</u> living there. A megacity can be a <u>single</u> city, or a <u>conurbation</u> — where neighbouring towns and cities have spread and <u>merged</u> together.

   - <u>World city</u> — a city that has an <u>influence</u> over the <u>whole world</u>. World cities are centres for <u>trade</u> and <u>business</u>. Lots of <u>people</u> and <u>goods</u> from <u>international</u> destinations pass through them. They also tend to be hubs of <u>culture</u> and <u>science</u>, with <u>international media</u> centres.

2) In 1950 most of the <u>biggest</u> and most <u>influential</u> cities were in <u>advanced countries</u>. There were only <u>2</u> megacities — Tokyo and New York.

3) By 2014 there were <u>28</u> megacities and this number is still growing — it's predicted to rise to <u>41</u> by 2030. More than <u>two-thirds</u> of current megacities are in <u>poorer</u> countries (<u>EDCs</u> and <u>LIDCs</u>), mostly in <u>Asia</u>, e.g. <u>Jakarta</u> in Indonesia and <u>Mumbai</u> in India.

4) In 1950, the only <u>world cities</u> were London, Paris, Tokyo and New York.

   2014

   Key
   - ACs
   - LIDCs
   - EDCs
   - □ Megacity

5) The number of world cities has also <u>increased</u>, but it's difficult to put an <u>exact number</u> on how many there are. Most are still in <u>ACs</u> but some, e.g. <u>Dubai</u>, <u>Moscow</u> and <u>Rio de Janeiro</u>, are in <u>EDCs</u>.

Zip wires and bouncy pavements — that would be a mega city...

What better way to start a new section than learning the page and then having a crack at an exam question:

1) Compare the patterns of urban growth in ACs and LIDCs.   [4]

Urbanisation in LIDCs

The lure of the city lights can be strong, but many dreams have been crushed by the problems of urban growth.

Urbanisation is Caused by Rural-Urban Migration and Internal Growth

1) Rural-urban migration is the movement of people from the countryside to the cities. The rate of rural-urban migration in LIDCs is affected by push factors (things that encourage people to leave an area) and pull factors (things that encourage people to move to an area). Rapid urbanisation in LIDCs is being caused by a combination of push and pull factors:

Push factors

1) Natural disasters, e.g. floods and earthquakes, can damage property and farmland, which people can't afford to repair.

2) Mechanisation of agricultural equipment — farms require fewer workers so there are fewer jobs.

3) Drought (see p.7) can make land unproductive, so people can no longer support themselves.

4) Conflict or war can cause people to flee their homes.

Pull factors

1) There are more jobs in urban areas that are often better paid.

2) Access to better health care and education.

3) To join other family members who have already moved.

4) People think they will have a better quality of life.

2) Urbanisation is also caused by internal growth (when the birth rate is higher than the death rate).

3) The birth rate tends to be higher in cities because it's normally young people that move to urban areas (to find work). These people then have children in the cities — increasing the urban population.

4) In LIDCs, better healthcare can be found in cities than in rural areas. This means people living in urban areas live longer, reducing death rates and increasing the proportion of people in urban areas.

Rapid Urbanisation can cause Lots of Problems in LIDCs

Cities offer lots of opportunities for the people migrating there — e.g. better access to education, healthcare and employment. The growing population can also help increase the wealth and economic development of the city, as well as the country it's in. However, very rapid growth puts pressure on cities, causing problems:

Economic Consequences

1) There may not be enough jobs for everyone, leading to high levels of unemployment.

2) Lots of people work in the informal sector, where the jobs aren't taxed or regulated by the government. People often work long hours in dangerous conditions for little pay.

3) People may not have access to education so they are unable to develop the skills needed to get better jobs.

Social Consequences

1) There aren't enough houses for everyone — many people end up in squatter settlements that are badly built and overcrowded.

2) Infrastructure can't be built fast enough — people often don't have access to basic services, e.g. clean water, proper sewers or electricity. This can cause poor health.

3) There can be high levels of crime.

Environmental Consequences

If cities grow rapidly, waste disposal services, sewage systems and environmental regulations for factories can't keep pace with the growth.

1) Rubbish often isn't collected or it may end up in big rubbish heaps. This can damage the environment, especially if it's toxic.

2) Sewage and toxic chemicals can get into rivers, harming wildlife.

3) The road system may not be able to cope with all the vehicles. Congestion causes increased greenhouse gas emissions and air pollution.

My internal growth mainly comes from my love of cream cakes...

This is important stuff — the consequences of rapid urban growth can be applied to most fast-growing cities in LIDCs. You also need to know why people move to the city in the first place and what internal growth is. So get learnin'.

Suburbanisation

Trends in urbanisation are a bit different in richer countries. There are three main types of movement, so gear up for a three-page dash through them. First up is suburbanisation — basically people moving to the suburbs.

Suburbanisation is Taking Place in Advanced Countries

Suburbanisation is the movement of people from city centres to the outskirts.
It's caused by a combination of push and pull factors:

Push Factors

1) Urban areas can be overcrowded, polluted, have high crime rates and may have little green, 'natural' space. Some people believe that their quality of life is lower in the inner city than it would be in the suburbs.

2) As countries develop, governments often clear low quality city centre housing and provide new houses outside the city for residents. E.g. slum clearances in England between 1950 and 1970 moved people to council estates on the outskirts of urban areas.

3) Deindustrialisation in city centres (when manufacturing moves out of an area) leads to people having to leave cities in search of employment in new industrial areas.

4) As unemployment increases in the city, people have less money to spend there, so local shops and services may be forced to close. This means there are fewer local services for people living in the city centre.

Pull Factors

1) Suburban areas can offer a lower population density, more open green spaces and a perception of being safer and more family-friendly.

2) Planning laws may be more relaxed outside city centres, so it's easier to build houses. In the UK, developers build new housing estates on the edges of urban areas, offering large, modern houses with gardens.

3) Improvements in public transport and increasing car ownership mean that people can live in the suburbs and commute in to the city to work.

4) Rents are often cheaper on the outskirts of cities, which attracts businesses. Jobs and services then become available in the suburbs — encouraging people to move there.

Suburbanisation has Social, Economic and Environmental Consequences

Economic

1) There are fewer people living in inner city areas and parts of cities that are mainly offices can be deserted after work hours. Shops, restaurants and other amenities may struggle for customers and close.

2) As businesses leave, unemployment increases, which leads to lower living standards and poverty.

Social

1) As people and businesses move out to the suburbs, buildings in the city centre are abandoned and may become derelict. This can lead to the city centre becoming run down.

2) Wealthier middle-class people may move to the suburbs where there is a better quality of life. The people left behind are poorer and are often foreign immigrants. This can lead to economic and ethnic segregation.

Environmental

1) New housing estates are often built on open countryside, which affects wildlife habitats.

2) As urban areas spread, more ground is concreted over. This can increase surface run-off (when water flows quickly overland) and the risk of flooding.

3) Most people who live in the suburbs own cars and may commute into the city to work. This means that the number of cars on the roads increases, causing congestion and air pollution.

Superbanisation — when the buildings start wearing capes and pants...

The inner city's bad, so people leave, which makes the inner city even worse — doesn't make for a particularly cheerful read I'm afraid, but you need to know the causes and consequences of suburbanisation in ACs. Hop to it...

Counter-Urbanisation

Sometimes people want to move out of the big smoke and set up a cosier life in a more rural area.
That's what counter-urbanisation is — it's nothing to do with building model towns out of board game pieces...

Counter-Urbanisation *is Taking Place Around Some Cities in ACs*

Counter-urbanisation is the movement of people away from large urban areas
to smaller settlements and rural areas. As well as the push factors from the
previous page, it's also caused by these
push and pull factors:

Push Factors

1) Suburbs and city centres often
   have problems with traffic
   congestion and parking.
2) Housing in central urban areas and
   the suburbs is often very expensive.
   People feel they are not getting value
   for money and move further from the
   city, where prices are often lower.

Pull Factors

1) Houses in smaller settlements and rural areas are
   often bigger and have more outside space than
   those in city centres and the suburbs.
2) Improved communication services (e.g. high-speed
   internet connections) make it easier for people to
   live in rural areas and work from home.
3) Improvements to communication services also
   mean that some companies no longer need to be
   in a city centre and can move to rural areas where
   land is cheaper. This creates jobs in rural areas.
4) Increased car ownership and improved public
   transport mean that people can live further
   from the city and commute to work.

There are Consequences *to Counter-Urbanisation*

Lots of the impacts of counter-urbanisation on cities are similar to those caused by suburbanisation
(see previous page). There are also impacts on rural areas:

Social

1) In some villages, the existing houses are improved,
   e.g. farm buildings are renovated. But some
   developments (e.g. unattractive new housing) can
   affect the character of rural settlements.
2) It can lead to the creation of commuter
   settlements — where people live in rural areas
   but continue to work in the city. This may force
   shops and services in rural areas to close because
   of reduced demand — people spend most of their
   time away from the area at work.
3) There is more demand for houses, so house
   prices increase. Younger people may not be able
   to afford to buy a house, which can mean the
   population is dominated by older people.
4) Schools in rural areas may close if the new
   residents are older people rather than families with
   children.
5) Rural roads and infrastructure may struggle
   to cope with the additional traffic.

Economic

1) Some services in rural areas see an
   increase in business (e.g. pubs that have
   restaurants). This is because the newer
   residents are often professionals or retired
   people who have higher disposable incomes.
2) But some rural shops and services (e.g. bus
   services) may close — wealthier residents
   who own cars are more likely to travel to
   use shops and services in urban areas.
3) Farmers are able to make money by selling
   unwanted land or buildings for housing.

Environmental

1) Most people in rural areas own a car, and
   the additional traffic can cause an increase
   in air pollution and congestion.
2) New housing estates are often built on open
   countryside, which affects wildlife habitats.

I was hoping for a page about mathematicians flocking to cities...

It seems that the suburbs just aren't green enough for some. Get this page learnt, then test your knowledge:
1) Explain why counter-urbanisation takes place in many advanced countries. [4]

Topic 5 — Urban Futures

Re-Urbanisation

These last few pages are a bit like the hokey-cokey. In to the city, out, in, out, shake it all about...

Some Cities in ACs are Experiencing Re-Urbanisation

Re-urbanisation is the movement of people back into urban areas. And you guessed it, it's caused by these push and pull factors:

> Greenfield sites are sites that have never been built on. Brownfield sites have been developed before but left derelict.

Push Factors

1) There may be a lack of jobs in some rural or suburban areas.

2) Rural areas provide fewer leisure or entertainment facilities (e.g. nightlife).

3) Counter-urbanisation may cause high house prices in rural areas (see p.55).

Pull Factors

1) The movement of industry and businesses out of cities as a result of deindustrialisation (see p.54) may leave land derelict. Government policies often favour redevelopment of brownfield sites in city centres over development of greenfield sites. People are attracted back to the city by new developments (e.g. high quality apartments).

2) Most universities are based in urban areas, so young people move there for education, and many stay.

3) Young, single people often want to live close to their work in areas with good entertainment services (e.g. bars and nightclubs). For example, Notting Hill in London attracts young, affluent workers because it is a lively area that is well connected to the city centre.

4) Once re-urbanisation has started it tends to continue — as soon as a few businesses invest and people start to return, it encourages other businesses to invest.

Re-Urbanisation has Social, Economic and Environmental Consequences

Economic

1) As people move back into the city centre, new shops and services open, which boosts the economy in the city.

2) But jobs created in new businesses may not be accessible to the original residents, many of whom are unskilled or semi-skilled.

3) Tourism in the city may increase if the city centre is improved. Increased tourism brings money into the city which can be spent on improving the area even more, e.g. building new attractions or improving public transport.

Social

1) As shops and businesses return, jobs are created. This means there is less unemployment, which can help to reduce certain types of crime, e.g. theft.

2) Local state schools can benefit from the increased number of students. However, wealthier people moving into an area may choose to send their children to private schools or better-performing schools away from the city centre.

3) Original residents in the area being re-urbanised are often on low incomes and may not be able to afford housing as prices increase. They may have to move to cheaper areas of the city.

4) There may be tension between the original residents and the new residents, which could lead to crime or violence.

5) Shops and services catering to the newer, more wealthy residents (e.g. cafés and designer clothes shops) may replace shops and services targeted at original residents (e.g. grocery stores and launderettes).

Environmental

1) Re-developing derelict brownfield sites in cities instead of greenfield sites in the open countryside protects countryside wildlife habitats.

2) But some brownfield sites have been derelict for a long time, so redeveloping them can destroy urban wildlife habitats.

To urbanise or not to urbanise — that is the question...

... and I wish people would blimmin' well make their minds up. Anyhow, whether you're in or you're out, you need to learn the causes and consequences of re-urbanisation, otherwise you might find your head spinning in your exam.

London — Case Study

London — where the streets are paved with gold and everyone has tea with the Queen on a Friday afternoon.

London is a *World City* in *South East England*

1) London is the UK's capital city and is an essential part of the UK's economy. Over 20% of the UK's income comes from London. It is also the centre of the UK's transport system — with road, rail, air and shipping links.

2) London has a major influence on its surrounding area. Companies are attracted to the region by the proximity to London, which increases jobs and wealth. The South East and East of England are the two biggest regional economies in the UK outside London.

3) It's important globally too — it's a world city and, along with New York, one of the two most important financial centres in the world. There are more foreign banks in London than anywhere else.

London [map label]

If you include the whole urban area of London, the population is about 14 million — London is a megacity.

The Population of London is Large and Growing

1) The population of London is now over 8.5 million people and it's growing because:
   - International migration — around 100 thousand more people arrived in London than left in 2014.
   - National migration — within the UK, young adults move to the city for work or to study but there is also counter-urbanisation (see page 55) as older people and families move out of the city.
   - Internal population growth — the young population means there are more births than deaths in the city.

2) There are several top-class universities, e.g. UCL, LSE and Imperial College, so the city has a large student population. Students come from all over the world — nearly 20% of the students are from overseas.

3) Population growth has meant that average population density is very high — over 5000 people per km².

4) Migration has been a major part of life in London for centuries. As a result it is now the most ethnically diverse city in the UK — less than half of the city's population is White British and more than half of new babies each year are born to international immigrants.

5) London's character has been strongly influenced by migration — people with the same ethnicity tend to settle in the same place, creating distinctive areas, e.g. Brick Lane is famous for its curry houses due to the Bangladeshi community, and Southall has a large Indian market.

Chinatown

There are *Distinctive Ways of Life* in London

1) London's West End is home to many theatres where the world's top musicals and plays are regularly performed. Some of the UK's most popular museums and art galleries are in London e.g. the British Museum and the National Gallery. The city is also a centre for fashion — London Fashion Week is one of the four biggest fashion events in the world.

2) London has very high ethnic diversity, and some areas, e.g. Chinatown, have a high proportion of people from one ethnic background. Lots of food, music and goods from that culture can be found in the area and many people are attracted to these areas to shop and eat.

3) There are also many big festivals celebrating different cultures and ethnic backgrounds, for example, the annual Afro-Caribbean Notting Hill Carnival, Chinese New Year parade, Proms and Eid in the Square.

4) Housing in richer areas (mainly west London and the suburbs, e.g. Sutton) tends to be modern apartments or large houses with gardens. In poorer areas (mainly the inner city and east London, e.g. Newham) the housing density is higher and many buildings have been split to house multiple families.

5) Many leisure facilities are available for people in London — cinemas, concert venues, clubs and pubs are all popular and the city is also home to some of the best restaurants and shopping areas in the UK. There are many large parks in the centre of the city, e.g. Hyde Park, and there are many popular visitor attractions, such as the Tower of London and the London Eye.

6) London has many world-class sports facilities and hosted the Olympic Games in 2012. Each year there are lots of popular mass participation sporting events around London, e.g. the London Marathon.

7) London's wealth means that it consumes a huge amount of resources — food, water and energy etc. E.g. Londoners consume nearly 7 million tonnes of food every year, most of which is imported.

London — Case Study

Modern London faces lots of Challenges

1 Housing Availability

1) London's population has been growing rapidly, but homes have not been built at the same pace.

2) As a result, the supply of homes is not enough to meet the demand of those who want to live in London so house prices and rents are rising.

3) Average rents in London are about double the UK average and house prices are some of the least affordable in the world.

4) As a result, workers on lower incomes often can't afford to live near to where they work, many people can't afford to buy homes, and adults house-sharing is becoming more common.

2 Transport Provision

London has a very good transport system but the rising population and increasing number of commuters is stressing the transport network.

1) Roads are frequently congested. Average traffic speed between 7am and 7pm in central London is only 8 miles per hour.

2) About 1 million passengers arrive by train each day — many trains are overcrowded.

3) The London Underground is increasingly filled beyond its capacity — delays due to overcrowding more than doubled between 2013 and 2015.

3 Access to Services

London provides some of the best healthcare and education in the UK. However, its large population means that access to these services can be difficult, especially for poorer people.

1) Healthcare — healthcare is free on the NHS but services are often overwhelmed. Waiting times for appointments have increased and ambulances have to cope with increasing traffic.

2) Education — the best state schools, e.g. Holland Park, are very over-subscribed and difficult to get into. Wealthy parents are able to send their children to fee-paying schools, but many children from poorer families end up in under-performing schools.

4 Inequality

1) London is home to the richest and the poorest people in the UK and the gap is widening. Average income in Kensington and Chelsea is more than £130 000 but less than £35 000 in Newham. More than 25% of the population are living in poverty, due to unemployment and low wages.

2) Unhealthy lifestyles, e.g. drinking, smoking and poor diets, are more common in deprived areas — life expectancy is about 5 years lower in poorer areas of the city than in wealthier areas.

There are Sustainable Solutions to London's Transport Problem

A sustainable solution means improving things for people today without negatively affecting future generations. The Mayor's Transport Strategy is an initiative that aims to improve London's transport network and make it more sustainable by easing congestion and reducing air pollution. For example:

1) A new railway, Crossrail (the Elizabeth line), is being built east to west across the city to increase rail capacity in central London by 10%. The Bakerloo Line is to be extended to Lewisham.

2) Rail and Underground capacity is being increased by running more trains every hour, increasing the number of carriages on trains and making parts of the Underground service 24 hour.

3) More dedicated bus lanes are to be created and roads have been made more suitable for cyclists by constructing two-way Cycle Superhighways throughout the city, e.g. between the Oval and Pimlico. Bikes are already available to hire easily using self-service machines.

4) Congestion charges have been introduced to discourage drivers from entering the city centre.

After Crossrail, work will start on Angrybus and Furiousferry...

You don't have to learn this case study — you might have studied a different example, so by all means go ahead and learn that one instead. You can still have a go at this lovely little exam-style question though.

1) For a named city in an AC, outline one initiative used to make it more sustainable.　[4]

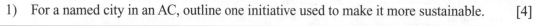

Topic 5 — Urban Futures

Lagos — Case Study

Lagos is a great example of the growth in cities due to migration and the benefits and problems this causes.

Lagos is the Biggest City in Africa

Nigeria

Lagos

1) Lagos is a city on the coast of Nigeria built around the western shore of a large lagoon.

2) Nigeria is a low-income developing country (LIDC) despite having the biggest economy in Africa (because most people are really poor but there are a few who are mega rich). The city's population is around 21 million, and is one of the fastest-growing urban areas in the world. The population of Lagos is growing by over 500 000 people a year.

3) The city was under British rule during colonial times and was a centre of trade. It was the national capital until 1991, and it remains the main financial centre for the whole of West Africa.

4) Lagos has an international port and airport, making it an important centre for regional and global trade. The city contains 80% of Nigeria's industry and lots of global companies are located there.

Migration is Causing the City to Grow Rapidly

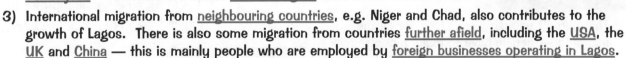

1) The population of Lagos is growing rapidly, largely due to rural-urban migration. Large numbers of migrants arrive in the city every year, creating an outwards urban sprawl of the city into the surrounding countryside and engulfing nearby towns.

2) The majority of people come from within Nigeria, and they come seeking better jobs — incomes are about 4 times higher than those in rural areas.

3) International migration from neighbouring countries, e.g. Niger and Chad, also contributes to the growth of Lagos. There is also some migration from countries further afield, including the USA, the UK and China — this is mainly people who are employed by foreign businesses operating in Lagos.

4) Migration has impacted the city's character. From its origins as a small fishing settlement inhabited by the Yoruba people (one of Nigeria's ethnic groups), it now has a very diverse population with people from each ethnic group within Nigeria, as well as many people with different nationalities.

5) The city has become overcrowded, congested and polluted. Lagos's location on the coast means there isn't much space to expand so population densities are very high.

There are Distinctive Ways of Life in Lagos

1) Lagos has a big film industry, which produces popular 'Nollywood' films. There is also a thriving music scene, which has introduced music styles such as Afrobeat and Afro hip-hop.

2) Western-style fashion is becoming common among the richer inhabitants, but many people still retain their traditional dress and ways of life, e.g. fishing in the lagoon, or making crafts to sell.

3) There are around 250 different ethnic groups living in Lagos and there can be ethnic tension, particularly between those with different religions, e.g. Christians and Muslims.

4) About two-thirds of the population live in slums. For those who can afford proper housing, it's a mix of old and new — some of the old colonial buildings remain, alongside new high-rise flats and skyscrapers in the central business district. The very rich live in gated communities, e.g. on Banana Island.

5) Street parties, pool parties and nightclubbing are all popular leisure activities in Lagos, and there are many festivals held throughout the year (e.g. Lagos International Jazz Festival, Badagry Festival, Eyo Festival) celebrating music, food and local culture.

6) Shopping is also popular in Lagos — there are loads of street vendors, lots of markets specialising in different products and rows and rows of small shops. The central business district on Lagos Island has been modernised and has more western-style shops and supermarkets, selling international foods.

7) Consumption of all resources is rising in Lagos — as people get wealthier, they can afford to buy more consumer goods and use more resources. Consumption of energy is rapidly increasing in Nigeria, and Lagos is responsible for more than half of this increase.

Lagos — Case Study

Lagos *faces Challenges* in Housing, Health, Waste *and* Jobs

1 Squatter Settlements

Over 60% of the city's population live in slums, e.g. Makoko.

1) Houses in Makoko are flimsy, wooden huts built on stilts in the lagoon. These are illegally built — people face eviction if slums are demolished to clean up the city.

2) There is only one primary school in Makoko and many families can't afford to send their children to school.

3) Communal toilets are shared by 15 households and most of the waste goes straight into the lagoon below — it's always full of rubbish and raw sewage.

4) Water can be bought in Makoko from a communal water point but that is up to 3 km from some homes. The only electricity comes from illegal connections that often cut out.

5) There are high levels of crime in Makoko — the slum is patrolled by gangs called 'area boys' who both commit crimes and act as informal 'police' in the slum.

2 Health

1) Most of the city doesn't have access to proper sewers or clean water. This causes health problems, e.g. cholera.

2) Malaria is also a problem — the stagnant water provides a breeding ground for mosquitoes.

3) There aren't enough healthcare facilities and many people can't afford to pay for treatment.

4) Many rural migrants distrust western medicine and prefer to seek help from traditional healers.

3 Informal Sector Jobs

1) There aren't enough formal jobs for all the migrants — people have to make money any way they can, e.g. by scavenging in the Olusosun rubbish dump for items to sell.

2) About 60% of the population work in informal jobs, e.g. street sellers, barbers, carpenters.

3) There's no protection for informal workers — they often work long hours for little pay. Lots of people live on less than $1.25 per day.

4) Street-sellers' stalls are bulldozed to make way for new developments and road widening.

4 Waste Disposal

1) The huge population produces lots of waste — approximately 9000 tonnes per day.

2) Only about 40% of rubbish is officially collected and there are large rubbish dumps, e.g. Olusosun, which contain toxic waste.

3) Waste disposal and emissions from factories are not controlled, leading to air and water pollution.

Sustainable Solutions *can Help with the* Waste Management Problem

The Lagos State Integrated Waste Management Project is an initiative that is trying to improve sustainability by reducing the amount of waste that goes to landfill sites and reducing the air pollution landfill causes. Strategies include:

1) The World Bank is financing a project to collect waste from food markets to turn into compost. This stops the waste from going to landfill sites, where it releases methane (a greenhouse gas) as it decomposes. Instead, a useful product is created that can be used to fertilise farming land, increasing food supplies.

2) Where waste still ends up in rubbish dumps, the government aims to generate electricity from it by burning the methane released. This is already happening at Ikosi Fruit Market, where electricity generated from rotting fruit is used to provide lighting for the market. A larger-scale project is also underway at the landfill site at Olusosun — pipes are being placed into the rubbish to collect the methane so that it can be taken to generators. The electricity generated will be used to power the dump, which is open 24 hours a day.

Lagos — growing brick by brick...

If you've studied a different case study of an EDC or LIDC city in class and you'd rather write about that one instead, then no problem — just make sure you have enough information to cover the key points on these two pages.

Revision Summary

Well, that was a whole load of fun. I bet you're dying to go and tell someone about push and pull factors or rural-urban migration now — but if you can hold it in just a little bit longer, have a go at these questions to check you really know your suburbanisation from your re-urbanisation. Once you can answer them all in your sleep, feel free to go and share the joy with as many people you like. Although you should probably crack on with the next section instead.

Urban Growth (p.52-53) ☑

1) What is urbanisation?
2) Where is urbanisation taking place most rapidly?
3) Describe the trend in urbanisation in ACs.
4) What is a megacity?
5) Give two characteristics of a world city.
6) Describe the change in the global distribution of megacities since 1950.
7) Give three push factors that lead to rural-urban migration.
8) Give one factor, other than migration, that causes urbanisation.
9) List two environmental challenges caused by urban growth in LIDCs.
10) Describe the social challenges that have been caused by rapid urban growth in LIDCs.

Urban Trends in Advanced Countries (p.54-56) ☐

11) What is suburbanisation?
12) Give two pull factors that lead to suburbanisation.
13) Describe the environmental consequences of suburbanisation.
14) Define counter-urbanisation.
15) Give two push factors that lead to counter-urbanisation.
16) Describe the social consequences of counter-urbanisation.
17) What is re-urbanisation?
18) Give two pull factors that lead to re-urbanisation.
19) Describe the economic consequences of re-urbanisation.

Challenges and Opportunities in Cities — Case Studies (p.57-60) ☑

20) For a city in an advanced country (AC) that you have studied:
   a) Describe how international migration has affected the growth and character of the city.
   b) Describe the ways of life in the city.
   c) Outline the problems with the availability of housing in the city.
   d) Describe the challenges caused by inequality in the city.
   e) Outline one initiative that is making the city more sustainable.

21) For a city in a low-income developing country (LIDC) or an emerging and developing country (EDC) that you have studied:
   a) Describe the city's importance within its region.
   b) Describe the patterns of national and international migration.
   c) Give two distinctive characteristics of the ways of life in the city.
   d) Describe the challenges of squatter settlements in the city.
   e) Outline the challenges caused by waste disposal in the city.
   f) Outline one initiative that is making the city more sustainable.

Measuring Development

This topic is a little <u>tricky</u> — but take a <u>deep breath</u> and <u>believe in yourself</u> and you'll be <u>just fine</u>.

Development *is when a Country is Improving*

1) When a country <u>develops</u> it basically gets <u>better</u> for the people living there.
There are <u>different aspects</u> to development:

   • <u>Economic</u> development — <u>progress</u> in <u>economic growth</u>, e.g. how <u>wealthy</u> a country is, its level of <u>industrialisation</u> and use of <u>technology</u>.

   • <u>Social</u> development — improvement in people's <u>standard of living</u>, e.g. <u>better health care</u> and access to <u>clean water</u>.

   • <u>Environmental</u> development — advances in the <u>management</u> and <u>protection</u> of the <u>environment</u>, e.g. reducing <u>pollution</u> and increasing <u>recycling</u>.

An increase in economic development often leads to social and environmental improvements.

2) The level of development is different in <u>different countries</u>, e.g. France is more developed than Ethiopia.

I make this development about 25 m.

There Are Loads of Measures of Development

Development is <u>pretty hard to measure</u> because it <u>includes so many things</u>. But you can <u>compare</u> the development of different countries using '<u>measures of development</u>'.

Name	What it is	A measure of...	As a country develops, it gets...
Gross Domestic Product (GDP)	The <u>total value</u> of <u>goods</u> and <u>services</u> a <u>country produces</u> in a <u>year</u>. It's often given in US$.	Wealth	Higher
GDP per capita	The GDP <u>divided</u> by the <u>population</u> of a <u>country</u>. It's often given in <u>US$</u> and is sometimes called <u>GDP per head</u>.	Wealth	Higher
Gross National Income (GNI)	The <u>total value</u> of <u>goods</u> and <u>services</u> produced by a <u>country</u> in a <u>year</u>, including income from <u>overseas</u>. It's often given in <u>US$</u>.	Wealth	Higher
GNI per capita	The GNI <u>divided</u> by the <u>population</u> of a <u>country</u>. It's also often given in <u>US$</u> and is sometimes called <u>GNI per head</u>.	Wealth	Higher
Birth rate	The number of <u>live babies born per thousand</u> of the population <u>per year</u>.	Women's rights	Lower
Death rate	The number of <u>deaths per thousand</u> of the population <u>per year</u>.	Health	Lower
Life expectancy	The <u>average age</u> a person can <u>expect to live to</u>.	Health	Higher
Infant mortality rate	The number of <u>babies</u> who <u>die under 1 year old</u>, <u>per thousand babies born</u>.	Health	Lower
Literacy rate	The <u>percentage</u> of <u>adults</u> who <u>can read and write</u>.	Education	Higher
Human Development Index (HDI)	This is a number that's calculated using <u>life expectancy</u>, <u>education level</u> (e.g. average number of years of schooling) and <u>income per head</u>. Every country has an HDI value between <u>0</u> (<u>least developed</u>) and <u>1</u> (<u>most developed</u>).	Lots of things	Higher
Happy Index	This is calculated by dividing a country's <u>life expectancy</u>, <u>well-being</u> and <u>level of inequality</u> by its <u>environmental impact</u>. Countries are graded <u>green</u> (good), <u>amber</u> (medium) or <u>red</u> (bad).	Lots of things	No overall pattern

Measures of revision — they're called exams...

Economic measures (like GNI) aren't always reliable because they don't show up variations in income (e.g. a few rich people and lots of poor people). It's best to use several different measures to get an overall picture of development level.

Uneven Development

Now you know what <u>development</u> is all <u>about</u>, it's time to find out how it <u>varies</u> across the world...

Uneven *Development has Consequences*

Level of development is <u>different</u> in <u>different countries</u>. Comparing development measures for <u>different countries</u> shows the <u>consequences</u> of uneven development — <u>differences</u> in <u>wealth</u>, <u>health</u> and <u>education</u>. For example:

Wealth — People in <u>more developed countries</u> have a <u>higher income</u> than those in <u>less developed</u> countries. E.g. GNI per capita shows that <u>income</u> in the <u>UK</u> is around <u>20 times higher</u> than in <u>Chad</u>.

Health — <u>Better health care</u> means that people in more developed countries <u>live longer</u> than those in less developed countries. E.g. people in the <u>UK</u> live almost <u>30 years longer</u> than people in <u>Chad</u>.

Education — People in more developed countries tend to be <u>better educated</u> than those in less developed countries. E.g. people in the UK spend more than <u>twice as long</u> in <u>education</u> as people in <u>Chad</u>.

	Chad	UK
GNI per head (US $)	880	43 440
life expectancy (years)	51.6	80.7
education level (average years of school)	7.4	16.2

Levels *of Development Vary across the World*

The <u>most developed</u> countries are in <u>north America</u>, <u>Europe</u> and <u>Australasia</u>, and the least developed are in central <u>Africa</u> and parts of <u>Asia</u>. The International Monetary Fund (IMF) <u>classifies</u> countries by their <u>level</u> of <u>development</u>:

Low-Income Developing Countries (LIDCs)

<u>LIDCs</u> are the <u>poorest</u> countries in the world — <u>GNI per capita</u> is <u>very low</u> and most citizens have a <u>low</u> standard of living. Their economy is often based on <u>primary industry</u> (e.g. <u>agriculture</u>), and they <u>don't export</u> many goods. LIDCs don't have much <u>money</u> to spend on <u>development</u> (e.g. new schools, hospitals or roads), so their level of development stays <u>low</u>. Examples: Afghanistan, Somalia, Mali and Nepal.

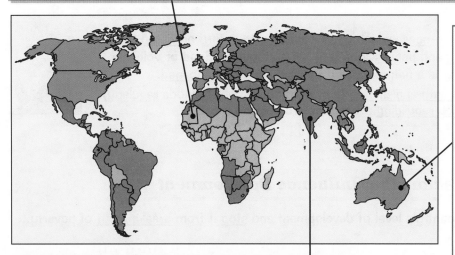

Advanced Countries (ACs)

ACs are the <u>wealthiest</u> countries in the world — <u>GNI per capita</u> is <u>high</u> and most citizens have a <u>high standard of living</u>. Their economy is based on <u>tertiary and quaternary industry</u> (e.g. <u>services</u>). ACs have lots of <u>money</u> to spend on improving <u>education</u>, <u>transport</u> and <u>health care</u>, so people tend to be <u>well-educated</u> and have a <u>high life expectancy</u>. Examples: UK, USA, France, Canada, Australia.

Emerging and Developing Countries (EDCs)

EDCs are generally <u>getting richer</u> as their <u>economy</u> is moving from being based on <u>primary industry</u> (e.g. mining) to <u>secondary industry</u> (manufacturing), and <u>exports</u> of manufactured goods are generally <u>high</u>. <u>Exports</u> and <u>increasing wages</u> mean that there's money to spend on <u>development</u>, so health care, education and transport are generally <u>improving</u>. This means that <u>standard of living</u> for many citizens is also <u>improving</u>. Examples: China, Brazil, Russia, India.

Uneven development — what happens if you do one-armed push-ups...

I used to think that 'developed' basically meant 'built up', and thought it sounded rather nice in all those undeveloped countries, with their forests and meadows. Turns out it doesn't mean that at all, and life isn't rosy in LIDCs.

Factors Affecting Development

You need to know the <u>reasons why</u> there are <u>global inequalities</u> — i.e. why <u>countries differ</u> in how <u>developed</u> they are. These same reasons can make it difficult for countries to <u>break out</u> of <u>poverty</u>.

Physical Factors can Affect How Developed a Country is

A country is more likely to be <u>less</u> developed if it has...

① A Poor Climate

1) If a country has a poor climate (<u>really hot</u> or <u>really cold</u> or <u>really dry</u>) not much will grow. This <u>reduces</u> the amount of <u>food produced</u>. In some countries this can lead to <u>malnutrition</u>, e.g. in Chad and Ethiopia. People who are malnourished have a <u>low quality of life</u>.

2) People also have <u>fewer crops to sell</u>, so <u>less money</u> to <u>spend on goods and services</u>. This also <u>reduces</u> their <u>quality of life</u>.

3) The government gets <u>less money from taxes</u> (as less is sold and bought). This means there's <u>less to spend</u> on <u>developing the country</u>, e.g. to spend on <u>improving healthcare</u> and <u>education</u>.

② Few Natural Resources

1) Countries <u>without</u> many <u>raw materials</u> like <u>coal</u>, <u>oil</u> or <u>metal ores</u> tend to <u>make less money</u> because they've got <u>fewer products to sell</u>.

2) This means they have <u>less money</u> to <u>spend on development</u>.

3) Some countries <u>do</u> have a lot of raw materials but still <u>aren't very developed</u> because they don't have the <u>money</u> to <u>develop</u> the <u>infrastructure</u> to <u>exploit them</u> (e.g. roads and ports).

③ A Poor Location

1) In countries that are <u>landlocked</u> (don't have any coastline) it can be <u>harder</u> and <u>more expensive</u> to <u>transport goods</u> into and out of the country.

2) This means it's harder to <u>make money</u> by <u>exporting goods</u>, so there's <u>less</u> to spend on development.

3) It's also harder to <u>import goods</u> that might <u>help</u> the country to <u>develop</u>, e.g. medicine and farm machinery.

④ Lots of Natural Hazards

1) A natural hazard is a <u>natural process</u> which <u>could</u> cause <u>death</u>, <u>injury</u> or <u>disruption</u> to humans or <u>destroy property</u> and possessions (e.g. an earthquake, flood or volcanic eruption). A <u>natural disaster</u> is a natural hazard that has actually <u>happened</u>.

2) Countries that <u>have a lot of natural disasters</u> (e.g. Bangladesh, which floods regularly) have to <u>spend a lot of money rebuilding</u> after disasters occur.

There are also Human Factors that Influence Development

<u>Human factors</u> can also affect a country's level of development and <u>stop</u> it from <u>breaking out</u> of poverty...

Conflict

1) <u>War</u>, especially <u>civil wars</u>, can <u>slow</u> or <u>reduce</u> levels of development. E.g. <u>health care</u> becomes much <u>worse</u> and things like <u>infant mortality increase</u> a <u>lot</u>.

2) <u>Money</u> is spent on <u>arms</u> and <u>fighting</u> instead of <u>development</u>, people are <u>killed</u> and <u>damage</u> is done to <u>infrastructure</u> and <u>property</u>.

3) Countries have to spend money <u>repairing</u> this <u>damage</u> when the fighting <u>ends</u>.

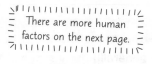
There are more human factors on the next page.

Debt

1) LIDCs often <u>borrow money</u> from <u>other countries</u> and <u>international organisations</u>, e.g. to help them cope with the aftermath of a natural disaster.

2) This money has to be <u>paid back</u> (usually with <u>interest</u>), so any money the country makes <u>can't</u> be used to <u>develop</u>.

Topic 6 — Dynamic Development

Factors Affecting Development

Politics

1) <u>Corrupt</u> governments can <u>hinder development</u>, e.g. by <u>taking money</u> that's intended for building <u>new infrastructure</u> or <u>improving facilities</u> for people. They might also prevent a <u>fair election</u> from happening, so there is <u>no chance</u> for a <u>democratically elected government</u> (chosen by the people) to gain power.

2) If a government is <u>unstable</u> (i.e. likely to lose power at any time), companies and other countries are <u>unlikely to invest</u> or want to <u>trade</u>, meaning that level of development stays <u>low</u>.

3) Governments need to invest in the <u>right things</u> to help a country <u>develop</u>, e.g. <u>transport</u> and <u>schools</u>. If they invest in the <u>wrong areas</u>, the country <u>won't</u> develop as quickly.

Trade

1) Trade is the <u>exchange</u> of <u>goods</u> and <u>services</u>. Countries can <u>import</u> goods and services (<u>buy them in</u> from another country) or can <u>export</u> them (<u>sell them to</u> another country).

2) Countries that <u>export</u> goods and services of <u>greater value</u> than they <u>import</u> have a <u>trade surplus</u>, while countries that <u>import</u> goods and services of <u>greater value</u> than they <u>export</u> have a <u>trade deficit</u>. A trade deficit means a country has <u>less money coming in</u> than <u>going out</u>, so it tends to be <u>poorer</u>.

3) <u>World trade patterns</u> (who trades with whom) seriously influence a country's <u>economy</u> and so affect their <u>level of development</u>. If a country has <u>poor trade links</u> (it trades a small amount with only a few countries) it <u>won't make a lot of money</u>, so there'll be <u>less to spend on development</u>.

4) <u>What</u> a country trades also affects its level of development — exporting <u>primary products</u> (e.g. wood, stone) is <u>less profitable</u> than exporting <u>manufactured goods</u> (e.g. cars, phones). Countries that export mostly <u>primary products</u> tend to be <u>less developed</u>.

Education

1) Educating people produces a more <u>skilled workforce</u>, meaning that the country can produce more <u>goods</u> and offer more <u>services</u> (e.g. ICT). This can bring <u>money</u> into the country, through <u>trade</u> or <u>investment</u>.

2) Educated people also <u>earn more</u>, so they pay more <u>taxes</u>. This provides <u>money</u> that the country can spend on <u>development</u>.

Tourism

<u>Tourism</u> can provide <u>increased income</u> as there will be <u>more money</u> entering the country. This money can be used to <u>increase</u> the <u>level of development</u>.

There's more about aid on p.67.

Disease and Healthcare

1) In some LIDCs, <u>lack of clean water</u> and <u>poor health care</u> mean that a large number of people suffer from <u>diseases</u> such as <u>malaria</u> and <u>cholera</u>.

2) People who are ill <u>can't work</u>, so they're not contributing to the <u>economy</u>. They may also need <u>expensive medicine</u> or <u>health care</u>.

3) Lack of economic <u>contribution</u> and increased <u>spending</u> on health care means that there's <u>less money</u> available to spend on <u>development</u>.

Aid

1) Aid is <u>help given</u> by one country to another. Some countries receive <u>more</u> than others, so they can develop <u>faster</u>.

2) Aid can be spent on <u>development projects</u> (e.g. building <u>schools</u> or improving <u>water supplies</u>), helping to increase development.

3) However, if countries come to <u>rely</u> on aid it might <u>stop</u> them from developing <u>trade links</u> that could be a <u>better</u> way of developing.

We don't need no education — unless we want to develop...

So, there are loads of things than can hinder a country's development. Make sure you learn 'em all.

1) Explain how a country's level of development can be affected by physical factors. [4]

Increasing Development — Stages and Goals

The next few pages are jam-packed with useful info for your <u>development case study</u>, so learn them well...

Rostow's Model shows Five Stages of Economic Development

1) <u>Rostow's</u> model <u>predicts</u> how a country's <u>level of economic development changes</u> over <u>time</u> — it describes how a country's economy changes from relying mostly on <u>primary</u> industry (e.g. agriculture), through <u>secondary</u> industry (e.g. manufacturing goods) to <u>tertiary</u> and <u>quaternary</u> industry (e.g. services and research).

2) At the same time, people's <u>standard of living improves</u>.

3) <u>Stage 1</u> is the <u>lowest</u> level of development and <u>Stage 5</u> is the <u>highest</u>.

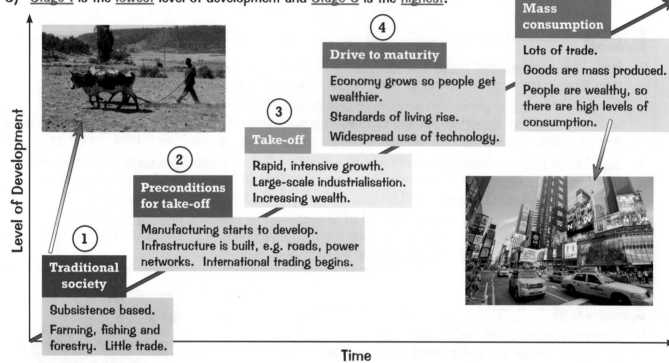

Level of Development (y-axis) / **Time** (x-axis)

⑤ Mass consumption
Lots of trade.
Goods are mass produced.
People are wealthy, so there are high levels of consumption.

④ Drive to maturity
Economy grows so people get wealthier.
Standards of living rise.
Widespread use of technology.

③ Take-off
Rapid, intensive growth.
Large-scale industrialisation.
Increasing wealth.

② Preconditions for take-off
Manufacturing starts to develop.
Infrastructure is built, e.g. roads, power networks. International trading begins.

① Traditional society
Subsistence based.
Farming, fishing and forestry. Little trade.

The Millennium Development Goals Aimed to Help LIDCs Develop

1) The <u>Millennium Development Goals</u> (<u>MDGs</u>) aimed to <u>improve life</u> in <u>LIDCs</u>. They were targets set by the United Nations (UN) in <u>2000</u> — all UN member states agreed to try to achieve the goals by <u>2015</u>.

2) There were <u>eight MDGs</u>, which aimed to:

   1) <u>Halve</u> the number of people living in <u>extreme poverty</u> or suffering from <u>hunger</u>.
   2) Make sure that <u>all children</u> had a <u>primary education</u>.
   3) <u>Increase</u> the number of <u>girls</u> and <u>women</u> in <u>education</u> and in <u>paid employment</u>.
   4) <u>Reduce death rates</u> in <u>children</u> under five years old by <u>two-thirds</u>.
   5) <u>Reduce death rates</u> amongst <u>women</u> caused by pregnancy or childbirth by <u>three-quarters</u>.
   6) Stop the <u>spread</u> of major <u>diseases</u>, including HIV/AIDS and malaria.
   7) <u>Protect</u> the <u>environment</u> and make sure development was <u>sustainable</u>, while <u>improving quality of life</u>.
   8) Make sure that countries <u>around the world</u> worked <u>together</u> to help LIDCs develop.

3) By <u>2015</u>, the UN had gone some way to achieving these goals, but success was <u>variable</u> in different parts of the world. The UN has set a new series of <u>Sustainable Development Goals</u> (<u>SDGs</u>) to achieve by <u>2030</u>.

My development goal is to retire somewhere sunny by the time I'm 30...

All this stuff might seem a bit dry and theoretical now, but you need to understand the theory to make sense of your LIDC case study. If you don't read it properly now, don't come crying to me when pages 69-72 make no sense...

Increasing Development — Aid

There are lots of different things that can <u>help</u> a country to develop, but none of them are <u>trouble-free</u>...

Aid can Help Countries to Develop

1) Aid is <u>given</u> by one country to another, either as <u>money</u> or as <u>resources</u> (e.g. food, doctors).

2) Money can be spent on development projects, e.g. building <u>schools</u> to <u>improve literacy</u> rates, making <u>dams</u> to <u>provide clean water</u> or providing <u>farming education</u> and <u>equipment</u> to <u>improve agriculture</u>.

3) There are <u>different types</u> of aid, all with <u>advantages</u> and disadvantages for development:

Type of Aid	What it is	Advantages	Disadvantages
'Top-down'	When an <u>organisation</u> or <u>government receives</u> the aid and <u>decides</u> how it should be <u>spent</u>.	• Often used for <u>large projects</u>, e.g. <u>dams</u> for hydroelectric power (HEP) or <u>irrigation schemes</u>. • These can solve <u>large scale</u> problems and improve the lives of <u>lots</u> of people. • Projects can improve the country's <u>economy</u>, helping with <u>long-term development</u>.	• The country may have to <u>pay back the money</u> (if it's a loan). • Large projects are often <u>expensive</u>. • They <u>may not benefit everyone</u> — e.g. HEP may not supply power to remote areas. • If governments are <u>corrupt</u>, they may use the <u>money</u> for their <u>own purposes</u>, so it doesn't help development.
'Bottom-up'	Money is given <u>directly to local people</u>, e.g. to build or maintain a well.	• <u>Local people</u> have a <u>say</u> in how the money will be <u>used</u>, so they get what they <u>need</u>. • Projects often <u>employ</u> local people, so they <u>earn money</u> and <u>learn new skills</u>.	• Projects may be <u>small-scale</u>, so they <u>don't benefit everyone</u>. • Different organisations (e.g. charities) may <u>not work together</u>, so projects may be <u>inefficient</u>.
Short-term	Aid sent to help countries cope with <u>emergencies</u>, e.g. natural disasters.	• Gives <u>immediate relief</u>, so the country <u>recovers faster</u>. • Money allocated for <u>development</u> doesn't have to be used to cope with the <u>emergency</u> instead.	• Often doesn't help with <u>longer-term</u> recovery, e.g. rebuilding <u>infrastructure</u>. This may <u>restrict</u> further development. • <u>Food aid</u> may <u>limit</u> the <u>price</u> farmers can charge for their crops, so their <u>income</u> is <u>reduced</u>.
Long-term	Aid given over a <u>long period</u> to help countries <u>develop</u>.	• Most projects aim to be <u>sustainable</u>, e.g. by helping people <u>meet their own needs</u>. • Projects can <u>improve life</u> for <u>lots</u> of people in the <u>long-term</u>. • May help to build <u>trade links</u> between the <u>donor</u> and <u>recipient</u> countries.	• May make the <u>recipient country dependent</u> on aid. • Aid is sometimes '<u>tied</u>' — money has to be spent on <u>goods</u> and <u>services</u> from the <u>donor</u> country, which may be <u>more expensive</u> than from other sources.
Debt relief	A country <u>doesn't</u> have to pay back <u>part</u> or <u>all</u> of the money it has <u>borrowed</u>.	• <u>Frees up money</u> that can be spent on <u>development</u>. • Donor countries can <u>specify</u> how the cancelled debt should be spent, e.g. on <u>health care</u> or <u>education</u>.	• Donor countries may be <u>reluctant</u> to cancel debts for countries with <u>corrupt governments</u>. • Imposing conditions can mean that the money <u>isn't</u> used where it's most <u>needed</u>.

"I'd like some long-term, bottom-up debt relief, please Dad..."

I outlined the major advantages to him — that I'd get to choose how I spent the money (buying a yacht) and that I'd learn valuable new skills (how to sail a yacht) — but he still wouldn't pay off my student loan.

Increasing Development — Trade and TNCs

Trade has Advantages and Disadvantages...

For more on trade, see p.65.

1) Trade between an <u>LIDC</u> and <u>other countries</u> can help the LIDC to <u>develop</u> by:

- <u>Creating jobs</u> and <u>bringing money</u> into the country. This improves people's <u>standard of living</u>.
- Increasing the amount of <u>money</u> a country has to spend on things like <u>health care</u> and <u>education</u>, and on <u>development projects</u>, such as <u>improving transport infrastructure</u>.

2) However, there are <u>problems</u> with countries <u>relying</u> on trade to help them <u>develop</u>:

- Some LIDCs <u>can't afford</u> the <u>technology</u> to produce goods <u>quickly</u> and <u>cheaply</u> (e.g. agricultural machinery). This means they might not be able to <u>match the prices</u> of other countries.
- <u>Conflict</u> can make the <u>supply</u> of goods <u>unreliable</u>, so countries may not have goods to trade.
- In countries where <u>diseases</u> such as HIV/AIDS are a major problem, money has to be spent on <u>treating people</u>, so there's <u>less money</u> to invest in <u>developing trade</u>.
- Trade can have a <u>negative effect</u> on people. E.g. to keep <u>prices</u> low, <u>wages</u> and <u>working conditions</u> may be very <u>poor</u>. So increased trade <u>won't</u> necessarily improve <u>quality of life</u> for everyone.
- LIDCs often export <u>primary products</u> such as grain or wood. These products don't create much <u>profit</u>, so they don't provide much <u>money</u> for development. They can also be <u>unreliable</u>, e.g. if crops <u>fail</u> because of <u>drought</u>.
- Countries are often dependent on trading <u>one product</u>, e.g. coffee or cotton. If the <u>demand</u> for that product <u>falls</u>, the country's income can <u>decrease sharply</u>.

... and so do Trans-National Companies

1) TNCs (trans-national companies) are <u>companies</u> that are located in or <u>produce and sell products</u> in <u>more than one country</u>. E.g. Sony is a TNC — it makes electronic products in China and Japan.

2) TNC <u>factories</u> are usually located in <u>poorer countries</u> because <u>labour is cheaper</u>, and there are fewer environmental and labour regulations, which means they make <u>more profit</u>.

3) They can <u>improve</u> the <u>development</u> of countries they work in by <u>transferring</u> <u>jobs</u>, <u>skills</u> and <u>money</u> to less developed countries, <u>reducing</u> the <u>development gap</u>.

4) TNC <u>offices</u> and <u>headquarters</u> are usually located in <u>richer countries</u> because there are <u>more people</u> with <u>administrative skills</u> (because <u>education is better</u>).

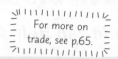

TNC Inc. — Profit vs Loads: Moved factories abroad

TNCs have <u>advantages</u> and <u>disadvantages</u>:

Advantages	Disadvantages
TNCs <u>create jobs</u> in all the countries they're located in.	<u>Employees in poorer countries</u> may be <u>paid lower wages</u> than employees in <u>richer countries</u>.
<u>Employees in poorer countries</u> get a <u>more reliable income</u> compared to jobs like farming.	<u>Employees in poorer countries</u> may have to work <u>long hours</u> in <u>poor conditions</u>.
TNCs <u>spend money</u> to <u>improve</u> the <u>local infrastructure</u>, e.g. airports and roads.	Most TNCs <u>come from richer countries</u> so the <u>profits go back there</u> — they <u>aren't reinvested</u> in the <u>poorer countries</u> the TNC operates in.
<u>New technology</u> (e.g. computers) and <u>skills</u> are <u>brought to poorer countries</u>.	The <u>jobs created in poorer countries aren't secure</u> — the TNC could relocate the jobs to another country at any time.

Don't confuse TNCs with T&Cs — this stuff is much more interesting...

While TNCs have some downsides, they certainly have some positive effects too. Have a good read of this page so it all sinks in. And, unlike Terms and Conditions, you won't even need to squint. By reading this, you agree that any eye strain from squinting is your responsibility.

LIDC Development — Case Study

Now you know all the theory of how development works, it's time to get to grips with what it looks like out there in the real world — yep, it's case study o'clock in the Democratic Republic of the Congo.

The Democratic Republic of the Congo is One of the World's Poorest Countries

1) The Democratic Republic of the Congo (DRC) is a huge country in central Africa. It is nearly landlocked — it just has a tiny stretch of coastline.

2) It has a population of around 79 million. A high birth rate is causing the population to grow quite rapidly, so there are increasing numbers of people who need food, clean water, education etc.

3) The DRC has very rich natural resources, including copper, gold, oil and diamonds. Its fertile soil and climate make it ideal for growing crops such as coffee, sugar and cotton.

4) The DRC also has rich deposits of minerals ores such as coltan and wolframite, which are used in laptops, mobile phones and cameras.

5) Despite this, it is a very poor country with a low level of development.

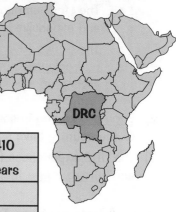

GNI per capita	US $410
Life expectancy	59 years
Literacy rate	61%
HDI	0.43

Political and Social Factors Have Hindered Development

1) The DRC was a Belgian colony from 1885 to 1960. By 1960, the country was quite developed in some ways — industry was booming, and education and health care were improving.

2) However, most of the massive wealth created from mines and farms was passed back to other countries. Native people were not allowed to vote, and were allowed only a very basic education.

3) The DRC gained independence from Belgium in 1960, and there was conflict over who would lead the country. In 1965, Mobutu Sese Seko seized power. His rule prevented the DRC from developing:

- Corruption was very widespread — President Mobutu allowed armed forces to loot the country, taking goods and money. This led to huge inequality in wealth — a small number of very rich people, and a huge number of very poor people.

- Large companies paid bribes to gain access to mineral resources. Much of the resulting wealth left the country, so it didn't benefit the local people.

- Mobutu forced many foreign-owned businesses to leave the country, leading to loss of jobs and wealth. He refused to pay back debts to Belgium, who cancelled development projects in the DRC.

- There was conflict over leadership for much of his rule. This caused damage to crops, property and infrastructure, forced people to flee their homes and made it hard for them to access medical care.

4) Mobutu was overthrown in 1997. This led to civil war, which lasted until 2003.

5) Joseph Kabila, who became president in 2001, promised to focus on improving infrastructure, health, education, housing, jobs and access to resources such as water and power.

Peace is fragile and fighting still continues in some areas.

6) There have been signs of economic growth since 2012, but development remains relatively slow.

'Conflict Minerals' Have also Held Back Development

1) Growing global demand for electronic products has increased demand for minerals ores such as coltan and wolframite. In parts of the DRC, armed groups force people to work in dangerous conditions to mine the mineral ores.

2) Fighting over ownership of the mines has caused the deaths of millions of people, causing these resources to become known as 'conflict minerals'.

3) Many companies are now buying minerals from other countries, where forced labour and war aren't an issue. This makes it difficult for the DRC to sell the resources it has, which is hindering economic development.

Topic 6 — Dynamic Development

LIDC Development — Case Study

The Environment Creates Challenges for Development

1) Although the DRC is rich in resources (see p.69), its geography makes it hard for them to be exploited:

   - The country is so large that goods have to be transported thousands of miles.
   - The small amount of coastline limits ocean transport. Building roads and railways is difficult and expensive because much of the country is covered in forest and there are lots of rivers.
   - The Congo River, which runs east to west across the country, has the potential to provide hydroelectric power for large parts of Africa. However, the difficult terrain means that setting up infrastructure to transmit this electricity is very difficult.

2) Food production in some areas is difficult, causing malnutrition and poverty — the centre and south of the country have a long dry season, and droughts can occur between April and November.

3) The DRC experiences frequent floods — this can ruin crops, as well as destroying settlements and infrastructure that require money to rebuild. This hinders further development.

The Millennium Development Goals have been Partially Met in the DRC

The DRC has made some progress towards meeting the MDGs (see p.66) — most measures of development show some improvement since 2000, but the DRC is still one of the least developed countries in the world.

1 Reduce Poverty and Hunger

1) The percentage of people living in poverty decreased from 71% in 2005 to 63% in 2012.

2) However, the number of people suffering from malnutrition increased from 51% in 2000 to 66% in 2015.

2 Provide Education For All

The percentage of children who completed a primary school education increased from 35% in 1999 to 72% in 2013.

3 Promote Gender Equality

1) The percentage of girls finishing primary school doubled from 32% in 1999 to 65% in 2013. However, the percentage of boys finishing primary school grew more over the same period, so inequality has increased.

2) There are fewer women than men in paid work, and on average they earn less than men doing the same job.

4 Reduce Child Death Rates

1) The death rate of children under five decreased from about 176 per thousand births in 2000 to about 120 per thousand births in 2013.

2) More than 70% of children are now vaccinated against measles, compared to less than 20% in 1999.

5 Reduce Maternal Death Rates

1) The number of women dying in childbirth decreased from around 870 per 100 000 births in 2000 to around 690 per 100 000 births in 2015.

2) The availability of health care for mothers before and during childbirth has increased since 1990.

6 Stop the Spread of Diseases

1) The percentage of people with HIV/AIDS has decreased from about 5% to about 1% since 2000. This is partly due to better education and increased access to contraception.

2) The proportion of people with malaria halved between 2000 and 2015, due partly to a huge increase in the availability of mosquito nets.

7 Make Development Sustainable

1) About 50% of the population have access to clean water — a small increase from 2000.

2) There are efforts to preserve the rainforests, e.g. the government has created protected areas and put bans on new logging operations.

8 Promote International Links

1) In 2008, China gave the DRC US $6 billion to spend on infrastructure, in return for access to some of its mineral resources.

2) Other countries have invested in trade (see p.71) and offered aid (see p.72).

LIDC Development — Case Study

Rostow's Model *May Help to Show* How *the DRC will Develop*

See p.66 for more on Rostow's model

1) The DRC has an economy that's based on both primary goods (e.g. metal and mineral extraction, agriculture) and secondary goods (e.g. shoes and cement).

2) The DRC appears to be at Stage 2 of Rostow's model of development ⟹ 'Preconditions for take-off'.

3) Rostow's model suggests that Stage 3 ('Take-off') is the next step for the DRC, with rapid industrialisation and increasing wealth. This should trigger increased trade and investment, leading to further development.

> In Stage 2, a country starts to manufacture goods and has surplus produce to trade. It develops infrastructure, e.g. transport networks.

4) However, the DRC doesn't fit neatly into Stage 2 and may not develop as Rostow's model suggests:

- Transport infrastructure is very poor, with few paved roads and limited railways. This limits the country's potential for exports and trade, which will slow its development.

- Only around 10% of people have access to electricity, and this value is much lower in rural areas. Power cuts are common. This makes it hard for industry to operate, which hinders development.

The DRC is *Increasing* its *Trade Links*

1) Until recently, the DRC had a trade deficit (it imported more than it exported). More money was being sent to other countries than was being received from them, which weakened the DRC's economy.

2) The DRC now exports roughly as much as it imports (about US $12.4 billion of goods each year).

3) The DRC exports mostly primary products, including crude oil, minerals, wood and coffee. Minerals and metals, such as diamonds, gold and copper, account for about 90% of exports.

4) The DRC's main imports are manufactured goods, such as machinery, vehicles and electrical equipment.

5) Until recently, many countries were reluctant to trade with DRC because of human rights violations, corruption and conflict. Since 1997, trade links have increased and the DRC now trades with a number of countries — its main trading partners are Belgium, China, Italy, France and Australia. The DRC is also a member of several trade communities, designed to increase free trade in Africa.

Trade Brings *Benefits* and *Problems* to the DRC

1) The increase in trade in the DRC has had significant advantages for the country:

- The economy of the DRC grew by 7% from 2010 to 2012, and this growth rate is expected to increase. Increased wealth improves standard of living and gives opportunities for investment in e.g. education and healthcare.

- Establishing links with other countries makes them more likely to invest in the DRC (e.g. by locating branches of TNCs there) or to offer aid, which can be used for development.

2) However, it has also caused some problems:

- The DRC's reliance on trading primary goods, e.g. minerals, makes it vulnerable to falling prices — in 2008 and 2009, global economic problems caused a sharp fall in the value of these products, which hindered economic growth in DRC.

- The DRC's reliance on importing manufactured goods makes it vulnerable to increased prices. These goods are generally more valuable than primary products, so the DRC has to pay a lot for them — this has also limited its economic development.

- Demand from richer countries for mineral ores such as coltan and wolframite (see p.69) led to uncontrolled exploitation of these resources. Their extraction often involved human rights abuses such as slavery, and helped to fund armed rebels in the DRC. There are now international efforts to make extraction and trade of these mineral ores safe, legal and profitable for the DRC.

LIDC Development — Case Study

Few TNCs are Located in the DRC

1) Relatively few TNCs currently operate in the DRC, but their number is increasing — particularly mining companies such as Anglo American (based in the UK and South Africa) and Banro (based in Canada).

2) TNCs have helped economic development in the DRC, but they have also caused problems:

Advantages

1) TNCs provide employment — Banro employs at least 1500 people in the DRC.

2) TNCs have set up development projects in the DRC — e.g. in 2014, Banro finished building a marketplace in Luhwindja, to provide jobs for local people and improve the local economy.

3) TNCs bring money into the DRC through taxes and spending on goods and services — Banro contributes almost US $120 million to the DRC economy each year through local spending.

4) TNCs invest money in infrastructure, e.g. roads and bridges, which benefits local people.

Disadvantages

1) TNCs can pull out of the country, taking jobs and wealth with them — in 2009, mining company De Beers announced that it would stop looking for new diamond reserves in the DRC.

2) Some profits from TNCs leave the DRC, e.g. some of Banro's profits return to Canada.

3) Some large mining companies have been accused of forcing small mines to close and people to leave their homes, to make way for large mines.

4) TNCs can cause environmental problems, e.g. construction of roads to give access to mines causes deforestation.

The DRC Receives a Lot of Aid

1) The DRC receives billions of dollars of aid every year — some of the highest amounts of any country. The main donors include the USA, UK, Belgium and the World Bank. Aid has pros and cons for the DRC:

Advantages

1) Aid funds projects to improve living conditions, health, education and infrastructure, e.g. the UK has funded the construction of 1700 km of new roads.

2) Emergency aid programmes have provided food and shelter for people who are affected by ongoing conflicts over land and resources.

Disadvantages

1) Some early aid was in the form of weapons to arm government forces. This promoted fighting and didn't directly benefit civilians.

2) Some aid has conditions, e.g. in 2008 China gave the DRC US $9 billion, but insisted that it be used to develop mining and infrastructure — this may not benefit the poorest people.

2) Both top-down and bottom-up aid projects have been used in the DRC:

	Project	Advantages	Disadvantages
'Top-down'	Proposed construction of Grand Inga Dam on Congo River, starting 2017. Cost: US $80 billion Donors: World Bank, African Development Bank and others	• Could provide cheap, clean energy for all of the DRC, plus extra to sell. • Will promote industry in the DRC, providing jobs and boosting the economy.	• Risk that money may be lost to corrupt officials/companies. • Little provision for transmitting energy to poor, rural communities. • Flooding of the Bundi Valley and relocation of 30 000 people.
'Bottom-up'	Involving teachers, students and parents in improving rural schools and increasing the number of children in education. Cost: £390 000 Donor: Comic Relief	• Local people have a say in how their schools should be improved. • Better-educated people earn more, so contribute more to economic development.	• Not enough funding to improve all schools, so not everyone benefits. • Some families need children to earn a living, so they can't afford to send them to school. • Doesn't tackle large-scale issues.

The Congo? Isn't that a dance? No, wait...

Phew, that's a lot to take in. Give it another read, and then have a go at this question.

1) For an LIDC you have studied, suggest how trade has influenced its level of development . [6]

Revision Summary

Hurrah, another section bites the dust. Hopefully you've now developed a good understanding of how countries are developing — luckily I've got a big stack of revision summary questions so you can be sure. All the answers are in the section you've just revised, so if you're struggling for an answer, head back to the page and learn it again. Once you've got them right, you can crack on and learn about the UK in the 21st century.

Development (p.62-63) ☑

1) What is economic development?
2) What is social development?
3) List five measures of development.
4) What is meant by 'uneven development'?
5) What do LIDC, AC and EDC stand for?
6) Where are most ACs found?

Factors Affecting Development (p.64-65) ☑

7) Give four physical factors that can affect how developed a country is.
8) For one physical factor, describe how it can affect development.
9) Give four human factors that can affect how developed a country is.
10) For one human factor, describe how it can affect development.

Increasing Development (p.66-68) ☑

11) Briefly describe the five stages of Rostow's model of economic development.
12) Describe two of the Millennium Development Goals.
13) Explain the difference between 'top-down' and 'bottom-up aid.'
14) What is the difference between short-term and long-term aid?
15) Give one advantage and one disadvantage of short-term aid.
16) Explain how debt relief can help a country to develop.
17) What is a TNC?
18) How can TNCs help the development of a country?
19) Give one disadvantage of TNCs for developing countries.

Development in the Democratic Republic of the Congo (p.69-72) ☑

20) True or false: the DRC is landlocked.
21) Explain how being a colony might have hindered development in the DRC.
22) Explain how political factors have affected development in the DRC.

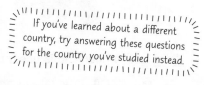
If you've learned about a different country, try answering these questions for the country you've studied instead.

23) What are 'conflict minerals'?
24) Describe two physical factors that have hindered development in the DRC.
25) For two Millennium Development Goals, describe how far they've been met in the DRC.
26) What stage of Rostow's development model does the DRC fall into? Explain your answer.
27) a) What are the DRC's main exports? What are its main imports?
    b) What effect might this have on its economy?
28) Give one advantage and one disadvantage to the DRC of increasing trade.
29) a) Name a TNC that operates in the DRC.
    b) Describe the advantages and disadvantages of TNCs to the DRC.
30) a) Describe one aid project taking place in the DRC.
    b) Describe the advantages and disadvantages of this aid project to the DRC.

Characteristics of the UK

Time to learn some stuff about the UK. I don't know if you've been, but I hear it's lovely at this time of year.

The Characteristics of the UK Change Across the Country

UK population density

Population density (the number of people living in a given area) varies:

- Population density is highest in cities, e.g. London, Glasgow, Birmingham — in London it's about 5500 people per km².
- It's also high in areas around major cities, or where there are clusters of cities, e.g. the south-east, Midlands and central Scotland.
- Mountainous regions such as northern Scotland and central Wales have low population densities.
- Other areas of low population density are north England and west Wales. Eden in Cumbria has a population density of about 24 people per km².

High population density can cause problems:

- There may be a shortage of available housing — e.g. in London, up to 60 000 new homes are needed every year to keep up with population growth. A shortage can drive up the price of houses, so some people can't afford to live there.
- There may be pressure on services such as health care and schools — there can be long waiting lists to see doctors, and children may have to attend a school a long way from home.

UK average annual rainfall

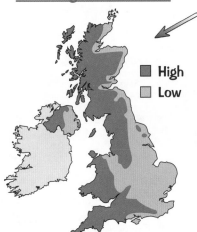

High
Low

The UK gets quite a lot of rain, but the amount varies hugely around the country:

> The UK's relief (see p.25) helps to determine patterns of population density, rainfall and land use.

- The north and west of the UK generally have high rainfall. E.g. Aultbea in northwest Scotland has an average annual rainfall of 1470 mm.
- The south and east of the UK generally have lower rainfall. E.g. London has an annual average rainfall of 560 mm.
- Rainfall tends to be higher in coastal areas than inland.
- Rainfall is also higher in areas of higher elevation — mountainous areas get more rainfall than low-lying areas.

Areas with high population density use a lot of resources, e.g. water. If the area also has low rainfall, this can cause water stress — there isn't enough water to meet people's needs. London experiences severe water stress.

Land use is how land is used, e.g. housing or farming. It varies across the UK:

UK land use

- Built-up areas
- Natural land
- Agricultural land
- Wetlands

- Most of the UK (about 70%) is agricultural land. Arable farming (growing crops) is more common in the south and east of the country, and grazing animals is more common in the north and west.
- Less than 10% of the UK is built on — buildings are concentrated in large urban areas, especially in south-east England, the Midlands and central Scotland. These urban areas are expanding.
- Forest covers about 13% of the land — some of this is natural and some has been planted and is managed by people.
- Some areas are not used as much by humans and have been left in a fairly natural state, e.g. mountainous or boggy areas in north Scotland.

Dry and not too busy — I'm off to Norfolk...

Don't worry too much about learning specific details on this page — the main thing to learn is the rough patterns of population density, rainfall, land use and relief (see p.25), and some of the issues these patterns can cause.

The Changing Population of the UK

Population change — it's everyone's favourite topic. Well, maybe not everyone's. Must be someone's though.

The UK's Population is Increasing

1) In 2001, the population of the UK was about 59 million. By 2015, it was about 65 million.
2) Population has increased every year since 2001, but growth rate has slowed down since 2011.
3) The changing population structure of the UK (the number of men and women in different age groups) is shown using population pyramids:

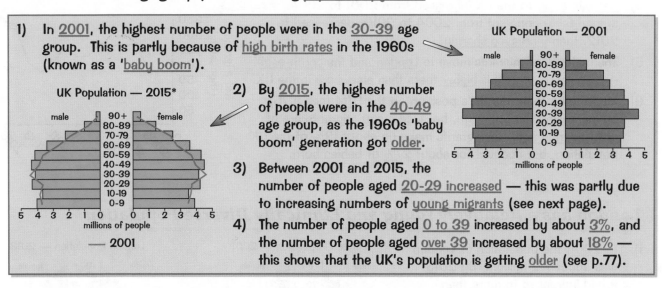

1) In 2001, the highest number of people were in the 30-39 age group. This is partly because of high birth rates in the 1960s (known as a 'baby boom').

2) By 2015, the highest number of people were in the 40-49 age group, as the 1960s 'baby boom' generation got older.

3) Between 2001 and 2015, the number of people aged 20-29 increased — this was partly due to increasing numbers of young migrants (see next page).

4) The number of people aged 0 to 39 increased by about 3%, and the number of people aged over 39 increased by about 18% — this shows that the UK's population is getting older (see p.77).

UK Population — 2015*
male / female, 90+, 80-89, 70-79, 60-69, 50-59, 40-49, 30-29, 20-29, 10-19, 0-9
5 4 3 2 1 0   0 1 2 3 4 5
millions of people
— 2001

UK Population — 2001
male / female, 90+, 80-89, 70-79, 60-69, 50-59, 40-49, 30-39, 20-29, 10-19, 0-9
5 4 3 2 1 0   0 1 2 3 4 5
millions of people

The UK is at Stage 4 of the Demographic Transition Model

1) The Demographic Transition Model (DTM) shows how a country's population is likely to change as it develops, based on changing birth and death rates.

2) At stage 1, birth and death rates are high, and population is low. As a country develops, healthcare improves, so death rate falls and population grows. Over time, better education and increased access to contraception means that birth rate falls, so population growth begins to slow down.

Natural population increase — birth rate, death rate, population size
Natural population decrease

	Stage 1	Stage 2	Stage 3	Stage 4	Stage 5
Birth rate	High and fluctuating	High and steady	Rapidly falling	Low and fluctuating	Slowly falling
Death rate	High and fluctuating	Rapidly falling	Slowly falling	Low and fluctuating	Low and steady
Population growth rate	Zero	Very high	High	Zero	Negative
Population size	Low and steady	Rapidly increasing	Increasing	High and steady	Slowly falling
When was the UK at this stage?	Before 1760	1760 to 1870	1870 to 1950	1950 to present	In the near future?

3) In the UK:

- Birth rate and death rate have fallen over the past 300 years — it has been through stages 1-3 of the DTM.

The DTM doesn't account for migration — see next page.

- Birth rate is now 12 births per thousand people and death rate is 9 deaths per thousand people. These are both quite low, but population is still growing slowly — this shows that the UK is at stage 4 of the DTM.

4) The UK hasn't yet reached stage 5 — when death rate is higher than birth rate, and population size starts to decrease.

What's all this nonsense about deaf rats?

The Changing Population of the UK

There's Lots of Migration to the UK

The difference between the number of people moving to and away from the UK is called net migration.

1) Roughly <u>half</u> the UK's <u>population growth</u> (see previous page) is driven by <u>natural increase</u> (more births than deaths), and about half by <u>migration</u>.

2) In 2015, <u>over 600 000</u> people moved to the UK, mostly from <u>China</u>, <u>Australia</u>, <u>India</u> and <u>Poland</u>. About <u>300 000</u> people moved overseas, mostly to <u>Australia</u>, <u>France</u> and <u>China</u>.

3) The <u>number</u> of people moving <u>to</u> the UK has been greater than the number <u>leaving</u> in <u>every year</u> since 2001.

4) <u>Net migration</u> to the UK <u>increased</u> from 2001 to 2004, <u>stayed fairly constant</u> from 2004 to 2010, decreased to 2012, then <u>increased sharply</u>.

5) The majority of migrants move to <u>London</u> and the <u>south-east</u> — <u>population growth</u> is <u>higher</u> there than elsewhere in the UK.

6) Migration affects the UK's position on the <u>DTM</u> (see p.75) by <u>increasing</u> the <u>birth rate</u>, because many migrants are of <u>child-bearing age</u>. Immigrants make up about <u>13%</u> of the UK population, but account for about <u>27%</u> of babies born.

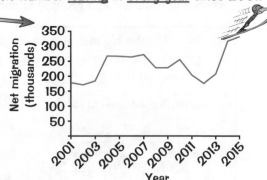

London has a Relatively Young and Ethnically Diverse Population

1) In <u>2001</u>, the population of London was about <u>7.2 million</u>. By <u>2015</u>, it had increased to more than <u>8.5 million</u>. This is <u>faster</u> growth than <u>anywhere else</u> in the UK.

2) Growth was <u>higher</u> amongst groups of <u>working age</u> (20-69 years) than for those <u>under 20</u> or <u>over 69</u> — lots of people move to London from elsewhere in the UK or from overseas for <u>work</u>. The <u>highest</u> population growth was in the <u>40-49</u> age bracket, which increased by almost <u>30%</u>.

3) The percentage of <u>men</u> in all age groups <u>increased more</u> than the percentage of <u>women</u> between 2001 and 2013, although the <u>total number</u> of women remained slightly higher.

4) Just like the rest of the UK, population growth in London is driven by <u>natural increase</u> and <u>migration</u>. People who migrate to London from <u>other countries</u> increase the city's <u>ethnic diversity</u>.

Ethnic Diversity

1) Across the UK as a whole, about <u>13%</u> of the population were <u>born</u> in another country. In <u>London</u>, this value is about <u>37%</u>.

2) Ethnic diversity in London has <u>increased</u> between 2001 and the present — in 2001, <u>60%</u> of the population were <u>white British</u>, but by 2011 this had <u>fallen</u> to <u>45%</u>.

3) The change was driven by an <u>increase</u> in the percentage of <u>white non-British</u> people (particularly from <u>Poland</u> and <u>Romania</u>), as well as <u>Black African</u> and <u>Asian</u> people.

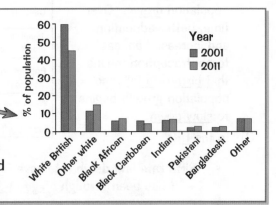

The population of London's growing — would you Adam and Eve it...

Maybe it's because I'm a Londoner, that I love population stats so. Mmm, tuneful. Once you're clear what's happening to the population of the UK and London, and why, proceed to the next page in an orderly fashion. No pushing at the back.

The UK's Ageing Population

An <u>ageing population</u> is one that has an increasingly <u>high proportion</u> of <u>older people</u>. Ageing populations can face some sticky <u>economic</u> and <u>social</u> problems. They also tend to consume a high quantity of teacakes.

The UK has an *Ageing Population*

In the UK, around <u>18%</u> of the population are <u>over 65</u>. The proportion of <u>older</u> people is <u>increasing</u> because:

1) <u>Birth rates</u> are <u>low</u> because couples are having <u>fewer</u> children — in the UK, the average number of children per family <u>decreased</u> from <u>2.9</u> in 1964 (the peak of the 1960s 'baby boom') to <u>1.8</u> in 2014. Also, more women are choosing <u>not to have children</u> than in the past.

2) People are <u>living longer</u> due to better <u>medical</u> care and a <u>healthier lifestyle</u> (e.g. not smoking). Life expectancy in the UK <u>increased</u> from <u>72 years</u> in 1964 to <u>81 years</u> in 2015.

The *Number* of Older People *Varies Around the UK*

1) The <u>proportion</u> of older people <u>isn't the same</u> everywhere in the UK.

2) It's <u>lower</u> in <u>Northern Ireland</u> and <u>Scotland</u> than in <u>England</u> and <u>Wales</u>.

3) It's generally <u>lower</u> in <u>big cities</u>, such as London, Bristol and Manchester — people often live in cities to be closer to their <u>jobs</u>, so a higher proportion of the population is of <u>working age</u>.

4) The percentage of older people is <u>high</u> in <u>coastal areas</u>, especially in <u>east</u> and <u>south-west England</u>, because lots of people move there when they <u>retire</u>.

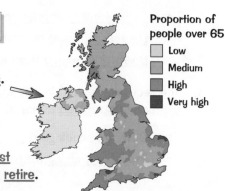

Proportion of people over 65
- Low
- Medium
- High
- Very high

The *Ageing Population Has Social* and *Economic Effects*

I've got loads of time to kill... zombies.

Social

1) <u>Healthcare services</u> are <u>under pressure</u> because <u>demand</u> for medical care has <u>increased</u>.

2) Some people act as <u>unpaid carers</u> for older family members in their free time, so they have <u>less leisure time</u> and are more <u>stressed</u>.

3) People may not be able to <u>afford</u> to have lots of children when they have dependent older relatives. This may lead to a further <u>drop in birth rate</u>.

4) Many retired people do <u>voluntary work</u>, e.g. in hospitals. This <u>benefits</u> the community.

Economic

1) <u>Taxes</u> for working people <u>rise</u> to pay for <u>healthcare</u> and services such as <u>pensions</u> and <u>retirement homes</u>.

2) Older people who <u>aren't working</u> pay <u>less tax</u>, so their economic contribution <u>decreases</u>.

3) However, some older people <u>look after</u> their grandchildren, so their children can <u>work</u>.

4) Many older people have <u>disposable income</u>, which they spend on goods and services that <u>boost</u> the economy.

There are *Different Responses* to the UK's *Ageing Population*

1) As the number of older people <u>increases</u>, the government may need to <u>increase taxes</u> or <u>cut spending</u> in other areas (e.g. education or defence) to fund more <u>support</u> and <u>medical care</u>.

2) The government is <u>raising</u> the <u>age</u> at which people can claim a <u>pension</u> — people <u>stay in work longer</u>, so they contribute to <u>taxes</u> and <u>pensions</u> for <u>longer</u>.

3) The government is encouraging people to <u>save more money</u> to help pay for their <u>retirement</u>. For example, in 2015 the government launched <u>savings accounts</u> for over-65s, known as 'pensioner bonds' — these offer a <u>higher rate of interest</u> than many savings accounts, so older people can <u>save more</u>.

4) The UK government currently offers a <u>winter fuel allowance</u> to <u>all</u> older people. In future, this may <u>only</u> be given to older people who <u>can't afford</u> to heat their homes, meaning <u>less money</u> is spent overall.

Being old isn't a crime, but my aunt has knitted some criminal jumpers...

'Live long enough to be a burden on your children' — I thought it was just a phrase... Check that you have a good grasp of the causes, distribution, effects and responses to the UK's ageing population by jotting down a few points for each.

The Changing Economy of the UK

The UK's economy is changing all the time — as if understanding economics wasn't hard enough already...

Changes to the Economy Have Been Driven by Politics

1) Between 1997 and 2007, the UK economy grew strongly and unemployment decreased. This was partly because of the government's priorities:

> *Investment in technology and education boosted growth of quaternary industries (see below).*

- Encouraging investment in new technologies, e.g. computing industries.
- Investing in university education, leading to a more skilled workforce.

2) However, in early 2008 the UK entered a recession. Businesses failed, GDP decreased and unemployment increased. The government had to change their priorities to end the recession:

- Supporting businesses so they didn't collapse — their collapse would increase unemployment.
- Decreasing taxes on goods to encourage spending and international trade.
- Borrowing money from e.g. private companies and overseas investors.

> *Getting people into work means there are fewer people claiming benefits and more paying taxes.*

3) The recession ended in late 2009. The government had to focus on paying off money borrowed during the recession and helping people to find jobs:

- Cutting spending on public services such as pensions, education and defence to raise money.
- Providing training for job-seekers and support for new businesses to decrease unemployment.

The UK's Employment Sectors Have Changed

1) Since 2001, jobs in quaternary industries (e.g. education and research, ICT) have increased most, while jobs in secondary industries (e.g. manufacturing) have decreased.

2) Over the same period, the number of people employed in primary production (e.g. farming and mining) and tertiary industries (e.g. retail) stayed fairly steady.

3) The biggest increases have been in professional and technical jobs (e.g. law, computing, research and development).

4) Employment in manufacturing decreased most, partly due to cheaper materials and labour being available overseas.

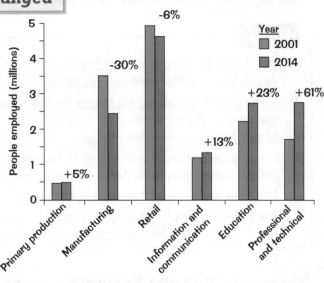

Working Hours Have Decreased Since 2001

1) Overall, working hours are decreasing — the average number of hours worked in a week was 34.7 in 2001 and 33.1 in 2014. The number of hours worked decreased slightly more for men than for women over this time.

> *Since 1998, the maximum working time per week is 48 hours, and workers are entitled to at least 5.6 weeks of holiday each year.*

2) There has been an increase in people doing part-time jobs and zero-hours contracts (where the employee isn't guaranteed any hours of work).

3) However, the number of families with both parents in full-time work has increased since 2003, when the government increased financial support for low-income working parents.

Politics? Economics? I thought this was a Geography book...

This is the kind of stuff examiners love to ask about, so check your understanding with this question.

1) Using the graph above, describe how UK employment in different sectors has changed since 2001.   [3]

UK Economic Hubs

Time to find out about the <u>economic centres</u> of the UK. Buckle your seatbelt — you're in for a wild ride.

An Economic Hub is an Economically Important Place

1) <u>Economic hubs</u> are places where <u>economic activity</u> is <u>concentrated</u> — e.g. they often have lots of <u>businesses</u>. They have economic <u>influence beyond</u> the hub itself, for example companies located in the hub may <u>trade</u> with companies in <u>other countries</u>.

2) Economic hubs occur at a <u>range of scales</u> — e.g. they can be an entire <u>region</u>, a <u>town</u> or <u>city</u>, or a <u>single street</u> within a city. For example:

Economic shrub

- <u>Region</u> — <u>South Wales</u> is home to lots of new <u>digital</u> and <u>media companies</u>, which are rapidly increasing their <u>takings</u> and <u>staff numbers</u>. This is helping to <u>boost</u> the <u>economy</u> of <u>Wales</u> and the <u>UK</u> as a whole.
- <u>City</u> — <u>London</u> is an economic hub for the UK, and has a <u>global economic influence</u>, e.g. through <u>trade</u> and <u>financial markets</u>. The <u>headquarters</u> of many <u>banks</u> and other <u>businesses</u> (both UK-based and global) are located there, and the city creates <u>22%</u> of the UK's GDP.
- <u>Part of city</u> — <u>Electric Works</u>, a large office building in central <u>Sheffield</u>, is home to many <u>digital</u>, <u>creative</u> and <u>media companies</u>.

The UK's Core Economic Hubs are Often in Cities

1) Many of the main economic hubs in the UK have a high concentration of <u>tertiary</u> and <u>quaternary</u> industries (see p.78). These are often based in <u>cities</u>, or in <u>science</u> or <u>business parks</u> on the <u>outskirts</u> of cities where there are <u>good transport links</u> and links with <u>universities</u>.

2) Economic hubs are <u>concentrated</u> in the <u>south-east</u> of <u>England</u> — cities like <u>London</u>, <u>Brighton</u> and <u>Cambridge</u> are experiencing more <u>rapid growth</u> in <u>new businesses</u> and <u>jobs</u> than cities <u>elsewhere</u> in the UK. However, the UK <u>government</u> is encouraging investment <u>outside</u> the south-east, and many <u>companies</u> are setting up sites in other areas. Some <u>examples</u> of current economic hubs and some of the <u>industries</u> located in them are:

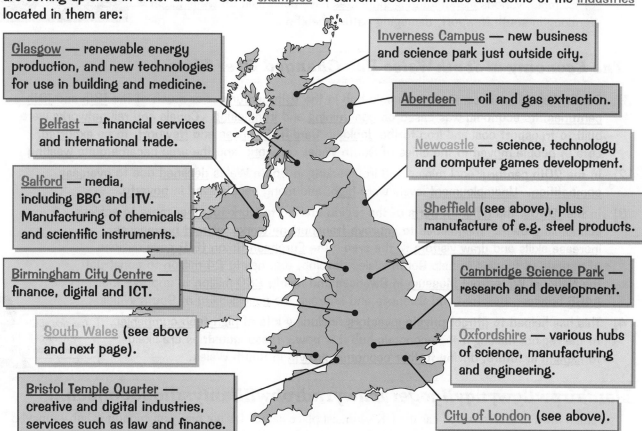

<u>Glasgow</u> — renewable energy production, and new technologies for use in building and medicine.

<u>Belfast</u> — financial services and international trade.

<u>Salford</u> — media, including BBC and ITV. Manufacturing of chemicals and scientific instruments.

<u>Birmingham City Centre</u> — finance, digital and ICT.

<u>South Wales</u> (see above and next page).

<u>Bristol Temple Quarter</u> — creative and digital industries, services such as law and finance.

<u>Inverness Campus</u> — new business and science park just outside city.

<u>Aberdeen</u> — oil and gas extraction.

<u>Newcastle</u> — science, technology and computer games development.

<u>Sheffield</u> (see above), plus manufacture of e.g. steel products.

<u>Cambridge Science Park</u> — research and development.

<u>Oxfordshire</u> — various hubs of science, manufacturing and engineering.

<u>City of London</u> (see above).

UK Economic Hubs

South Wales *is an Economic Hub*

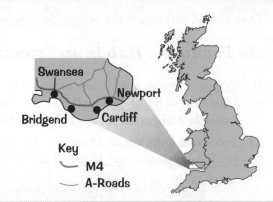

Key
- ⌣ M4
- ⌣ A-Roads

1) Wales is <u>less wealthy</u> than the UK as a whole. However, <u>South Wales</u> is much <u>richer</u> than other parts of Wales — e.g. GDP per capita in Cardiff is £22 000 compared to £15 500 in Wales as a whole.

2) The <u>difference</u> in wealth between South Wales and the rest of Wales is caused by the large number of <u>companies</u> that have located in the <u>south</u>, and the high number of <u>visitors</u> the area attracts:

- <u>Manufacturing</u> — e.g. <u>Ford cars</u> have a production plant in <u>Bridgend</u> that employs about <u>2000 people</u>.
- <u>Services</u> — e.g. insurance providers <u>Admiral</u> have their headquarters in <u>Cardiff</u>, as well as offices in <u>Newport</u> and <u>Swansea</u>, and employ over <u>5000 people</u> in South Wales.
- <u>Digital</u> — digital companies in South Wales grew by <u>87%</u> between 2010 and 2013 — much faster than in the UK as a whole. <u>TechHub</u> in Swansea was set up in 2016 to provide <u>office space</u>, <u>networking opportunities</u> and <u>advice</u> for new digital companies.
- <u>Media</u> — over <u>50 000 people</u> are employed in media and creative industries in Wales as a whole, with the highest concentration in <u>South Wales</u>. The head office of <u>BBC Cymru Wales</u> is in <u>Cardiff</u>, and programmes made there, such as <u>Doctor Who</u> and <u>Casualty</u>, are <u>exported worldwide</u> (see p.82).
- <u>Tourism</u> — <u>600 000 people</u> visit <u>Cardiff</u> each year, contributing <u>£130 million</u> to the <u>local economy</u>.

3) Most companies are based in the cities, creating <u>inequalities in wealth</u> between the cities and <u>surrounding</u> areas. However, growth has a <u>positive effect</u> on the whole region by <u>creating jobs</u>, <u>attracting visitors</u> and prompting <u>further development</u>, e.g. out-of-town shopping centres.

4) Through <u>business investment</u>, <u>employment</u> and <u>exports</u>, South Wales contributes significantly to the economy of <u>Wales</u> and the <u>UK</u> as a whole.

5) Economic growth in South Wales has had <u>environmental impacts</u> on the region. For example, various <u>manufacturing industries</u> have been built on <u>wetlands</u> at ⟱ Wentloog in south Newport, damaging natural habitats.

The Economy *of South Wales Has Changed Over Time*

1) South Wales first became an economic hub in the <u>18th century</u>. For much of the <u>18th</u> and <u>19th</u> <u>centuries</u>, its economy was based on <u>coal mining</u> and <u>ironmaking</u>. <u>Canals</u> and <u>rail networks</u> were built to transport coal and iron to the <u>docks</u> in <u>Cardiff</u>, <u>Swansea</u> and <u>Newport</u>, to be <u>exported</u>. Lots of people <u>moved</u> to the cities of South Wales for <u>work</u>, and the area became quite <u>wealthy</u>.

2) In the <u>20th century</u>, coal mining and ironworking in South Wales <u>declined</u> due to <u>overseas</u> <u>competition</u>. <u>Unemployment</u> levels were <u>high</u>, and many people lived in <u>poverty</u>.

3) In the <u>1990s</u>, the <u>different parts</u> of the region started to <u>work together</u> more to achieve economic growth. They aimed to <u>improve transport networks</u>, <u>attract businesses</u>, <u>increase skills</u> and <u>draw visitors</u> to the area. The <u>European Union (EU)</u> gave millions of pounds of funding to help South Wales develop, e.g. nearly <u>£4 million</u> to construct the <u>National Waterfront Museum</u> in Swansea and nearly <u>£80 million</u> to improve the <u>A465</u> between Hereford and Swansea and improve the <u>accessibility</u> of South Wales.

4) This has helped to <u>attract private investors</u>, including lots of <u>high-tech companies</u>, to the region, making it the economic hub it is now. These industries are likely to <u>expand</u> in future, driving <u>further economic growth</u> in South Wales.

Can you spell out your address again?

Llanfairpwllgwyngyllgogerychwyrndrobwllllantysiliogogogoch...

... is a small town in Wales, which has the UK's longest place name. It's not really an economic hub — maybe because it's too long to fit on a business card. Writing it down and looking at it can give hours of fun, though*.

* This isn't legally binding — please don't sue us if you don't have fun.

The UK's Role in the World

The UK may be a relatively <u>small</u> state, mostly surrounded by <u>water</u>, but that hasn't stopped us getting involved in things all around the world. It gives us something other than the weather to <u>talk</u> about, I suppose.

The UK is a *Member* of *Several International Organisations*

1) Lots of <u>international organisations</u> have been set up to try to <u>avoid conflict</u>, and to ensure that member countries <u>work together</u> to help <u>resolve</u> conflict elsewhere.

2) The <u>UK</u> is a member of several international <u>groups</u>, such as:

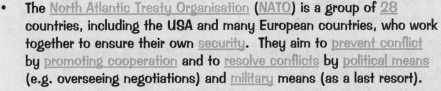

- The <u>North Atlantic Treaty Organisation</u> (<u>NATO</u>) is a group of <u>28</u> countries, including the USA and many European countries, who work together to ensure their own <u>security</u>. They aim to <u>prevent conflict</u> by <u>promoting cooperation</u> and to <u>resolve conflicts</u> by <u>political means</u> (e.g. overseeing negotiations) and <u>military</u> means (as a last resort).

  > The UK is a former member of the European Union (EU), which was set up after WWII to prevent further conflict in Europe. In 2020, the UK left the EU.

- The <u>United Nations</u> (<u>UN</u>) is made up of <u>193</u> member states. It was founded in 1945, at the <u>end of WWII</u>, to <u>maintain peace</u>. The UN tries to solve issues that can't be dealt with by individual countries, e.g. helping countries <u>develop sustainably</u> and delivering <u>aid</u> during crises.

- The <u>Group of Seven</u> (<u>G7</u>) has <u>seven</u> members — the US, Canada, France, the UK, Japan, Germany and Italy. Members meet once a year to discuss relevant <u>issues</u>, including <u>economic policies</u>, <u>conflict</u>, <u>energy supply</u> and <u>security</u>, and come to <u>agreements</u> about how best to approach them.

The UK has been *Involved* in *Trying to Resolve Conflict* in *Ukraine*

1) <u>Ukraine</u> is a country in eastern Europe — it is bordered by <u>Russia</u> to the north and east. Ukraine was <u>governed</u> by Russia until 1991.

2) In <u>2013</u>, backed by <u>Russia</u>, the Ukraine government decided not to form closer <u>trade links</u> with the <u>EU</u>, but to strengthen their ties with Russia <u>instead</u>. This was <u>unpopular</u> with many Ukrainians, who wanted to build a closer <u>relationship</u> with <u>western Europe</u>, and there were <u>protests</u> and <u>violence</u>. The president was <u>removed</u> from office and a <u>pro-EU</u> president was <u>elected</u>.

3) In <u>2014</u>, the <u>Russian President</u>, Vladimir Putin, <u>took control of Crimea</u> (part of Ukraine) and moved large numbers of Russian <u>troops</u> to the <u>Russia-Ukraine border</u>. Years of <u>fighting</u> between the <u>Ukrainian army</u> and <u>pro-Russian Ukrainians</u> followed.

> In 2022, the conflict worsened when Russia invaded Ukraine.

4) <u>International organisations</u> in which the <u>UK</u> plays a part have reacted in <u>various ways</u>:

NATO | NATO supports <u>negotiations</u> between the two sides to try to settle the conflict. In 2015, they created a <u>rapid-response force</u> of around <u>5000 soldiers</u> stationed in surrounding countries to try to <u>deter</u> future attempts by Russia to gain territory. The rapid-response force is being led by different countries in rotation — the <u>UK</u> led it in <u>2017</u>, as well as <u>supplying troops</u> and <u>RAF jets</u>.

UN | The <u>UN</u> supports <u>peace talks</u> between Russian and Ukrainian leaders and <u>provides aid</u> (e.g. food, medicine and blankets) to people forced to <u>leave their home</u> because of fighting. In 2015, the UK gave £15 million in aid to Ukraine, as well as <u>military support</u> and <u>training</u> for the Ukrainian <u>army</u>.

G7 | <u>G7</u> used to be <u>G8</u> — the other countries <u>forced Russia out</u> in 2014, after its seizure of Crimea. The UK, along with the other G7 countries, has imposed <u>sanctions</u> on Russia — e.g. <u>restricting</u> the <u>money</u> that Russian banks can borrow and <u>limiting trade</u> with Russia. By threatening the Russian <u>economy</u>, they hope to convince Russia to agree to a <u>ceasefire</u> and the <u>withdrawal</u> of troops.

Let's all keep fighting for world peace...

To read this page, you'd think that all people do is fight. There's more to the UK's role in the world than fighting or trying to stop other countries from fighting, but you don't need to know about it, so feel free to carry on in blissful ignorance.

UK Media Exports

Media exports — that doesn't just mean putting a load of CDs on a plane and sending them off to the other side of the world. Nope, with this newfangled internet malarkey, media products can be exported really easily.

The UK Exports Lots of Media Products

Social media

1) Media products are things like films, TV and radio shows, music and books.

2) The UK produces lots of media and exports it all over the world. This makes a big contribution to the UK's economy — in 2012, media industries employed nearly 1.7 million people and exported over £17 billion of products worldwide.

3) Some examples of media products that have been exported from the UK are:

- TV drama series — e.g. 'Downton Abbey' is watched by around 120 million people in more than 100 countries, including the USA and China.

- TV reality shows — e.g. 'The X Factor UK' is watched by more than 360 million people in 147 territories, and 51 countries have produced their own national version.

- Films — UK films are distributed all over the world, but are most popular in New Zealand, Australia and Europe. For example, 'The King's Speech' took over US $400 million at the box office, of which two-thirds was outside the UK.

- Music — UK artists account for nearly 14% of global album sales each year. Adele, Ed Sheeran and One Direction were three of the biggest-selling artists in the world in 2015.

- Books — e.g. the 'Harry Potter' series by J. K. Rowling has been translated into 68 languages and has sold more than 400 million copies in more than 200 territories.

The UK's Media Exports Have a Global Influence

Media produced in the UK and reflecting life here are distributed all over the world, and some successful British artists have become internationally famous. This means that media exports have a big influence:

- Most exported UK media are in English, so people in other countries develop a better understanding of the English language. However, the accents and phrases they learn may not be representative of the UK as a whole.

- The different lifestyles, values and beliefs of UK residents become more widely known and understood. However, this can be misleading — e.g. most people in the UK don't have servants or live in a house like Downton Abbey.

- Media exports affect the way the UK is perceived in other countries — e.g. in some films and TV shows it is portrayed as an ugly, industrial country, while in others it is shown as scenic and rural.

- Seeing the UK portrayed positively in different media makes people want to come here — either to work, to study or just to visit. For example, tourism in the UK increased after the 2012 Olympic Games in London, which was broadcast on TV around the world.

- Exports of similar media products may increase, strengthening the UK's economic influence.

- UK media exports can inspire people or companies in other countries to create or develop new media products — e.g. the quiz show 'The Weakest Link' started in the UK but the format was bought by more than 40 other countries, including the USA, Australia and France.

- Some people copy the clothes or hairstyles of celebrities they admire, so British celebrities have an impact on fashion around the world, and can boost sales of products that they use or endorse.

I wish I hadn't copied the hairstyle of that pig in the film...

It doesn't always pay to copy celebs — that little tuft of hair was so cute on him, but it just looked silly on me. And don't get me started on the trouble I got into when I walked down my local high street wearing the outfit he wore in the film...

Multicultural UK

It's not just the UK that influences the rest of the world — the rest of the world influences what life's like here.

Ethnic Groups Influence Life and Culture in the UK

1) The UK is a multicultural country — for centuries, people have moved here from all over the world. High proportions of ethnic minorities come from India, Pakistan and Africa.

2) People moving to the UK bring their own culture, which they share — e.g. by setting up businesses such as shops and restaurants or building religious centres.

3) People from the same ethnic background often settle in the same area of a city, creating a distinctive character in that area (because of e.g. the architecture and types of businesses that people create there).

China Town in Liverpool

4) Ethnic groups have influenced food, media and fashion in the UK:

Food

1) Food that originates in other countries has become a staple for many Brits, e.g. curry and pizza.

2) Restaurants producing authentic ethnic food are popular with people of that ethnic background, and of many other ethnic backgrounds, including white British people.

3) Different national dishes need different ingredients, so shops specialising in those ingredients often open in areas with a high number of people from a particular ethnic background — e.g. London Road in Sheffield has a large Asian community, and lots of shops selling Indian and Chinese produce.

4) In recent years, mainstream supermarkets have increased the amount of ethnic food that they sell — many large supermarkets have a 'world food' aisle, and even small supermarkets offer ready-made curry paste, noodles and other ingredients for ethnic dishes.

Media

People from ethnic minorities have made the media scene in the UK more diverse. This has helped different groups to understand and empathise with each other. For example:

1) People from ethnic minorities have written, acted in and produced a number of successful TV shows, such as 'The Kumars' and 'Youngers'.

2) Music styles including soul, reggae and dubstep all have roots in Black African and Caribbean music. They have been extremely influential in shaping music in the UK.

3) Authors from other cultures write books exploring their heritage or experiences in the UK, e.g. 'Yoruba Girl Dancing' by Nigerian writer Simi Bedford.

4) There have been numerous crossovers between traditional British culture and ethnic culture — e.g. several Shakespeare plays, including 'Hamlet', have been performed as Bollywood musicals.

Fashion

1) As with food, in areas with a high population of people from an ethnic minority background, shops selling traditional clothes for those countries are likely to open. E.g. Stratford Road in Birmingham has a lot of shops selling saris and other traditional Indian clothes.

2) As these clothes become more common, people from other cultures start to wear them. Asian and middle-eastern fashion has become popular in the UK, e.g. harem trousers and kaftans.

3) Fashion houses and high-street shops start to sell their own versions of these clothes, often combining traditional and UK styles — e.g. Indonesian-style batik prints on strapless tops.

4) Hair styles are also influenced by other cultures — e.g. dreadlocks were popularised by Jamaican people, and are now worn by lots of white British people.

Curry favour with the examiner — learn the details on this page...

Just a few questions to go and you'll have finished this section. Start with this one, then try the next page.

1) Describe how ethnic groups have affected **either** food, media **or** fashion in the UK.   [4]

Revision Summary

Phew, who knew there was so much to know about the UK in the 21st century... you'd think it'd be enough just to look out the window or wander down your local high street, but unfortunately it's all a bit more complicated than that. There's a lot to get your head round in this section, so make sure you're clear on the basics by working your way through these questions — try to do them without looking back at the pages (unless you get really stuck, in which case I'll allow you a quick peek).

UK Characteristics (p.74) ☑

1) Which areas of the UK have a high population density? *South east*
2) Give two problems that high population density might cause. *housing crisis, water stress*
3) Briefly describe the pattern of rainfall across the UK. *heavy relife in NW, sparse in SE*
4) What is meant by 'water stress'? *not enough water to sustain a population*
5) What is most land in the UK used for? *agriculture*
6) Roughly what percentage of the UK is built on? *10 %*

Changing UK Population (p.75-77) ☑

7) Briefly describe what has happened to the number of people in the UK since 2001. *increasly*
8) True or false: There are more older people in the UK now than there were in 2001. *true*
9) a) What stage of the DTM is the UK at? *4*
   b) What does this tell you about birth rate and death rate in the UK? *higher moving in dearart*
10) 'The UK has positive net migration.' What does this mean? *more people moving in dearart*
11) How might migration affect the UK's position on the DTM? *increase in births*
12) True or false: Population growth in London is slower than in the UK as a whole. *false*
13) Name two areas of the UK where the proportion of older people is high. *east + south west engla*
14) a) Give two social effects of an ageing population on the UK. *Healthcare services under pressure, voluntary work*
    b) Give two economic effects of an ageing population on the UK. *Taxes rise + disposable income*
15) Give one way that the UK government has tried to overcome the negative effects of an ageing population. *raising age at which you can claim a pension*

Changing UK Economy (p.78-80) ☑

16) Briefly describe how the economy of the UK has changed between 2001 and now. *recesion*
17) Give one example each of an industry in the primary, secondary, tertiary and quaternary sectors.
18) a) What has happened to the number of people employed in secondary industries since 2001?
    b) What has happened to the number of people employed in quaternary industries since 2001?
19) Describe how average working hours have changed since 2001.
20) What is an economic hub?
21) Give three examples of economic hubs in the UK.
22) Give two examples of major industries in South Wales.
23) How is industry in South Wales different now compared to the 19th century?

> If you've studied an economic hub other than South Wales, you can answer about that instead.

UK's Global Significance (p.81-83) ☑

24) Give two examples of international organisations that the UK is a member of.
25) a) Give an example of an international conflict that the UK has been involved in trying to resolve.
    b) Describe one way in which an international organisation involving the UK has reacted to this conflict.
26) Name two media products that the UK exports.
27) Give two ways in which media exports may have influenced people in other countries.
28) a) Give one example each of ethnic food, media and fashion.
    b) For each example, give one way in which it has influenced UK life or culture.

Resource Supply and Demand

Resources are just all the things that we <u>use</u> — and in this case we're talking about <u>food</u>, <u>water</u> and <u>energy</u>.

Everyone Needs Food, Energy and Water

<u>Resources</u>, such as <u>food</u>, <u>energy</u> and <u>water</u>, are needed for <u>basic human development</u>:

1) <u>Food</u> — without <u>enough nutritious food</u>, people can become <u>malnourished</u>. This makes them more likely to get <u>ill</u>, and may stop them from <u>working</u> or doing well at <u>school</u>.

2) <u>Energy</u> — a good supply of energy is needed for a <u>basic standard of living</u>, e.g. to provide <u>lighting</u> and <u>heat</u> for cooking. It's also essential for <u>industry</u> and <u>transport</u>.

3) <u>Water</u> — people need a constant supply of <u>clean</u>, <u>safe water</u> for <u>drinking</u>, <u>cooking</u> and <u>washing</u>. Water is also needed to <u>produce food</u>, <u>clothes</u> and lots of other products.

Demand for Resources is Increasing

<u>Consumption</u> of food, water and energy around the world is <u>increasing</u>. There are <u>two</u> main reasons for this:

① Rising Population

1) The global population is <u>increasing</u> — in <u>2011</u> it was just over <u>7 billion</u> and it's expected to reach <u>9 billion</u> by <u>2040</u>. <u>More people</u> require <u>more resources</u>.

2) Increased demand for one resource can increase demand for another — e.g. <u>more people</u> means that <u>more food</u> needs to be grown, which increases demand for <u>water</u>.

② Economic Development

1) <u>Economic development</u> means that people are getting <u>wealthier</u>, especially in emerging and developing countries (EDCs — see p.63).

2) Wealthier people have <u>more disposable income</u>, which affects their <u>resource consumption</u>:

- They have <u>more money</u> to spend on <u>food</u> and they often buy <u>more</u> than they <u>need</u>.

- They can afford <u>cars</u>, <u>fridges</u>, <u>televisions</u> etc., all of which use <u>energy</u>. Manufacturing these goods and producing energy to run them also uses a lot of <u>water</u>.

- More people can afford flushing toilets, showers, dishwashers etc. This <u>increases water use</u>.

Supply of Resources isn't Increasing Fast Enough

Many countries are trying to <u>increase supplies</u> of food, water and energy. However, there are also lots of factors that <u>limit</u> these supplies, meaning that <u>supply can't meet demand</u>. For example:

1) <u>Climate</u> — some countries have very <u>low rainfall</u>, so <u>water supplies</u> are limited. This also limits how much <u>food</u> they can grow. <u>Climate change</u> may change <u>rainfall patterns</u>, affecting <u>water availability</u> and <u>crop growth</u> (see p.22).

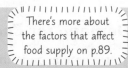

There's more about the factors that affect food supply on p.89.

2) <u>Geology</u> — some countries don't have reserves of <u>fossil fuels</u> such as coal and oil, and may not have a suitable <u>landscape</u> for generating <u>renewable energy</u> from e.g. wind or hydropower. Geology can also limit <u>water supply</u> — when rain falls on <u>permeable rock</u>, e.g. sandstone, it <u>flows</u> into the rock and can form <u>underground water stores</u> that are <u>hard</u> to get to.

3) <u>Conflict</u> — war can disrupt <u>transport</u> of <u>resources</u>, e.g. by damaging roads, water pipes or power lines.

4) <u>Poverty</u> — some countries <u>can't afford</u> the <u>technology</u> (e.g. agricultural machinery, nuclear power plants) to <u>exploit</u> the <u>natural resources</u> that are available.

5) <u>Natural hazards</u> — events such as tropical storms, earthquakes and volcanic eruptions can <u>damage</u> <u>agricultural land</u> and <u>destroy infrastructure</u> such as <u>water pipes</u> and <u>power lines</u>.

Global food consumption — keep eating till you're a perfect sphere...

Wow, that was a mighty quick dash through some pretty big ideas. Don't worry, there's plenty more coming up on resources — but if you can get your head round this lot, you'll be off to a flying start with the rest of the topic.

Human Use of the Environment

We humans change the environment to get more food, energy and water, but it's not trouble-free...

Farming *is Becoming More Mechanised*

1) Since the 1960s, there has been a growth in large-scale, industrial farming where processes are increasingly done by machines, e.g. tractors and combine harvesters, rather than people.

2) Industrial farming can increase the amount of food that can be produced, because processes such as milking, ploughing and harvesting can be done more quickly.

3) However, changes to farms have had impacts on ecosystems and the environment:

- Field sizes have increased so that food can be produced more cheaply. Removal of hedgerows has led to a decline in biodiversity.

- The amount of chemicals used in food production has been increasing — large quantities of artificial fertilisers and pesticides are applied to crops, and animals are given special feed to encourage growth. If they enter water courses (e.g. rivers), these chemicals can harm or kill organisms.

- Increased use of heavy machinery, e.g. in planting and harvesting, can cause soil erosion.

Commercial Fishing *Methods Increase Fish Catches*

1) Global demand for fish is increasing. Most fish and seafood is provided by commercial fishing methods — these include trawling (towing huge nets behind boats) and dredging (dragging a metal frame along the seabed to harvest shellfish such as oysters and scallops).

2) Since the 1950s, fishing has become increasingly mechanised — this means that boats can now carry bigger nets and haul in bigger catches than used to be possible, helping to meet demand for fish.

3) Fish farms (aquaculture) are also being used to breed fish and shellfish in contained spaces.

4) Commercial fishing is having a number of impacts on ecosystems and the environment:

- Over-fishing of some fish (e.g. cod) means that some species are now endangered. Decreasing the number of one species in an ecosystem can have knock-on impacts on other species (see p.40).

- Dredging can damage seafloor habitats and disturb organisms such as sea urchins and starfish.

- Fish farms are often overcrowded, and the large number of fish produce a lot of waste. If this waste is released into the natural environment, it can cause large blooms of algae. The algae absorb a lot of oxygen from the water, causing other plants and animals to die.

Demand for *Energy is Increasing Deforestation*

1) Deforestation is the removal of trees from forests. Increasing energy demand increases deforestation — trees are burnt as fuel or cleared to make way for power stations.

2) In some countries where a large river runs through an area of forest (e.g. the Amazon River in the Amazon rainforest in Brazil), forest is being destroyed to make way for hydroelectric power (HEP) stations. HEP provides renewable energy that will help us meet our increasing energy needs. However, the initial construction of HEP stations involves building a dam, which floods large areas of forest.

3) Deforestation has many environmental impacts:

- Trees remove CO_2 from the atmosphere, and burning vegetation to clear forest releases CO_2. So deforestation means more CO_2 in the atmosphere, which adds to global warming (see p.19).

- Forests provide an important habitat — around underline{70%} of all land-based plant and animal species live in forests. If the forests are cut down, these habitats are lost and species may die out.

- Removing trees exposes the soil and makes it easier to erode — eroded soil can enter rivers and streams, damaging the habitats of fish and other freshwater organisms.

- Trees intercept rainfall, so removing them makes flooding more likely — this can damage habitats.

Human Use of the Environment

Mining has Environmental Impacts

1) <u>Fossil fuels</u>, e.g. <u>coal</u>, <u>gas</u> and <u>oil</u>, are a major source of <u>energy</u>. They are <u>removed</u> from the ground by <u>mining</u>.

2) <u>Surface mining</u> is where large areas of vegetation, soil and rock are <u>stripped away</u> so that miners can reach the materials they want. <u>Sub-surface mining</u> involves <u>digging deep shafts</u> below the ground surface.

3) Recently, a technique called <u>fracking</u> has been developed to <u>extract shale gas</u> — natural gas that is trapped underground in <u>shale rock</u>. <u>Liquid</u> is <u>pumped</u> into the rock at <u>high pressure</u>. This causes the rock to <u>crack</u> (fracture), releasing the <u>gas</u>, which is then <u>collected</u> as it comes out of the production well.

4) Mining has lots of <u>impacts</u> on the <u>environment</u> and <u>ecosystems</u>:

- <u>Waste</u> from mines can <u>pollute soil</u>, <u>groundwater</u>, <u>drinking water</u> and <u>air</u>. Pollutants include mercury and lead, which are <u>very toxic</u> to plants, animals and people.
- Habitats are <u>destroyed</u> to make way for mines, leading to <u>loss of biodiversity</u>.
- Mining uses a huge amount of <u>water</u> (a <u>limited resource</u>).
- Coal, oil and gas are <u>not sustainable</u> energy sources. They're <u>non-renewable</u>, and release CO_2 when they're burned — this contributes to <u>global warming</u> (see p. 19).

Reservoirs Can Provide a Reliable Water Supply

1) <u>Seasonal variations</u> in rainfall or <u>unpredictable</u> rainfall can cause a <u>water shortage</u> at certain times of year. One way of coping with this problem is by <u>increasing storage</u>.

2) Building a <u>dam</u> across a river <u>traps</u> a large amount of water behind the dam, creating a <u>reservoir</u> — this provides a <u>reliable</u> source of water <u>all year</u>. However, dams and reservoirs have <u>environmental impacts</u>:

- Reservoirs <u>flood</u> large amounts of land, <u>destroying habitats</u> and <u>agricultural land</u>.
- Reservoirs impact local <u>ecosystems</u>. Water is often <u>released</u> through the dam at <u>regular intervals</u> making the river flow much more <u>uniform</u> — this often <u>reduces species diversity</u>. Dams also act as a <u>barrier</u> to species' <u>movements</u>, e.g. <u>salmon</u> that migrate upstream to lay their eggs.
- The <u>natural flow</u> of <u>sediment downstream</u> is disrupted, <u>reducing</u> the <u>fertility</u> of areas downstream.
- Reservoirs create <u>new</u> aquatic environments, which can become home to <u>non-native species</u>.

Water Transfer Moves Water to Places Where It's Needed

1) Water is often not <u>where</u> it is most <u>needed</u>. E.g. the <u>south</u> and <u>east</u> of the UK is much <u>drier</u> than the <u>north</u> and <u>west</u>, and has a <u>higher population density</u>, so there isn't always <u>enough water</u> to go round.

2) <u>Water transfers</u> use <u>canals</u> and <u>pipes</u> to move water from a river that has <u>surplus</u> water to a river that has a water <u>shortage</u>. This can cause <u>problems</u> for <u>ecosystems</u> and the <u>environment</u>:

1) <u>Large-scale engineering works</u> are needed to create new <u>channels</u>. These can <u>damage ecosystems</u>.

2) There may be <u>water shortages</u> in areas where the water is coming <u>from</u>, particularly in <u>dry years</u>. This can put <u>pressure</u> on <u>local ecosystems</u>.

3) Lots of <u>energy</u> is needed to <u>pump</u> the water over <u>long distances</u> if there isn't a natural downhill route. This can <u>release greenhouse gases</u>, adding to <u>climate change</u>.

4) Water transfer schemes often involve building <u>dams</u> and <u>reservoirs</u> (see above).

> Water transfer has definitely improved my commute...

Water management techniques — cross your legs and jiggle...

Have a go at this handy exam-style question to check that you've got to grips with these pages.

1) Describe the environmental impacts of increasing food supply. [4]

Food Security

I worked in <u>food security</u> for a while — I had to stand by the exit from my local supermarket and look threatening. Probably would have been more effective if I was taller than 5 foot 1...

Food Security is When People Have Enough to Eat

Food Security

- <u>Food security</u> is when people have access to enough <u>nutritious food</u> to stay <u>healthy</u> and <u>active</u>.
- Countries that <u>produce a lot</u> of food or are <u>rich</u> enough to <u>import</u> the food they need have <u>food security</u>.

Food Insecurity

- <u>Food insecurity</u> is when people <u>aren't</u> able to get enough food to <u>stay healthy</u> or lead an <u>active life</u>.
- Countries that <u>don't grow enough</u> to feed their population and <u>can't afford to import</u> the food they need have <u>food insecurity</u>.

Food Security is Affected by Physical and Human Factors

Food <u>security</u> is affected by <u>how much</u> food is being <u>produced</u> and whether people can <u>access</u> food supplies. Food production and accessibility are affected by both <u>physical</u> and <u>human</u> factors:

Physical Factors

1) <u>Climate</u> — countries with climates that are too cold or have too little rainfall <u>can't grow much food</u>. <u>Extreme</u> weather events (e.g. <u>floods</u> and <u>droughts</u>) also affect food supply.

2) <u>Water stress</u> — crops and livestock need <u>water</u> to <u>survive</u>. Areas that have <u>low rainfall</u> or where water for <u>irrigation</u> is <u>scarce</u> struggle to grow <u>enough</u> food.

3) <u>Pests and diseases</u> — pests <u>reduce yields</u> by <u>consuming</u> crops, e.g. rats cause big problems by eating stored grain, and huge <u>locust swarms</u> eat all the vegetation in their path. <u>Diseases</u> affect <u>most</u> crops and livestock and can cause a lot of <u>damage</u> if they spread through crops and herds, e.g. <u>37%</u> of the world's wheat crops are under threat from a disease called <u>wheat rust</u>.

Human Factors

1) <u>Poverty</u> — people living in <u>poverty</u> often <u>can't afford</u> to <u>buy</u> food and often don't have their own <u>land</u> where they can <u>grow food</u>. Poverty also affects people's ability to <u>farm</u> the land <u>effectively</u>, e.g. they may not be able to buy the <u>fertilisers</u> or <u>pesticides</u> they need. At a <u>global scale</u>, poverty means that countries which can't grow enough <u>can't afford</u> to <u>import food</u> from countries with a surplus.

2) <u>Technology</u> — the <u>mechanisation</u> of farm equipment (see p.86) increases the amount of food that can be grown by making the process more <u>efficient</u>. <u>New technologies</u> (e.g. genetic engineering — see p.90) can <u>protect</u> plants from <u>disease</u> and <u>increase</u> their <u>yields</u>.

3) <u>Conflict</u> — fighting may <u>damage</u> agricultural land or make it <u>unsafe</u>, making it difficult to grow enough food. <u>Access</u> to food becomes difficult for people who are forced to <u>flee</u> their homes. Conflicts also make it difficult to <u>import</u> food because <u>trade routes</u> are <u>disrupted</u> and <u>political relationships</u> with supply countries may <u>break down</u>.

4) <u>Over-farming</u> — grazing too much <u>livestock</u> can decrease <u>vegetation</u> cover and cause <u>soil erosion</u>. Intensive <u>arable farming</u> can use up <u>soil nutrients</u> and make the land <u>infertile</u>. In both cases, the land can no longer be used to <u>produce food</u>, unless it's given enough time to <u>recover</u>.

5) <u>Food prices</u> — the prices of certain foods change depending on <u>supply</u> and <u>demand</u>. If the price of basics such as corn and rice <u>increases too much</u>, poorer people <u>can't afford</u> them and go hungry.

Any food I try to eat using chopsticks is pretty insecure...

If you're asked about the causes of food insecurity (and you're feeling brainy) think about how one factor could affect others — e.g. an outbreak of disease might cause a shortage of a certain food, which would increase its price. Cunning.

Access to Food

This page is all about which countries <u>have food</u>, which <u>don't</u>, and what might happen when there's <u>not enough</u>...

Access *to Food Varies Around the World*

1) A country's <u>access to food</u> depends on how much it can <u>grow</u> and how much it can afford to <u>import</u>. Generally, <u>richer</u> countries have <u>better access</u> to food — if they can't grow it themselves, they can buy it.

2) There are several ways of showing <u>how</u> access to food <u>varies globally</u>. For example:

The <u>daily calorie intake</u> of people in different countries shows the <u>amount</u> that people <u>eat</u>.

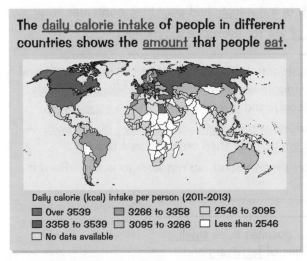

Daily calorie (kcal) intake per person (2011-2013)
- Over 3539
- 3358 to 3539
- 3266 to 3358
- 3095 to 3266
- 2546 to 3095
- Less than 2546
- No data available

The <u>Global Hunger Index</u> shows how many people are suffering from <u>hunger</u> or <u>illness</u> caused by lack of food. The index gives a value for each country from 0 (<u>no hunger</u>) to 100 (<u>extreme hunger</u>). Countries are divided into <u>categories</u> depending on the <u>severity</u> of the problem.

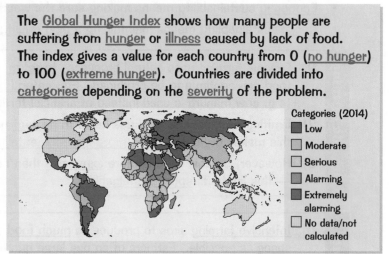

Categories (2014)
- Low
- Moderate
- Serious
- Alarming
- Extremely alarming
- No data/not calculated

3) Both measures show a <u>similar pattern</u>:

- <u>More developed</u> areas like <u>Europe</u> and <u>North America</u> eat <u>a lot</u>.
- <u>Less developed</u> areas like <u>Africa</u>, <u>Central America</u> and parts of <u>Asia</u> consume <u>less</u> food per person, and more people suffer from <u>hunger</u> and <u>hunger-related illnesses</u>.
- <u>EDCs</u> (see p.63) are eating <u>more</u> and hunger is <u>decreasing</u> as <u>wealth increases</u>, e.g. China.

The Global Hunger Index doesn't calculate values for advanced countries (see p.63).

4) However, neither method shows up <u>variations</u> within countries — even in a country with a <u>high calorie intake</u> and a <u>low score</u> on the world hunger index, <u>some</u> people may have <u>limited access</u> to food.

Malthus and Boserup Had Different Theories About Food Supply

Malthus and Boserup both came up with theories about how <u>population growth</u> and <u>food availability</u> are <u>related</u>:

Malthus's Theory

- <u>Thomas Malthus</u> was an 18th-century economist. He thought that <u>population</u> would increase <u>faster</u> than <u>food supply</u>. This would mean that eventually there would be <u>too many people</u> for the <u>food</u> available.
- He believed that, when this happened, people would be killed by catastrophes such as <u>famine</u>, <u>illness</u> and <u>war</u>, and the population would <u>return</u> to a level that could be <u>supported</u> by the food available.

Boserup's Theory

- <u>Ester Boserup</u> was a 20th-century economist. Her theory was that <u>however big</u> the world's population grew, people would always produce <u>sufficient food</u> to meet their needs.
- She thought that, if <u>food supplies</u> became <u>limited</u>, people would come up with <u>new ways</u> to <u>increase production</u> (e.g. by making technological advances) in order to <u>avoid hunger</u>.

Neither theory has been proved completely <u>right</u> or completely <u>wrong</u>. There have been <u>famines</u> in some areas, but on a <u>global scale</u>, food production has <u>so far kept up</u> with population growth.

Famine, illness, war — Malthus sounds like a proper fun sponge...

Don't be put off by all the theory — basically, Malthus thought that the size of the population was controlled by food availability, whereas Boserup thought that food availability was controlled by the size of the population. Simple(ish).

Increasing Food Production

Mmm, increased food production = <u>more food</u>. Grab your knife and fork, and dig in.

Attempts to Increase Food Security *Can be Sustainable*

1) There are lots of ways that <u>food production</u> can be <u>increased</u> to help achieve food <u>security</u>.
2) They can be <u>environmentally</u>, <u>economically</u> and <u>socially sustainable</u>:
   - <u>Environmental</u> sustainability means keeping the environment in a <u>healthy state</u> in the <u>long-term</u>.
   - <u>Economic</u> sustainability means making sure the wealth of <u>individuals</u> and <u>countries</u> continues to <u>grow</u>.
   - <u>Social</u> sustainability means maintaining a <u>high quality of life</u> for everyone <u>indefinitely</u>.

Organic Farming

1) <u>Organic farming</u> uses <u>natural processes</u> to <u>return</u> nutrients to the soil, so that soil stays <u>fertile</u> and <u>food</u> can continue to be produced. E.g. <u>natural products</u> are used instead of <u>artificial chemicals</u> (e.g. cow manure is used instead of artificial fertilisers), and <u>animals</u> aren't given <u>vaccinations</u>.
2) Limiting artificial chemical use helps to <u>protect</u> natural <u>ecosystems</u> and <u>preserve biodiversity</u> — this makes organic farming <u>more environmentally sustainable</u> than conventional farming.
3) However, organic food is more <u>expensive</u> than non-organic food, so not everyone can afford it — this limits its <u>social sustainability</u>.

Mechanisation (see p.86) is also an example of intensification of farming.

Intensive Farming

1) <u>Intensive farming</u> aims to produce as <u>much food</u> as possible in as <u>small a space</u> as possible. Farmers often use large quantities of <u>fertilisers</u> and <u>pesticides</u> to <u>maximise crop yields</u>. They may also keep animals inside in small spaces and give them food with <u>added antibiotics</u> and <u>growth hormones</u> to prevent disease and encourage growth.
2) <u>Artificial chemicals</u> (e.g. fertilisers, pesticides and antibiotics) can make their way into <u>natural ecosystems</u> and <u>disrupt</u> their <u>balance</u> — i.e. <u>harming</u> some species and <u>favouring</u> others. This <u>reduces</u> the <u>environmental sustainability</u> of intensive farming.
3) These chemicals are also <u>expensive</u> and have to be applied <u>year after year</u> to maintain crop yields — this increases the <u>cost</u> of food production, so it becomes <u>less economically sustainable</u>.

Genetic Modification

1) <u>Genetically modified</u> (GM) crops allow <u>more food</u> to be grown in <u>smaller areas</u> with <u>fewer resources</u>. For example, GM crops can be designed to have <u>higher yields</u>, <u>resistance</u> to <u>drought</u>, <u>disease</u> or <u>pests</u> (increasing yields and reducing the need for pesticides) or <u>higher nutritional values</u>.
2) <u>Increasing yields</u> and growing more <u>nutritious</u> food increases <u>food security</u>, which makes GM crops more <u>socially sustainable</u>. <u>Decreased</u> use of <u>artificial chemicals</u> means that the <u>cost</u> of food production <u>decreases</u>, so GM crops may be <u>economically sustainable</u> for poorer farmers.
3) However, there are <u>environmental concerns</u> about GM crops, which <u>reduce</u> their sustainability:
   - They may <u>reduce biodiversity</u> because fewer varieties of crops are planted.
   - GM plants may <u>interbreed</u> with wild plants and pass on their <u>genes</u> or <u>disrupt ecosystems</u>.

Hydroponics

1) <u>Hydroponics</u> is a method of growing plants <u>without soil</u> — plants are grown in a <u>nutrient solution</u>, and are <u>monitored</u> to make sure they get the right amount of nutrients. This <u>maximises</u> crop <u>yield</u>.
2) <u>Less water</u> is required than for plants grown in soil, and <u>reduced risk</u> of <u>disease</u> and <u>pests</u> means less need for pesticides. This increases their <u>environmental sustainability</u>.
3) However, hydroponics is very <u>expensive</u>, so it is currently only used for <u>high-value crops</u>. Not everyone can <u>afford</u> to buy these crops, which makes them <u>less socially sustainable</u>.

I'd like hydroponically grown tomato sauce on my GM chips, please...

If you're asked to write about how sustainable a method of increasing food supply is, think about whether it'll help produce more food in the long-term, without costing too much, harming people or damaging the environment.

Ethical Consumerism

It's not just food <u>production</u> that can be made more sustainable — <u>consumption</u> is just as important.

Ethical Consumerism *Can Help to Increase Food Security*

1) <u>Ethical consumerism</u> means choosing to buy goods that have been produced with <u>minimal harm</u> to <u>people</u> and the <u>environment</u>. It's also about how we <u>use goods</u> — e.g. whether we <u>throw</u> lots of food <u>away</u>.

2) Ethical consumerism can help to <u>increase food security</u> and <u>sustainability</u> by:
   - <u>reducing damage</u> to <u>agricultural land</u> caused by food production, so land remains <u>fertile</u>.
   - making food production <u>profitable</u>, so farmers can <u>afford</u> to carry on <u>producing</u> it.
   - paying <u>more money</u> to poorer countries for goods, so <u>poverty decreases</u>.
   - <u>reducing</u> the amount of <u>greenhouse gases</u> emitted by <u>transport</u> and <u>waste disposal</u>. This may help to limit climate change and therefore prevent <u>decreases in food production</u> (see p.22).

There are *Lots of Ways* of Making Food Consumption More Ethical

Buy Fair Trade Products

1) Companies who want to <u>sell products</u> labelled as 'fair trade' have to <u>pay farmers</u> a <u>fair price</u>. This helps farmers in <u>poorer countries</u> make enough to improve their <u>quality of life</u>.

2) Food produced under fair trade schemes is <u>ethical</u> and <u>sustainable</u> because:
   - <u>Buyers</u> pay <u>extra</u> on top of the fair price to <u>help develop</u> the area where the goods come from, e.g. to <u>build schools</u> or <u>health centres</u>. This makes buying fair trade products more <u>socially sustainable</u>.
   - Only producers that <u>treat their employees well</u> can <u>take part</u> in the scheme, e.g. all employees must have a <u>safe working environment</u>. This <u>improves</u> the workers' <u>quality of life</u>.
   - There are <u>rules</u> about how fair trade food is grown — farmers must use <u>environmentally friendly methods</u> that e.g. protect <u>biodiversity</u>, limit <u>greenhouse gas emissions</u> and preserve <u>soil health</u>.

Reduce Waste

1) Globally, <u>one third</u> of food that is produced is <u>wasted</u> — reducing this will make <u>more food available</u>, so <u>less</u> needs to be <u>grown</u> to feed people. This will <u>increase</u> environmental and social <u>sustainability</u>.

2) Schemes such as '<u>Think.Eat.Save</u>' and '<u>Love Food Hate Waste</u>' encourage <u>individuals</u>, <u>businesses</u> and <u>governments</u> to be <u>less wasteful</u> with food. E.g. by helping people <u>plan</u> their meals better and sharing recipe ideas for <u>using up leftovers</u>. They also encourage people to <u>compost waste</u> rather than putting it in the <u>bin</u> (food in <u>landfill</u> sites produces <u>methane</u>, which is a greenhouse gas).

3) Consumers can also choose food that has <u>less packaging</u> — this reduces the amount of <u>resources</u> that are used, and means that <u>less plastic</u> etc. goes into <u>landfill</u>, increasing environmental <u>sustainability</u>.

Buy Local and Seasonal Food

Buying organic food is also an example of ethical consumerism (see p.90).

1) In many <u>wealthy countries</u>, people expect to buy the foods they like <u>all year round</u>. This means that foods have to be <u>imported</u> for all or part of the year.

2) Consumers can choose to eat more food that has been <u>produced locally</u> (e.g. choosing potatoes that have been grown on a nearby farm). They can also <u>eat seasonally</u> — this means eating foods that grow locally at that <u>time of year</u> (e.g. only eating strawberries in summer, when they are grown in the UK).

3) Local and seasonal consumption <u>reduces</u> the amount of food that is <u>imported</u>, which reduces <u>greenhouse gas emissions</u> from transport. This makes it more <u>environmentally sustainable</u>.

Send me cake and I'll give you some revision tips — that's a fair trade...

There you were, enjoying a non-fair trade banana from Brazil before tossing the peel on the street, and I go and make you feel guilty about it. If you're not feeling guilty, you probably haven't read the page — I advise that you do so now.

Small-Scale Food Production

Increasing food security isn't just about giant farms and international schemes. Sometimes, <u>less is more</u>.

Individuals *and Communities* Can Increase *Food Production*

1) <u>Small-scale</u> food production (e.g. growing fruit and vegetables in the <u>garden</u>) is an alternative to large-scale agriculture. It relies on <u>individuals</u> and <u>communities</u>, rather than governments or large organisations — because of this, it's known as a '<u>bottom-up</u>' approach.

2) It can help to <u>increase food security</u>:
   - Food is grown in <u>gardens</u>, on <u>balconies</u> etc., so overall <u>food production increases</u>.
   - People can grow exactly what they <u>want</u> and pick it <u>fresh</u> each day, which <u>reduces waste</u>.
   - Methods are often <u>organic</u> and <u>non-intensive</u> — this helps keep the land <u>fertile</u>.
   - People are less reliant on expensive <u>imported food</u>, helping <u>poorer people</u> to eat <u>healthily</u>.

3) Small-scale approaches are usually <u>less damaging</u> to the <u>environment</u> than large-scale farming methods.

Small-Scale Approaches *Make Food Supplies More Sustainable*

Permaculture

1) <u>Permaculture</u> is all about sustainable food production and consumption. People are encouraged to <u>grow their own food</u> and <u>change</u> their <u>eating habits</u> — eating <u>fewer animal products</u> and <u>more fruit and vegetables</u>, and buying <u>local</u>, <u>organic</u> or <u>fair trade food</u> wherever possible.

2) <u>Food</u> is grown in a way that recreates <u>natural ecosystems</u> — this <u>protects</u> the soil and wildlife, so it's <u>environmentally sustainable</u>. It also means that the growing site is <u>low maintenance</u>, so food can be grown with <u>less time</u> and <u>effort</u> — this increases its <u>social sustainability</u>.

3) Food <u>production</u> is designed to keep <u>soils healthy</u> so that crops can continue to grow. For example, <u>mixed cropping</u> is used, which involves having plants of <u>different heights</u> and <u>different types</u> in one area. This means the available <u>space</u> and <u>light</u> are used <u>better</u>, there are <u>fewer pests</u> and <u>diseases</u> and <u>less watering</u> is required. Using <u>few resources</u> increases environmental <u>sustainability</u>.

Urban Gardens

1) <u>Urban gardens</u> use spaces such as <u>empty land</u>, <u>roof tops</u> and <u>balconies</u> in towns and cities to grow food. Many urban gardens are <u>community projects</u>, where people <u>work together</u> to grow food and improve their <u>environment</u>.

2) Urban gardens make food <u>locally available</u>, <u>reducing</u> the need to <u>transport</u> food <u>long distances</u>. This means it is often <u>fresher</u> and <u>more nutritious</u> and can also be <u>cheaper</u> — improving the <u>food security</u> of <u>poorer residents</u>.

3) They add <u>greenery</u> to cities, making them <u>healthier</u> and <u>more attractive</u> places to live, so they're <u>socially sustainable</u>. It also makes urban areas <u>less dependent</u> on buying food produced by <u>large-scale agriculture</u> — this can help make it <u>economically</u> and <u>environmentally sustainable</u>.

Allotments

1) <u>Allotments</u> are areas of land in villages, towns or cities that are divided into <u>plots</u> and <u>rented</u> to individuals or small groups of people to <u>grow plants</u>, including <u>fruit</u> and <u>vegetables</u>.

2) Many people in towns and cities have <u>little</u> or <u>no garden</u>, so an allotment lets them <u>grow food</u>.

3) Like urban gardens, allotments are <u>environmentally</u> and <u>socially sustainable</u> because they allow people to grow <u>cheap</u>, <u>healthy</u> food <u>close to home</u>.

Urban gardens — more beet crops than beat drops...

Make sure you're familiar with what each of these strategies involves and how it's sustainable.

1) How effective is small-scale food production as a way to sustainably improve food security?   [6]

UK Food Security — Case Study

We're off to the UK — for a case study about food security. I know it's exciting, but try to remain calm.

Food Consumption *Has Decreased Since 1940...*

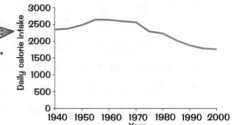

1) Average daily calorie intake in the UK increased from about 2350 in 1940 to about 2600 in 1960, then decreased to about 1750 by 2000.

2) However, this data doesn't include calories from drinks, sweets or meals out. If you include these food types, calorie intake in 2000 was around 2150 — this is still lower than in 1940.

3) There are several reasons for this decrease in consumption:

- People were more active in the past, so they needed more calories — fewer people have physical jobs now, and more people own cars and use them instead of e.g. walking or cycling.

- There's more awareness of and concern about obesity and good nutrition now — e.g. the government regularly publishes recommendations that people eat less high-calorie food such as fat and sugar.

- There have been spikes in the cost of food — e.g. the price of wheat and rice peaked in 2008. This can make it difficult for the poorest people to afford food, so their consumption decreases.

...*but Food Availability Has Increased*

1) In the UK, food availability is high — most people have enough to eat. The UK produces about 60% of the food it needs and imports the rest. Food security is affected by where food comes from — e.g. home-grown food availability can decrease if crops fail, and imports can decrease if prices go up.

2) Food availability has changed over time:

- There was less food available during World War II — there were global food shortages, and imports to the UK were disrupted by German attacks on ships carrying food. The UK government introduced rationing of foods such as meat, cheese, eggs and sugar to make sure that everyone had enough.

- The Common Agricultural Policy (CAP) was introduced in the 1950s — it increased production of crops such as wheat by intensifying agriculture (see p.90). Since the 1990s, food production has been more sustainable, and yields have been fairly stable.

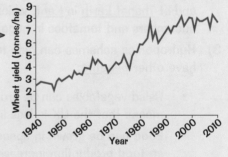

- Since the 1960s, there has been a growing demand for seasonal products (e.g. strawberries) all year round and high-value foods, such as exotic fruits, coffee and spices. Imports of these foods into the UK have increased, so they are constantly available — we produce only 22% of the fruit and vegetables we consume.

Food Banks Have Helped Increase Food Security in Newcastle

1) Although food availability in the UK is high, there are about 5 million people who don't have enough to eat.

2) One way of tackling this is with food banks — people and companies donate food, which is handed out to those in need. Recipients get a package containing enough nutritious food to last them for three days.

3) One city where food banks are needed is Newcastle — around 8% of people in the city have used one of the food banks there. West End food bank is the busiest in the country, giving food to around 1000 people each week. Food banks in Newcastle have helped increase food security:

- They help reduce hunger and improve people's diets — this also improves their health.
- Some shops and bakeries donate unsold fresh food at the end of the day, reducing waste.
- Some food banks give lessons in cooking and budgeting, to help people with limited money eat healthily.

4) However, food banks don't solve underlying problems, such as low wages and benefit cuts.

5) It's difficult for food banks to store fresh food, so a lot of the food that is given out is processed (e.g. biscuits, tinned soup) — this can have lots of added salt and sugar, which can cause health problems in the long-term.

Topic 8 — Resource Reliance

UK Food Security — Case Study

Intensification *Increased Food Supplies in the UK*

Intensification of farming from the 1940s to the 1980s was an attempt to increase food security by increasing production. The methods used included:

- Higher yielding crops and animals (developed by breeding individuals that gave higher yields initially).
- Monoculture — growing just one crop over a large area.
- Irrigation technologies, e.g. groundwater pumping, electric sprinklers.
- Chemicals, e.g. fertilisers, pesticides and herbicides.
- Mechanisation, e.g. use of machines for sowing, harvesting, weeding and spraying.

This was effective in increasing food security in the UK — in 1940, the UK imported 70% of its cereal crops, but by 1980 this had decreased to 20%. However, intensification also had negative impacts, such as:

1) Monoculture crops could be wiped out by a single pest, drought or disease, e.g. cereal crop yields decreased by about 500 000 tonnes because of drought in 1976.
2) Intensive methods caused environmental damage, for example:
   - Monoculture reduced biodiversity, especially of flowering plants and insects.
   - The chemicals used caused pollution of land and water, disrupting ecosystems.
   - Over-exploiting the land led to reduced soil fertility and increased soil erosion in some areas.

Hydroponics *Can Increase Food Security*

1) Recently, the UK government has promoted 'sustainable intensification', which aims to increase food security without damaging the environment. One method of sustainable intensification is using new technology, such as hydroponics (see p.90), to increase food production.
2) Hydroponics is used on a large scale in abandoned WWII tunnels under London, and at Thanet Earth in Kent, which produces over 10% of the UK's peppers, cucumbers and tomatoes in huge greenhouses.
3) Hydroponics schemes can help to increase food security in the UK, and they have other benefits:

   - Salad vegetables can be grown in the UK all year round, reducing reliance on imports. This means that the UK is less likely to be affected by e.g. shortages or price increases of food.
   - Food can be grown in spaces that would otherwise not be used (e.g. underground tunnels), so food production increases overall.
   - Many schemes aim to be environmentally sustainable — e.g. they recycle water and use natural predators to kill pests — this reduces the need for artificial pesticides.
   - They also create jobs, e.g. Thanet Earth employs 500 people.

4) However, they also have some disadvantages:

   - Schemes can be expensive to set up and run, which increases the cost of the food produced — this may mean that some people can't afford it.
   - Some schemes, e.g. Thanet Earth, have been built in rural areas, so natural habitats have been lost.
   - Schemes like Thanet Earth require a large amount of energy to power the greenhouses, as well as to package and deliver the produce to the shops.

This train has been delayed by pak choi on the line...

No, of course not — they haven't started growing veg in the tunnels that are in use just yet. In the exam, you might be asked about food security in a country you've studied — make sure you learn how it's changed over time and why.

Revision Summary

Mmmm, what a fantastic feast of facts that was. The good news is that you've reached the end of the topics in this book — congratulations. You win the amazing prize of going straight to the 'Geographical Exploration' section on p.96. Do not pass Go, do not collect £200. You can have a biscuit first though — reading about food has made me pretty hungry too.

Resource Use and Production (p.85-87) ☑

1) Give two ways that food is important to people's well-being.
2) Give two ways that energy is important to people's well-being.
3) Outline two reasons why demand for food, energy and water is increasing
4) How can climate limit food supply?
5) What impact might geology have on a country's energy supply?
6) Describe one way in which farming has changed since the 1960s.
7) Give two environmental impacts of commercial fishing.
8) Explain how increasing demand for energy can cause deforestation.
9) Give three environmental impacts of mining.
10) a) What is water transfer?
    b) Give one way in which it might damage ecosystems.

Food Supplies (p.88-89) ☑

11) Give a definition of food security.
12) Give two physical factors that affect the availability of food.
13) Explain how conflict can affect food security.
14) Briefly describe how food consumption varies around the world.
15) a) What did Malthus believe would happen to food supply as population increased?
    b) What did Boserup believe would happen to food supply as population increased?

Increasing Food Production (p.90-92) ☑

16) What is meant by environmental sustainability?
17) a) Give two ways that intensive farming can increase food supply.
    b) Give two ways in which intensive farming is unsustainable.
18) Apart from intensive farming, give two ways in which food supply can be increased.
19) What is ethical consumerism?
20) Describe two ways in which people can make their food consumption more ethical.
21) Describe how permaculture can sustainably increase food supply.

UK Food Security (p.93-94) ☑

22) True or false: daily calorie consumption in the UK is higher now than in 1940.
23) How has food availability in the UK changed since 1940?
24) How did the Common Agricultural Policy affect food availability?
25) a) Give one example of a <u>local</u> attempt to increase food security.
    b) How has it helped to increase food security?
26) a) Give one example of a <u>national</u> attempt to increase food security.
    b) Give one advantage of this attempt.
    c) Give one disadvantage of this attempt.

Geographical Exploration

Now before you get all <u>excited</u> and grab your <u>map</u>, <u>compass</u> and <u>binoculars</u>, it's not **THAT** kind of <u>exploration</u>...

Geographical Exploration is about *Analysing* and *Interpreting Information*

Paper 3 (the <u>Geographical Exploration</u>) tests you on a <u>range</u> of topics from the course.

1) In the <u>exam</u>, you'll be given a <u>resource booklet</u> with loads of information about a <u>country</u>.

2) You need to study <u>all</u> the information <u>carefully</u> and work out <u>what it all means</u>.

3) You'll have to answer <u>questions</u>, using the information you're <u>given</u> and your <u>knowledge</u> of Geography from the <u>rest of the course</u>:

- The questions might be about <u>physical</u> (Our Natural World) or <u>human</u> (People and Society) geography topics, or a <u>mix of the two</u>.
- They could cover <u>any</u> of the <u>content</u> you've studied during the course.
- Some questions will only use <u>one source</u>, but for others you'll have to use <u>several sources</u>.

4) There'll also be a <u>longer answer</u> question, where you'll need to <u>make a decision</u> about something related to the information you've been given, and <u>justify</u> that decision (see below).

There'll be *Lots* of Different Information Sources *in the Resource Booklet*

1) The booklet could include <u>several</u> different types of information, such as <u>maps</u>, <u>graphs</u>, <u>photographs</u>, <u>diagrams</u>, <u>statistics</u>, <u>newspaper articles</u> and <u>quotes</u> from people involved.

2) All the information will be <u>related</u> in some way — e.g. you might be given a <u>newspaper article</u> on a non-governmental organisation, <u>photos</u> of a city in an LIDC and a <u>data table</u> about measures of development in that LIDC.

3) The information you're given is there to <u>help you</u> answer the questions in the exam paper. Each question will be <u>linked</u> to certain parts of the <u>resource booklet</u>.

4) Some questions will probably ask you to <u>demonstrate geographical skills</u>, including reading <u>graphs and charts</u> (see pages 107-110) and calculating <u>statistics</u> (see pages 111-112).

5) Questions with <u>extended written answers</u> will ask you to refer to <u>information</u> in the resource booklet.

The *Final Question* is a *Decision-Making Exercise*

1) You'll be asked to <u>make a decision</u> about something using the <u>information</u>, e.g. suggesting a <u>strategy</u> for how an area could best be managed to meet the needs of <u>everyone</u> involved. There's <u>no single right or wrong answer</u> — but you need to be able to <u>justify</u> your decision, so make sure you can use the <u>information</u> to <u>support it</u>.

No decision is wrong, but some are ill-advised.

2) <u>Whatever</u> your decision is, you need to write a <u>balanced answer</u>. Try to think of the potential <u>economic</u>, <u>political</u>, <u>social</u> and <u>environmental impacts</u> of your decision, and how any <u>negative impacts</u> could be <u>reduced</u>.

3) The question is likely to be about a <u>complex issue</u> with <u>lots</u> of <u>different parties involved</u>. So think about <u>possible conflicts</u> that your decision might cause <u>between different groups</u> of people, or between <u>people</u> and the <u>environment</u>, and how they could be <u>resolved</u>.

Treadmill or cross-trainer — decisions, decisions...

Paper 3 might seem a bit daunting, but don't panic — just make sure you're comfortable writing about what you've learnt in the rest of the course, and use the information you're given. Do that and you're well on the way to exam success.

Fieldwork

Ah, fieldwork. Time to venture into the outside world armed only with a clipboard and a geographical hat*...

*Geographical hat not always supplied.

You have to Write About Two Geographical Enquiries in the Exam

1) Fieldwork is assessed in the second part (Section B) of Papers 1 and 2. There's no assessed coursework, but you need to be able to write about fieldwork that you have done in the exam.

2) You need to have done at least one human and one physical geographical enquiry. You will be asked about the physical one in Paper 1 and the human one in Paper 2.

'Geographical enquiry' is just fancy exam-speak for fieldwork.

3) The fieldwork part of the exam has two types of questions:

- In some questions you'll be asked about fieldwork techniques in unfamiliar situations. You might have to answer questions about techniques for collecting data, how to present data you've been given or how useful the different techniques are.

- In some questions you have to answer questions about your investigation — you might be asked about your question or hypothesis, methods, what data you collected and why, how you presented and analysed it, how you could extend your research and so on.

Geog rocks my world

For Each of your Enquiries, You'll Need to Know...

1 Why You Chose Your Question

You'll need to explain why the question or hypothesis you chose is suitable for a geographical enquiry.

You'll also need to know the geographical theory behind your question.

Make sure you know what the risks associated with collecting your data were, how they were reduced, and why the location you chose was suitable.

2 How and Why You Collected Data

You need to describe and justify what data you collected. This includes whether it was primary data (data that you collected yourself) or secondary data (data that someone else collected and you used), why you collected or used it, how you measured it and how you recorded it.

3 How You Processed and Presented Your Data

The way you presented your data, and why you chose that option, could come up.

You'll need to describe what you did (e.g. what maps, graphs and diagrams you used), explain why it was appropriate, and how you adapted your presentation method for your data. You might also be asked for a different way you could have presented your data.

There's more on analysing, concluding and evaluating on the next page.

4 What Your Data Showed

You'll need to know:

- A description of your data.
- How you analysed your data.
- An explanation of your data.

This might include links between your data sets, the statistical techniques you used, and any anomalies (odd results) in the data that you spotted.

You might have to link your data to geographical theory and case studies.

There's more on graphs and statistical techniques on pages 107-112.

5 The Conclusions You Reached

You'll need to summarise your data and explain how it provides evidence to answer the question or support the hypothesis you set at the beginning.

6 What Went Well, What Could Have Gone Better

You might be asked to evaluate your fieldwork:

- Were there problems in your data collection methods?
- Were there limitations in your data?
- What other data would it have been useful to have?
- How reliable are your conclusions?
- How did it improve your geographical understanding?

No, you can't get a tractor to do your field work for you...

If your fieldwork doesn't quite go to plan, make sure you can write about it and say why things went wrong.

Fieldwork

Analysis, conclusions and evaluations can be pretty tricky, so here's a load of stuff to help you with them.

You need to Describe and Explain what the Data Shows

You might be asked to do some calculations based on results you have been given in the exam.

Analysing and interpreting data is about:

1) Describing what the data shows — you need to describe any patterns and correlations (see pages 107-110) and look for any anomalies. Make sure you use specific points from the data and reference what graph, table etc. you're talking about. You might also need to make comparisons between different sets of data. Statistical techniques (see pages 111-112) help make the data more manageable, so it's easier to spot patterns and make comparisons.

2) Explaining what the data shows — you need to explain why there are patterns and why different data sets are linked together. Use your geographical knowledge to help you explain the results and remember to use geographical terms.

Conclusions are a Summary of the Results

Be careful when drawing conclusions. Some results show a link or correlation, but that doesn't mean that one thing causes the other.

A conclusion is a summary of what you found out in relation to the original question. It should include:

1) A summary of what your results show.

2) An answer for the question you are investigating, and an explanation for why that is the answer.

3) An explanation of how your conclusion fits into the wider geographical world — think about how your conclusion and results could be used by other people or in further investigations.

Evaluations Identify Problems in the Investigation

Evaluation is all about self assessment — looking back at how good or bad your study (or the data you are given in the exam) was. You need to be able to:

1) Identify any problems with the methods used and suggest how they could be improved. Think about things like the size of the data sets, if any bias (unfairness) slipped in and if other methods would have been more appropriate or more effective.

2) Describe how accurate the results are and link this to the methods used — say whether any errors in the methods affected the results.

3) Comment on the validity of your conclusion. You need to talk about how problems with the methods and the accuracy of the results affect the validity of the conclusion. Problems with methods lead to less reliable and accurate results, which affects the validity of the conclusion.

> Accurate results are as near as possible to the true answer — they have few errors.
> Reliable means that data can be reproduced.
> Valid means that the data answers the original question and is reliable.

For example:

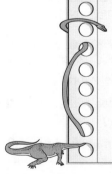

I concluded that the river flowed faster further downstream. However, one problem with my data collection method was that it was difficult to put the float in at exactly the same point each time. This reduced the accuracy of my measurements. To make my investigation more accurate, I could have placed a tape measure across the river to mark the exact point of entry. Another problem was that I only took two readings at each site and I only used one upstream site and one downstream site. To make my data more reliable I could have taken more readings at each site, and used a larger number of sites both upstream and downstream. These improvements would have produced a more valid conclusion.

Evaluation — could do with a hair cut, otherwise fine...

Bit of a weird one this — you need to remember how you analysed your data, the conclusion of your investigations and the evaluation for your studies. So make sure you have some points ready to go before you hit the exam. But you also need to be able to analyse, conclude and evaluate based on someone else's data that you might be given in the exam.

Answering Questions

This section is filled with lots of lovely <u>techniques</u> and <u>skills</u> that you need for your <u>exams</u>. It's no good learning the <u>content</u> of this book if you don't bother learning the skills you need to pass your exam too. First up, answering questions properly...

Make Sure you *Read the Question Properly*

It's dead easy to <u>misread</u> the question and spend five minutes writing about the <u>wrong thing</u>. Four simple tips can help you <u>avoid</u> this:

1) Figure out if it's a <u>case study question</u> — they helpfully say <u>CASE STUDY</u> in friendly capitals at the <u>start</u> of the question. If you see this you need to <u>include a case study</u> you've learnt about in your answer.

2) <u>Underline</u> the <u>command words</u> in the question (the ones that tell you <u>what to do</u>):

> Answers to questions with 'explain' in them often include the word '<u>because</u>' (or '<u>due to</u>').

> When writing about differences, '<u>whereas</u>' is a good word to use in your answers, e.g. 'ACs have a high level of development whereas LIDCs have a lower level'.

Command word	Means write about...
Describe	what it's <u>like</u>
Explain	<u>why</u> it's like that (i.e. give <u>reasons</u>)
Compare	the <u>similarities</u> AND <u>differences</u>
Discuss	give <u>both sides</u> of an argument
Suggest why	give <u>reasons</u> for
Evaluate	weigh up the <u>pros</u> and <u>cons</u>

> If a question asks you to describe a <u>pattern</u> (e.g. from a map or graph), make sure you identify the <u>general pattern</u>, then refer to any <u>anomalies</u> (things that <u>don't</u> fit the general pattern).
>
> E.g. to answer 'describe the global distribution of volcanoes', <u>first</u> say that they're mostly on plate boundaries, <u>then</u> mention that a few aren't (e.g. in Hawaii).

3) <u>Underline</u> the <u>key words</u> (the ones that tell you what it's <u>about</u>), e.g. volcanoes, tourism, migration, counter-urbanisation, debt relief.

4) If the question says '<u>using Fig. 2</u>', bloomin' well <u>make sure</u> you've talked about <u>what Figure 2 shows</u>. <u>Don't</u> just wheel out all of your <u>geographical knowledge</u> and forget all about the photo you're <u>supposed</u> to be <u>talking about</u>. <u>Re-read</u> the <u>question</u> and your <u>answer</u> when you've <u>finished</u>, just to check.

Some Questions are *Level Marked*

Questions worth <u>6 marks or more</u> with longer written answers are <u>level marked</u>, which means you need to do these <u>things</u> to get the <u>top level</u> and a <u>high mark</u>:

1) <u>Read</u> the question properly and figure out a <u>structure</u> for your answer before you start. Your answer needs to be well <u>organised</u> and <u>structured</u>, and written in a <u>logical</u> way.

2) If it's a <u>case study</u> question, include plenty of <u>relevant details</u>:

> • This includes things like <u>place names</u>, <u>dates</u>, <u>statistics</u>, names of <u>organisations</u> or <u>companies</u>.
>
> • Don't forget that they need to be <u>relevant</u> though — it's no good including the exact number of people killed in a flood when the question is about the <u>causes</u> of a flood.

3) <u>One</u> of the questions in each paper has <u>3 extra marks</u> available for <u>spelling</u>, <u>punctuation</u>, <u>grammar</u> and <u>specialist terminology</u> (SPaG). To get <u>top marks</u> you need to:

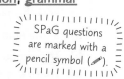

SPaG questions are marked with a pencil symbol (✏).

• Make sure your <u>spelling</u>, <u>punctuation</u> and <u>grammar</u> are <u>consistently correct</u>.

• Write in a way that makes it <u>clear</u> what you mean.

• Use a <u>wide range</u> of <u>geographical terms</u> (e.g. sustainable development) <u>correctly</u>.

Outline the similarities and differences between compare and discuss...

It may all seem a bit simple to you, but it's really important to understand what you're being asked to do. This can be tricky — sometimes the differences between the meanings of the command words are quite subtle, so get learnin'.

Labelling and Comparing

These next few pages give you some advice on what to do for specific types of questions.

You Might Have to Label Photos, Diagrams or Maps

If you're asked to label something:

1) Figure out from the question what the labels should do, e.g. describe the effects of an earthquake, label the features of a landform, identify human influences on the landscape, etc.

2) Add at least as many labels as there are marks.

3) When describing the features talk about things like the size, shape and relief. Make sure you use the correct geographical names of any features, e.g. wave cut platform, meander.

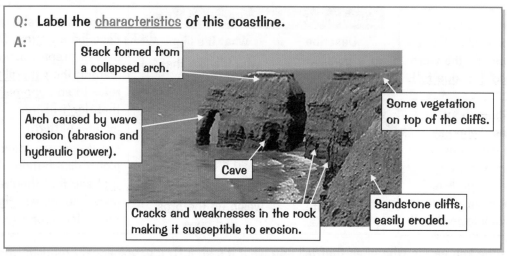

Q: Label the characteristics of this coastline.

A:

Stack formed from a collapsed arch.

Some vegetation on top of the cliffs.

Arch caused by wave erosion (abrasion and hydraulic power).

Cave

Sandstone cliffs, easily eroded.

Cracks and weaknesses in the rock making it susceptible to erosion.

Look at Shapes When You Compare Plans and Photos

You might be given two items, like a plan and an aerial photograph, and be asked to use them together to answer some questions. Plans and aerial photos are a bit like maps — they show places from above. Here are some tips for questions that use plans and photos:

1) The plan and photo might not be the same way up.

2) Work out how the photo matches the plan — look for the main features on the plan like a lake, a big road or something with an interesting shape, and find them on the photo.

3) Look at what's different between the plan and the photo and think about why it might be different.

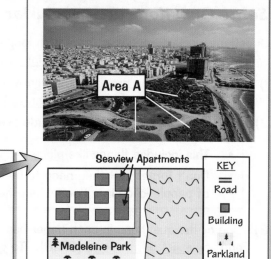

Area A

Seaview Apartments

KEY
Road
Building
Parkland
Sea

Madeleine Park

Q: Look at the development plan for Crystal Bay (2000) and the photo taken after development in 2009.

a) Name the area labelled A in the photo.

b) Give one difference you can see between the photo and the plan.

A: a) Madeleine Park

b) The roads have been built in slightly different areas. There's a small harbour area in front of the apartments.

It isn't only fashionistas that are interested in labels...

You might have to use plans or photos in your exam to answer all sorts of questions — take your time and read the question carefully so you know exactly what you should be doing. Up next is all manner of maps, whoop whoop.

Geographical Skills

Maps

Maps, glorious maps... there's nothing better. OS® maps are my personal favourite, but these aren't bad.

Latitude and Longitude are Used for Global Coordinates

1) The position of anywhere on Earth can be given using coordinates if you use latitude and longitude.

2) Lines of latitude run horizontally around the Earth. They measure how far north or south from the equator something is.

3) Lines of longitude run vertically around the Earth. They measure how far east or west from the Prime Meridian (a line of longitude running through Greenwich in London) something is.

4) Latitude and longitude are measured in degrees.

5) For example, the coordinates of London are 51° N, 0° W and New York is at 40° N, 74° W.

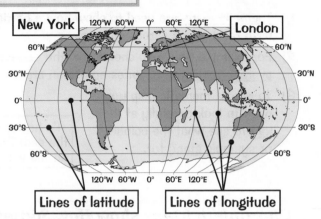

Describing Distributions on Maps — Describe the Pattern

1) In your exam you could get questions like, 'use the map to describe the distribution of volcanoes' and 'explain the distribution of deforestation'.

2) Describe the general pattern and any anomalies (things that don't fit the general pattern).

3) Make at least as many points as there are marks and use names of places and figures if they're given.

4) If you're asked to give a reason or explain, you need to describe the distribution first.

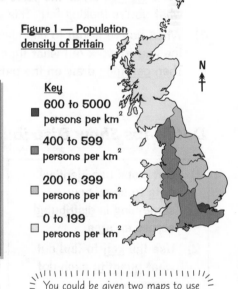

Figure 1 — Population density of Britain

Key

■ 600 to 5000 persons per km^2

■ 400 to 599 persons per km^2

■ 200 to 399 persons per km^2

□ 0 to 199 persons per km^2

Q: Use Figure 1 to explain the pattern of population density in Britain.

A: The London area has a very high population density (600 to 5000 per km^2). There are also areas of high population density (400 to 599 per km^2) in the south east, the Midlands and north west of England. These areas include major cities (e.g. Birmingham and Manchester). More people live in and around cities because there are better services and more job opportunities than in rural areas. Scotland and Wales have the lowest population densities in Britain (less than 199 per km^2)...

You could be given two maps to use for one question — link information from the two maps together.

Describing Locations on Maps — Include Details

1) In your exam you could get a question like, 'describe the location of cities in ...'.

2) When you're asked about the location of something say where it is, what it's near and use compass points.

3) If you're asked to give a reason or explain, you need to describe the location first.

Q: Use the maps to describe the location of the National Parks.

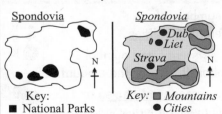

Spondovia

Key:
■ National Parks

Spondovia
●Dub
●Liet
Strava

Key: ■ Mountains
● Cities

A: The National Parks are found in the south west and north east of Spondovia. They are all located in mountainous areas. Three of the parks are located near to the city of Strava.

Describing maps — large, cumbersome, impossible to fold...

...but I love them really. Give me a paper map over some digital device — or worse, a GPS satnav type thing. Yuck. Make sure you're happy with latitude and longitude, then practise describing a map using lots of lovely details.

Maps

Geography: you stand accused of being mostly about <u>colouring in</u>. For my first witness I call — this page.

Thematic Maps **show Information about a** *Theme*

1) <u>Thematic maps</u> are used to show how a particular <u>theme</u> (e.g. weather, life expectancy, birth rate) <u>varies</u> across an <u>area</u>.

2) For example, this map shows how the <u>average temperature</u> varies across an area.

3) To <u>read</u> a thematic map you need to look carefully at the <u>key</u> to see what the colours or symbols <u>stand for</u>.

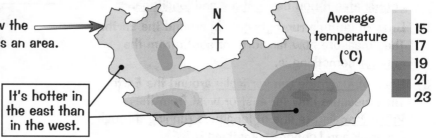

N

Average temperature (°C)

15
17
19
21
23

It's hotter in the east than in the west.

Choropleth Maps **show How Something** *Varies Between Different Areas*

1) <u>Choropleth maps</u> show how something varies between different areas using <u>colours</u> or <u>patterns</u>.

2) The maps in exams often use <u>cross-hatched lines</u> and <u>dot patterns</u>.

3) If you're asked to talk about all the parts of the map with a certain <u>value</u> or <u>characteristic</u>, look at the map carefully and put a <u>big tick</u> on all the parts with the <u>pattern</u> that <u>matches</u> what you're looking for. This makes them all <u>stand out</u>.

4) When you're asked to <u>complete</u> part of a map, first use the <u>key</u> to work out what type of <u>pattern</u> you need. Then <u>carefully</u> draw on the pattern, e.g. using a <u>ruler</u>.

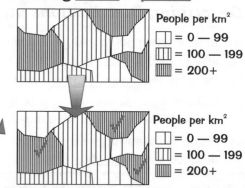

People per km²
= 0 — 99
= 100 — 199
= 200+

People per km²
= 0 — 99
= 100 — 199
= 200+

Dot Maps **Show Distribution** **and** *Quantity* **Using Identical Symbols...**

1) Dot maps use <u>identical dots</u> to show how something is <u>distributed</u> across an <u>area</u>.

2) Use the <u>key</u> to find out what <u>quantity</u> each dot represents.

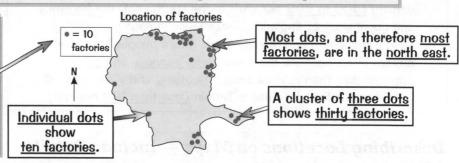

Location of factories

• = 10 factories

N

Individual dots show ten factories.

<u>Most dots</u>, and therefore <u>most factories</u>, are in the <u>north east</u>.

A cluster of <u>three dots</u> shows <u>thirty factories</u>.

...*Proportional Symbol Maps* **use Symbols of** *Different Sizes*

1) <u>Proportional symbol maps</u> use symbols of different <u>sizes</u> to represent different <u>quantities</u>.

2) A <u>key</u> shows the <u>quantity</u> each <u>different sized</u> symbol represents. The <u>bigger</u> the symbol, the <u>larger</u> the amount.

3) The symbols might be <u>circles</u>, <u>squares</u>, <u>semi-circles</u> or <u>bars</u>, but a <u>larger symbol</u> always means a <u>larger amount</u>.

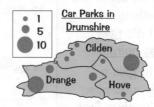

1
5
10

Car Parks in Drumshire

Cilden

Drange

Hove

Q: Which area of Drumshire has the most car parks?

A: Drange (20)

When it comes to maps, the key is, er, key...

No matter whether you've got identical dots, proportional symbols or straight lines, the key to correctly interpreting the map is to understand what each symbol means. The title helps here, but you really need to check the key carefully.

Maps

Two more <u>maps</u>, with two more ludicrous names — <u>isoline</u> and <u>sphere of influence maps</u>.
Isoline, I mean seriously... it sounds more like a coach tour company.

Isolines on Maps Link up Places with Something in Common

1) <u>Isolines</u> are lines on a map <u>linking</u> up all the places where something's the <u>same</u>, for example:
   - <u>Contour lines</u> are isolines linking up places at the same <u>altitude</u>.
   - Isolines on a <u>weather map</u> (called <u>isobars</u>) link together all the places where the <u>pressure's</u> the same.
2) Isolines can be used to link up lots of things, e.g. <u>average temperature</u>, <u>wind speed</u> or <u>rainfall</u>.
3) Isolines are normally <u>labelled</u> with their <u>value</u>. The <u>closer together</u> the <u>lines</u> are, the <u>steeper</u> the <u>gradient</u> (how quickly the thing is changing) <u>at that point</u>.

1 Reading Isoline Maps

1) <u>Find</u> the place you're interested in on the map and if it's on a <u>line</u> just <u>read</u> off the value.
2) If it's <u>between</u> two lines, you have to <u>estimate</u> the value.

Q: Find the average annual rainfall in Port Portia and on Mt. Mavis.

A: Port Portia is between the lines for 200 mm and 400 mm so the rainfall is likely to be around 300 mm per year.
Mt. Mavis is on an isoline so the rainfall is 1000 mm per year.

Average annual rainfall on Itchy Island (mm per year)

N

600
500   600
1000
500
Mt. Mavis
800
Port Portia
600
400
200

2 Completing Isoline Maps

1) Drawing an isoline's like doing a <u>dot-to-dot</u> — you just join up all the dots with the <u>same numbers</u>.
2) Make sure you don't <u>cross</u> any <u>other isolines</u> though.

Q: Complete on the map the isoline showing an average rainfall of 600 mm per year.

A: See the red line on the map.

Sphere of Influence Maps Show How Important Places Are

1) The <u>sphere of influence</u> of something is the area <u>affected</u> by it.
2) For example, the sphere of influence of a <u>local shop</u> could extend to just the <u>few surrounding streets</u>, if it's only people from the area who <u>normally</u> use it. But the sphere of influence of a <u>supermarket</u> could extend over a <u>larger area</u> because people are prepared to <u>travel further</u> to buy items they can't get at the <u>local shop</u>.
3) To <u>draw</u> a sphere of influence map, you need to know the <u>maximum distance</u> people are prepared to travel. You can then <u>draw a circle</u> whose <u>outer edge</u> lies at <u>that distance</u> from the thing you are <u>interested</u> in (i.e. the <u>shop</u> or <u>supermarket</u> in this example) in <u>every direction</u>.

Q: Where would people who live at point A normally shop?

A: At their <u>local shop</u>.

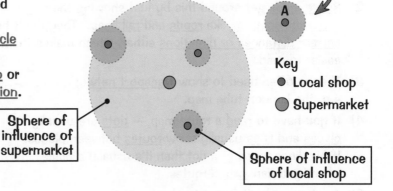

Sphere of influence of supermarket

Key
● Local shop
● Supermarket

Sphere of influence of local shop

A sphere of influence — an irresistible doughnut...

And there you have it — two more maps done and dusted. Make sure you know what they are and how to read them.
An atlas is a good place to find thematic maps if you fancy an interpretation practice session for your bedtime reading.

Maps

And here are the last few <u>jazzy maps</u>. Don't panic, these ones are pretty straightforward to <u>read</u> and <u>draw</u>.

Flow Lines *show* Movement

1) <u>Flow line maps</u> have <u>arrows</u> on, showing how things <u>move</u> (or are moved) from one place to another.

2) They can also be <u>proportional symbol maps</u> — the <u>width</u> of the arrows show the <u>quantity</u> of things that are <u>moving</u>.

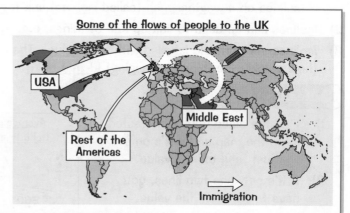

Q: From which <u>area</u> do the <u>greatest</u> number of people entering the UK come from?

A: <u>USA</u>, as this arrow is the largest.

Q: The number of people entering the UK from the <u>Middle East</u> is <u>roughly half</u> the number of people entering from the <u>USA</u>. Draw an <u>arrow</u> on the map to <u>show</u> this.

A: Make sure your arrow is going in the <u>right direction</u> and its <u>size</u> is appropriate (i.e. <u>half the width</u> of the USA arrow).

Desire Lines *show* Journeys

1) <u>Desire line maps</u> are a type of flow line as they show <u>movement</u> too.

2) They're <u>straight lines</u> that show <u>journeys</u> <u>between</u> two <u>locations</u>, but they <u>don't follow</u> <u>roads</u> or <u>railway lines</u>.

3) <u>One line</u> represents <u>one journey</u>.

4) They're used to show <u>how far</u> all the people have <u>travelled</u> to get to a <u>place</u>, e.g. a shop or a town centre, and <u>where</u> they've <u>come from</u>.

Route Maps *are* Simplified Maps

1) Some maps are <u>hard to read</u> because they show <u>too much detail</u>.

2) <u>Route maps</u> get around this by just showing the <u>most</u> <u>important features</u> like <u>roads</u> and <u>rail lines</u>. They don't have <u>correct distances or directions</u> either, which makes them easier to read.

3) They're often used to show <u>transport networks</u>, e.g. the London tube map.

4) If you have to <u>read</u> a route map — <u>dots</u> are usually <u>places</u> and <u>lines</u> usually show <u>routes</u> between places. If two lines cross <u>at a dot</u> then it's usually a place where you can <u>switch</u> routes.

5) As always, don't forget to check out the <u>key</u>.

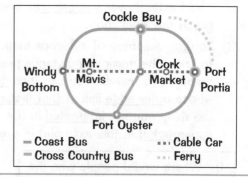

Q: How many different transport routes pass through Port Portia?

A: <u>Three</u> (coast bus, cable car and ferry).

Desire lines — I'm sure my palm reader mentioned those...

...unfortunately I'm not as good at seeing the future as she is* so I can't predict if any of these maps are going to come up in your exam. That's your lot for weird and wonderful maps anyway. Just ~~proper~~, sorry, OS® maps to go now.

*If you're wondering, I'm going to meet a short, fair stranger very soon...

Ordnance Survey Maps

Next up, marvellous <u>Ordnance Survey</u>® <u>maps</u>. Don't worry, they're easy once you know how to use 'em.

Learn These Common Symbols

Ordnance Survey (OS®) maps use lots of <u>symbols</u>. It's a good idea to learn some of the most <u>common ones</u> — like these:

Don't worry if you can't remember them all — you'll be given a <u>key</u> for each map.

▬	Motorway
▬	Main (A) road
▬	Secondary (B) road
⋈	Bridge
▬	Railway

-·-·-	County boundary
▦	National Park
╌╌	boundaries
▱	Building
⬤	Bus station

⫶⫶⫶	Footpaths
☀	Viewpoint
i	Tourist information centre
P	Parking
+ ♦ ●	Places of worship

You have to be able to Understand Grid References

You need to be able to use <u>four figure</u> and <u>six figure grid references</u> for your exam.

Q: Give the four figure and six figure grid reference for the place of worship.

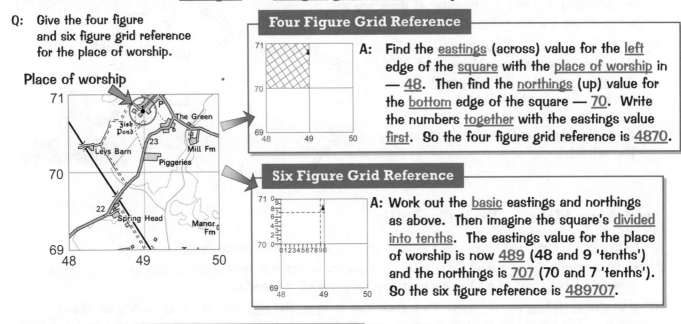

Four Figure Grid Reference

A: Find the <u>eastings</u> (across) value for the <u>left</u> edge of the <u>square</u> with the <u>place of worship</u> in — <u>48</u>. Then find the <u>northings</u> (up) value for the <u>bottom</u> edge of the square — <u>70</u>. Write the numbers <u>together</u> with the eastings value <u>first</u>. So the four figure grid reference is <u>4870</u>.

Six Figure Grid Reference

A: Work out the <u>basic</u> eastings and northings as above. Then imagine the square's <u>divided into tenths</u>. The eastings value for the place of worship is now <u>489</u> (48 and 9 'tenths') and the northings is <u>707</u> (70 and 7 'tenths'). So the six figure reference is <u>489707</u>.

You need to Know your Compass Points

You've got to know the compass — for giving <u>directions</u>, saying <u>which way</u> a <u>river's flowing</u>, or knowing what they mean if they say 'look at the river in the <u>NW</u> of the map' in the exam. Read it <u>out loud</u> to yourself, going <u>clockwise</u>.

North — East — South — West

OR

Never — Eat — Soggy — Wheat

You Might have to Work Out the Distance Between Two Places

To work out the <u>distance</u> between <u>two places</u> on a <u>map</u>, use a <u>ruler</u> to measure the <u>distance</u> in <u>cm</u> then <u>compare</u> it to the scale provided to find the distance in <u>km</u>.

Q: What's the distance from the bridge (482703) to the church (489707)?

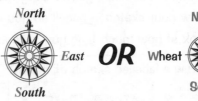

A: They're 2.2 cm apart on the map...
2.2 cm

...which means they're 1.1 km apart in real life.

Scale 1:50 000
2 centimetres to 1 kilometre (one grid square)
1.1 km   Kilometres

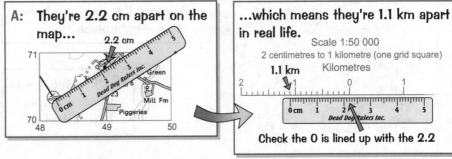

Check the 0 is lined up with the 2.2

Learn the common cymbals — and really annoy your neighbours...

I told you OS® maps aren't as bad as you thought. If a bedraggled walker who's been out in the rain for five hours with only a cup of tea to keep them going can read them, then so can you. Get ready for some more map fun...

Ordnance Survey Maps

Almost done with map skills now. Just this final page looking at contour lines and sketching from Ordnance Survey® maps or photographs to deal with then you're free, free I tell you... (well, free from maps anyway).

The Relief of an Area is Shown by Contours and Spot Heights

1) Contour lines are the browny-orange lines drawn on maps — they join points of equal height above sea level (altitude).

2) They tell you about the relief of the land, e.g. whether it's hilly, flat or steep.

3) They show the height of the land by the numbers marked on them. They also show the steepness of the land by how close together they are (the closer they are, the steeper the slope).

4) For example, if a map has lots of contour lines on it, it's probably hilly or mountainous. If there are only a few it'll be flat and often low-lying.

5) A spot height is a dot giving the height of a particular place. A trigonometrical point (trig point) is a blue triangle plus a height value. They usually show the highest point in that area (in metres).

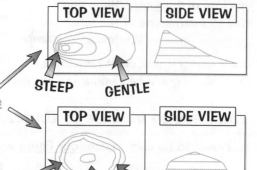

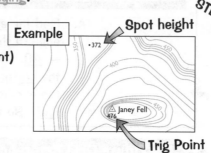

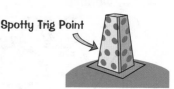

Spotty Trig Point

Sketching Maps — Do it Carefully

1) In the exam, they could give you a map or photograph and tell you to sketch part of it.

2) Make sure you figure out what bit they want you to sketch out, and double check you've got it right. It might be only part of a lake or a wood, or only one of the roads.

3) If you're sketching an OS® map, it's a good idea to copy the grid from the map onto your sketch paper — this helps you to copy the map accurately.

4) Draw your sketch in pencil so you can rub it out if it's wrong.

5) Look at how much time you have and how many marks it's worth to decide how much detail to add.

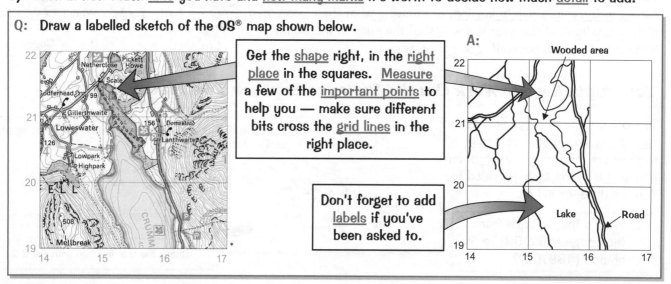

Q: Draw a labelled sketch of the OS® map shown below.

Get the shape right, in the right place in the squares. Measure a few of the important points to help you — make sure different bits cross the grid lines in the right place.

Don't forget to add labels if you've been asked to.

What a relief that's over...

When you're sketching a copy of a map or photo see if you can lay the paper over it — then you can trace it (sneaky). Anyway, that may be it for maps, but you're not quite free yet... It's time to rock the charts and graphs. Oh yeah.

Charts and Graphs

Stand by for <u>charts</u> and <u>graphs</u>. Make sure you can <u>interpret</u> (read) and <u>construct</u> (draw) each of them...

*Describing **what** Graphs **Show** — Include **Figures** from the Graph*

When <u>describing</u> graphs make sure you mention:

1) The general pattern — when it's <u>going up</u> and <u>down</u>, and any <u>peaks</u> (highest bits) and <u>troughs</u> (lowest bits).

2) Any <u>anomalies</u> (odd results).

3) Specific <u>data points</u>.

> Q: Use the graph to describe population change in Cheeseham.
>
> A: The population halved between 1950 and 1960 from 40 thousand people to 20 thousand people. It then increased to 100 thousand by 1980, before falling slightly and staying steady at 90 thousand from 1990 to 2000.

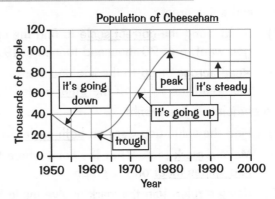

You might also see bar charts with horizontal bars.

*Bar Charts — Draw the Bars **Straight** and **Neat***

To <u>read</u> a bar chart:

1) Read along the <u>bottom</u> to find the <u>bar</u> you want.

2) To find out the <u>value</u> of a bar in a <u>normal</u> bar chart — go from the <u>top</u> of the bar <u>across</u> to the <u>scale</u>, and <u>read off</u> the number.

3) To find out the <u>value</u> of <u>part</u> of the bar in a <u>divided</u> bar chart — find the <u>number at the top</u> of the part of the bar you're interested in, and <u>take away</u> the <u>number at the bottom</u> of it.

To <u>complete</u> a bar chart:

1) First find the number you want on the <u>vertical scale</u>.

2) Then <u>trace</u> a line across to where the <u>top</u> of the bar will be with a <u>ruler</u>.

3) Draw in a bar of the <u>right size</u> using a <u>ruler</u>.

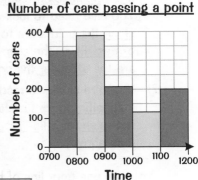

> Q: How many barrels of oil did Hoxo Plc. produce per day in 2015?
>
> A: 500 000 – 350 000 = <u>150 000 barrels</u> per day

> Q: Complete the chart to show that Froxo Inc. produced 200 000 barrels of oil per day in 2015.
>
> A: 150 thousand (2014) + 200 thousand = <u>350 000 barrels</u>. So draw the bar up to this point.

*Histograms **are a Lot Like** Bar Charts*

1) <u>Histograms</u> are very <u>similar</u> to <u>bar charts</u>, but they have a <u>continuous scale</u> of <u>numbers</u> on the <u>bottom</u> and there <u>can't</u> be any <u>gaps between the bars</u>.

2) You can use <u>histograms</u> when your <u>data</u> can be divided into <u>intervals</u>, like <u>this</u>: ⟹

3) You <u>draw</u> and <u>plot</u> them just like a <u>bar chart</u>, but you have to make sure that the bars are all the <u>correct width</u>, as well as the <u>correct height</u>.

Time	Cars
0700-0800	334
0800-0900	387
0900-1000	209
1000-1100	121
1100-1200	?

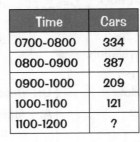

> Q: How many cars were recorded between 1100 and 1200?
>
> A: Trace a line from the top of the 1100-1200 bar and read the answer off — <u>200 cars</u>.

The top forty for sheep — the baaaaaaaaaaaaa chart...

Something to watch out for with bar charts (and line graphs on the next page) is reading the scale — check how much each division is worth before reading them or completing them. Don't assume each division is worth one...

Geographical Skills

Charts and Graphs

'More <u>charts</u> and <u>graphs</u>' I hear you cry — well OK, your weird wishes are my command.

Line Graphs — the Points are Joined by Lines

To read a line graph:

1) Read along the <u>correct scale</u> to find the <u>value</u> you want, e.g. 20 thousand tonnes or 1920.

2) Read <u>across</u> or <u>up</u> to the line you want, then read the value off the <u>other</u> scale.

To complete a line graph:

1) Find the value you want on <u>both scales</u>.

2) Make a <u>mark</u> (e.g. ×) at the point where the <u>two values meet</u> on the graph.

3) Using a <u>ruler</u>, <u>join</u> the <u>mark</u> you've made to the <u>line</u> that it should be <u>connected to</u>.

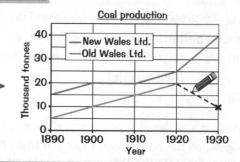

Coal production

Q: Complete the graph to show that Old Wales Ltd. produced 10 thousand tonnes of coal in 1930.

A: Find 1930 on the bottom scale, and 10 thousand tonnes on the vertical scale. Make a mark <u>where they meet</u>, then join it to the <u>blue</u> line <u>with a ruler</u>.

Scatter Graphs Show Relationships

<u>Scatter graphs</u> tell you how <u>closely related</u> two things are, e.g. altitude and air temperature. The fancy word for this is <u>correlation</u>. <u>Strong</u> correlation means the two things are <u>closely</u> related to each other. <u>Weak</u> correlation means they're <u>not very</u> closely related. The <u>line of best fit</u> is a line that goes roughly through the <u>middle</u> of the scatter of points and tells you about what <u>type</u> of correlation there is. Data can show <u>three</u> types of correlation:

1) <u>Positive</u> — as one thing <u>increases</u> the other <u>increases</u>.

2) <u>Negative</u> — as one thing <u>increases</u> the other <u>decreases</u>.

3) <u>None</u> — there's <u>no relationship</u> between the two things.

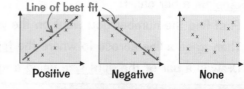

Line of best fit

Positive   Negative   None

① Reading Scatter Graphs

1) If you're asked to <u>describe</u> the <u>relationship</u>, look at the <u>slope</u> of the graph, e.g. if the line's moving <u>upwards</u> to the <u>right</u> it's a <u>positive correlation</u>. You also need to look at how <u>close</u> the points are to the <u>line of best fit</u> — the <u>closer</u> they are the <u>stronger</u> the correlation.

2) If you're asked to read off a <u>specific point</u>, just follow the <u>rules</u> for a <u>line graph</u> (see above).

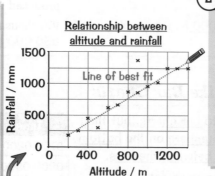

Relationship between altitude and rainfall

Line of best fit

② Completing Scatter Graphs

1) You could be asked to <u>draw</u> a <u>line of best fit</u> — just draw it roughly through the <u>middle</u> of the scatter of points.

2) If you're asked to <u>add a point</u> — just follow the <u>rules</u> for adding a point to a <u>line graph</u> (see above).

Q: Describe the relationship shown by the scatter graph.

A: Altitude and rainfall show a strong, positive correlation — as altitude increases, so does the amount of rainfall.

- You can use your <u>line of best fit</u> to make <u>predictions</u> by <u>reading off values</u> from the graph.

- If you're confident your best fit line will <u>continue</u>, you can <u>extend</u> it <u>beyond</u> the data you have collected. This means you can make <u>predictions outside the range</u> of data you <u>collected</u>.

Sorry darling, we've got no relationship — look at our scatter graph...

Line graphs and scatter graphs with a line of best fit are pretty similar, but don't get them confused — however much you might want to, it's not always ok to go around joining dots up. Study this page 'til you're seeing lines in your sleep.

Geographical Skills

Charts and Graphs

Happy days — the quick dash through <u>charts</u> and <u>graphs</u> continues. Don't say I never <u>treat</u> you...

Pie Charts *Show Amounts or Percentages*

The important thing to remember with pie charts is that <u>the whole pie = 360°</u>.

1 Reading Pie Charts

1) To work out the <u>%</u> for a wedge of the pie, use a <u>protractor</u> to find out how large it is in <u>degrees</u>.

2) Then <u>divide</u> that number by <u>360</u> and <u>times</u> by <u>100</u>.

3) To find the <u>amount</u> a wedge of the pie is <u>worth</u>, work out your <u>percentage</u> then turn it into a <u>decimal</u>. Then times the <u>decimal</u> by the <u>total amount</u> of the pie.

Pie Chart of Transport Type

0°
324°
270°
Bicycle
90°
Car
Pogostick
126°
180°

Q: Out of 100 people, how many used a pogostick?
A: 126 – 90 = 36°, so (36 ÷ 360) × 100 = 10%, so 0.1 × 100 = <u>10 people</u>.

2 Completing Pie Charts

1) To <u>draw</u> on a <u>new wedge</u> that you know the <u>%</u> for, turn the % into a <u>decimal</u> and <u>times</u> it by <u>360</u>. Then draw a wedge of that many <u>degrees</u>.

Q: Out of 100 people, 25% used a bicycle. Add this to the pie chart.
A: 25 ÷ 100 = 0.25, 0.25 × 360 = <u>90°</u>.

2) To add a <u>new wedge</u> that you know the <u>amount</u> for, <u>divide</u> your amount by the <u>total amount</u> of the pie and <u>times</u> the answer by <u>360</u>. Then <u>draw</u> on a wedge of that many <u>degrees</u>.

Q: Out of 100 people, 55 used a car, add this to the pie chart.
A: 55 ÷ 100 = 0.55, 0.55 × 360 = <u>198°</u> (198° + 126° = <u>324°</u>).

Dispersion Diagrams *Show the Frequency of Data*

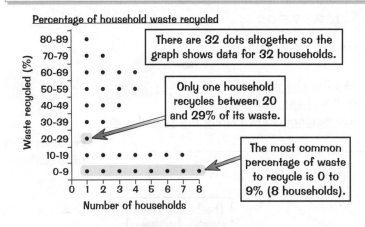

Percentage of household waste recycled

There are 32 dots altogether so the graph shows data for 32 households.

Only one household recycles between 20 and 29% of its waste.

The most common percentage of waste to recycle is 0 to 9% (8 households).

1) Dispersion diagrams are a bit like a cross between a <u>tally chart</u> and a <u>bar chart</u>.

2) The <u>range</u> of <u>data that's measured</u> goes on one axis. <u>Frequency</u> goes on the other axis.

3) <u>Each dot</u> represents <u>one piece</u> of <u>information</u> — the <u>more dots</u> there are in a particular category, the <u>more frequently</u> that event has happened.

4) The dispersion diagram on the left shows the <u>percentage</u> of <u>household waste</u> that's <u>recycled</u> for <u>households</u> in a <u>particular village</u>.

Population Pyramids *Show the Structure of a Population*

1) <u>Population pyramids</u> are a bit like <u>two bar charts</u> on their <u>sides</u>.

2) It's way of showing the <u>population</u> of a country by <u>age</u> and <u>gender</u>.

3) The <u>number of people</u> goes on the <u>horizontal axis</u>, and the <u>age groups</u> go on the <u>vertical axis</u>. The <u>left side</u> is the <u>male population</u> and the <u>right side</u> is the <u>female population</u>.

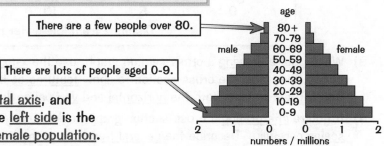

There are a few people over 80.

There are lots of people aged 0-9.

Pie charts aren't bad, but I prefer cake...

Hmm, who'd have thought pie could be so complicated. Don't panic though, a bit of practice and you'll be fine. And don't worry, there's only three more pages to go in the whole book, so take a deep breath and hang on in there.

Geographical Skills

Charts and Graphs

Yep, you guessed it — there are <u>even more</u> charts and graphs to learn. These are the <u>last ones</u>, I <u>promise</u>.

Radial Graphs *Often Show* Directional Data

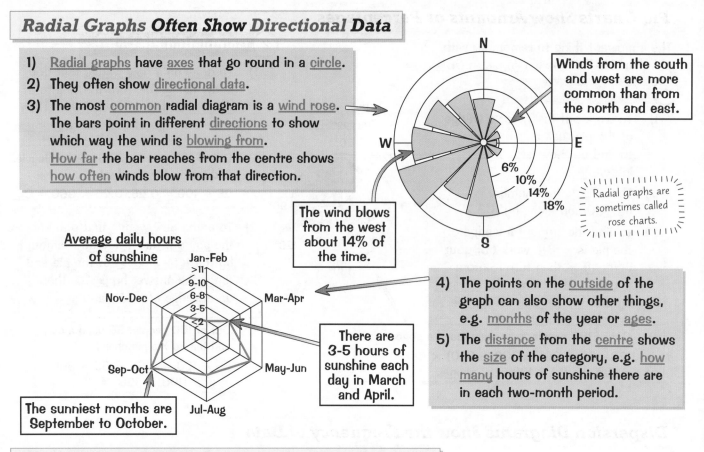

1) <u>Radial graphs</u> have <u>axes</u> that go round in a <u>circle</u>.

2) They often show <u>directional data</u>.

3) The most <u>common</u> radial diagram is a <u>wind rose</u>. The bars point in different <u>directions</u> to show which way the wind is <u>blowing from</u>. <u>How far</u> the bar reaches from the centre shows <u>how often</u> winds blow from that direction.

Winds from the south and west are more common than from the north and east.

The wind blows from the west about 14% of the time.

Radial graphs are sometimes called rose charts.

Average daily hours of sunshine

Jan-Feb >11 9-10 6-8 3-5 <2 Mar-Apr Nov-Dec Sep-Oct May-Jun Jul-Aug

There are 3-5 hours of sunshine each day in March and April.

The sunniest months are September to October.

4) The points on the <u>outside</u> of the graph can also show other things, e.g. <u>months</u> of the year or <u>ages</u>.

5) The <u>distance</u> from the <u>centre</u> shows the <u>size</u> of the category, e.g. <u>how many</u> hours of sunshine there are in each two-month period.

Cross-Sections *show the* Land *from* Sideways *on*

1) <u>Cross-sections</u> show what the landscape looks like if it's <u>chopped</u> down the <u>middle</u> and <u>viewed</u> from the <u>side</u>.

2) In geography, they're useful for showing things like the <u>change</u> in the <u>height</u> of the land, the <u>shape</u> of a <u>river channel</u> or the <u>shape</u> of a <u>beach</u>. They're often presented as a <u>graph</u> with <u>height</u> and <u>distance</u> shown along the <u>x-</u> and <u>y-axes</u>. For example:

cross-section of mountain

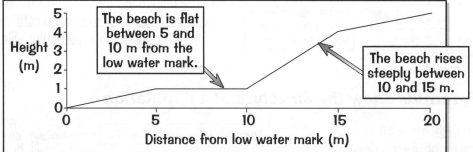

Height (m) — Distance from low water mark (m)

The beach is flat between 5 and 10 m from the low water mark.

The beach rises steeply between 10 and 15 m.

3) When you're <u>drawing</u> a cross-section graph, use the <u>x-axis</u> to plot the contour heights. <u>Join</u> all the points, then <u>label</u> the cross-section to show <u>features</u> of the landscape (e.g. valley sides, hilltops etc.) Don't forget to label both the <u>horizontal</u> and <u>vertical scales</u> (the x and y axes).

4) If you're <u>interpreting</u> a cross-section graph, make sure you look at both the <u>horizontal</u> and <u>vertical scales</u> carefully. Describe the <u>general trends</u>, e.g. the beach generally slopes upwards away from the sea, and then pick out the <u>key features</u>, e.g. where the land is <u>steepest</u> and where it is <u>flatter</u>.

A bit of revision helps to avoid cross sections in exams...

...or so I heard. Still, it can't hurt to be a little more prepared, so go back and learn this page 'til you've got radial graphs spinning in circles in your head and you're dreaming in cross-sections. Then direct yourself to the next page.

Geographical Skills

Statistics

EEEK, these pages are full of maths. In a geography book. Still, it should all be familiar from maths lessons...

Learn the Definitions for *Mode, Median, Mean, Range* and *Modal Class*

Mode, median and mean are measures of average and the range is how spread out the values are:

MODE = MOST common
MEDIAN = MIDDLE value (when values are in order of size)
MEAN = TOTAL of items ÷ NUMBER of items
RANGE = DIFFERENCE between highest and lowest

REMEMBER:
Mode = most (emphasise the 'mo' in each when you say them)
Median = mid (emphasise the m*d in each when you say them)
Mean is just the average, but it's mean 'cos you have to work it out.

Sample	1	2	3	4	5	6	7
River discharge (cumecs)	184	90	159	142	64	64	95

Q: Calculate the mean, median, mode and range for the river discharge data shown in the table above.

A:
- The mode is the most common value = 64.
- To find the median, put all the numbers in order and find the middle value: 64, 64, 90, 95, 142, 159, 184. So the median is 95.
- Mean = $\dfrac{\text{total of items}}{\text{number of items}}$ = $\dfrac{184 + 90 + 159 + 142 + 64 + 64 + 95}{7}$ = $\dfrac{798}{7}$ = 114
- The range is the difference between highest and lowest value, i.e. 184 – 64 = 120

When there are two middle numbers, the median is halfway between the two.

You also Need to Know *How to Find the Modal Class* and *Interquartile Range*

If your data is grouped you might need to find the modal class. This is just the group with the most values in.

Age	Number of people
0-19	21
20-39	37
40-59	27
60+	15

Q: Find the modal class of the population data shown in the table.
A: Modal class = 20-39 years

Remember, the modal class will be the group — not how many items are in that group.

As well as finding the median (the middle value in a list), you can also find the upper and lower quartiles — the values a quarter (25%) and three-quarters (75%) of the way through the ordered data.

Q: The number of shoppers in each shop in a village were counted. Find the median and the quartiles of the data set.

A: 2, 3, 6, 6, 7, 9, 13, 14, 17, 22, 22
Lower quartile   Median   Upper quartile

The interquartile range is the difference between the upper quartile and the lower quartile. It contains the middle 50% of values.

Q: Find the interquartile range of the number of shoppers.
A: 17 – 6 = 11

You Need to be Able to *Calculate Percentages*

To give the amount X as a percentage of a sample Y, you need to divide X by Y and multiply by 100.

Q: This year, 35 out of the 270 houses in Foxedapolice were burgled. Calculate the percentage of houses burgled in Foxedapolice.
A: 35 ÷ 270 × 100 = 13%

This page is mean — wish I was still on those maps pages...

Sheesh, I wasn't expecting so much stats in a geography book. But here it is, so you might as well learn it before it comes up in your exam. Practise by writing down a list of numbers and finding each of the averages.

Statistics

Ahh, you've reached the <u>last page</u>. Unfortunately, it's more <u>stats</u>. Sorry. Grab a calculator and let's smash it.

Make sure you can Work Out Percentage Change

Calculating <u>percentage change</u> lets you work out <u>how much</u> something has <u>increased</u> or <u>decreased</u>.
You use this <u>formula</u>:

$$\text{Percentage change} = \frac{\text{final value} - \text{original value}}{\text{original value}} \times 100$$

A <u>positive</u> value shows an <u>increase</u> and a <u>negative</u> value shows a <u>decrease</u>.

Q: Last year in Foxedapolice, only 24 houses were burgled, compared to 35 this year. Calculate the percentage change in burglaries in Foxedapolice.

A: $\frac{35 - 24}{24} \times 100 = \underline{46\% \text{ increase}}$ in the number of burglaries in Foxedapolice.

Percentiles Tell You Where in Your Data Set a Data Point Lies

1) Percentiles are useful if you want to compare the value of <u>one data point</u> to the <u>rest</u> of your data.

2) To find a percentile, you <u>rank</u> your data from smallest to largest, then <u>divide</u> it into <u>one hundred equal chunks</u>. Each chunk is <u>one percentile</u>.

3) This means that each percentile represents <u>one percent</u> of the data, and so the <u>value of a percentile</u> tells you what <u>percentage</u> of the data has a value <u>lower than</u> the data points in that percentile.

E.g. Sid the Stone is in the <u>90th percentile</u> for <u>weight</u> in his section of the river bed. This means that <u>90%</u> of the stones are <u>lighter</u> than Sid.

4) Percentiles can be used to give a more realistic idea of the <u>spread</u> of data than the <u>range</u> (see p.111) — by finding the range between the <u>10th</u> and <u>90th percentiles</u> in a data set (the middle 80% of the data), you can look at the spread of the data while ignoring any <u>outlying</u> results.

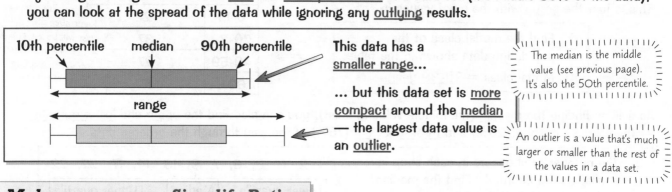

The median is the middle value (see previous page). It's also the 50th percentile.

An outlier is a value that's much larger or smaller than the rest of the values in a data set.

Make sure you can Simplify Ratios

A <u>ratio</u> shows how <u>two</u> amounts <u>compare</u> to each other — it's one way of showing a <u>proportion</u>.

Ratios are written like this ⟹ <u>1:10</u>. E.g. 'Droughts and storms occurred in the ratio <u>1:10</u>.' This means that for every <u>1 drought</u>, there were <u>10 storms</u>.

You might also be asked to <u>simplify</u> a ratio — this just means writing it using the <u>smallest numbers</u> possible.

E.g. If you're asked to simplify the ratio <u>45:60</u>, find the <u>highest number</u> that <u>both</u> sides can be <u>divided</u> by. 45 and 60 can both be divided by <u>15</u> — this gives the ratio <u>3:4</u>.

Q: Write the ratio 72:48 in its simplest form.

A: 72 and 48 can both be divided by 24 to give <u>3:2</u>.

Percentiles — the mathematician's choice for bathroom walls...

Once you've cracked this stats stuff, you can go and celebrate. Or read the whole book again. Or go back to your favourite topic — whatever you like. I'm going to read through the index, but I won't blame you if you don't join me.

Acknowledgements

With thanks to © iStock.com for images on pages 20, 41, 50, 59, 66,

Photograph on p.10 (Haweswater) © John Douglas/p.28 & p.30 (Old Harry) © Raymond Knapman/p.30 (Lulworth Cove) © Nick Macneill/ p.30 (Chesil Beach) © Eugene Birchall/p.30 (Swanage Bay) © Peter Trimming/p.31 (landslides) © Robin Webster/p.32 (sea wall) © David Dixon/p.32 (groynes) © N Chadwick/p.32 (beach replenishment) © Maurice D Budden/p.36 (Hell Gill Force) © Roger Templeman/p.36 (gorge) © Ian Greig/p.36 (Eden at Salkeld) © Greg Fitchett/p.36 (Eden floodplain) © Rose and Trev Clough/p.36 (v-shaped valley) © Mick Garratt/ p.37 (landslide) © Stephen Craven/p.37 (sandstone cliffs) © Andy Waddington/p.37 (Great Asby Scar) © Peter Standing/p.38 (reservoir) © Rose and Trev Clough/p.38 (River Eden) © Andy Connor/p.57 (Chinatown) © Colin Smith/p.80 (wetlands) © Steve Sheppard/p.83 (Chinatown, Liverpool) © Alan Walker/p.83 (London Road, Sheffield) © Basher Eyre/p.86 (tractor) © Walter Baxter/p.94 (greenhouse) © David Anstiss. Licensed for re-use under the Creative Commons Attribution-Share Alike 2.0 Generic Licence. (https://creativecommons.org/licenses/by-sa/2.0/)

Climate predictions on page 23/graph of net migration and 2013 population pyramid on on page 76/1964 birth rate and map of over-65s on page 77/working hours data on page 78/statistics regarding media industries on page 82/calorie intake data, graph of wheat yield and UK produce-growing data on page 93 contain public sector information licensed under the Open Government Licence v3.0. (http://www.nationalarchives.gov.uk/ doc/open-government-licence/version/3/)

Data used to construct the population density of the UK map on page 74, 2001 population pyramids on pages 75 and 76, ethnicity graph on page 76, population density map on page 101 and flow map of immigration on page 104 : Office for National Statistics licensed under the Open Government Licence v.3.0. (https://www.nationalarchives.gov.uk/doc/open-government-licence/version/3/)

Data used to construct graph on page 5: NOAA 2016; Vecchi and Knutson, 2011

Map on page 7: Aqueduct Global Maps 2.1 Indicators. Constructing Decision-Relevant Global Water Risk Indicators by Francis Gassert, Paul Reig, Tien Shiao, Matt Luck, Research Scientist, ISciences LLC and Matt Landis Research Scientist, ISciences LLC — April 2015. Licensed under a Creative Commons Attribution International 4.0 License (https://creativecommons.org/licenses/by/4.0/)

Map extract on page 8 created from OS Open Data. Contains OS data © Crown copyright and database right 2016.

Satellite image on page 9: Jeff Schmaltz, MODIS Rapid Response Team, NASA/GSFC

Photograph of flood defences on page 9: US Army Corps of Engineers

Photograph of Nepal earthquake damage on page 14 © Rajan Journalist. Licensed under the Creative Commons Attribution-Share Alike 4.0 International license (https://creativecommons.org/licenses/by-sa/4.0/deed.en)

Short term climate graph on page 19 adapted from Crown Copyright data supplied by the Met Office licensed under the Open Government Licence v3.0.

Sea-level rise data on page 23 © Crown Copyright 2009. Lowe, J. A., Howard, T. P., Pardaens, A., Tinker, J., Holt, J., Wakelin, S., Milne, G., Leake, J., Wolf, J., Horsburgh, K., Reeder, T., Jenkins, G., Ridley, J., Dye, S., Bradley, S. (2009), UK Climate Projections science report: Marine and coastal projections. Met Office Hadley Centre, Exeter, UK.

Topographic map of the United Kingdom on page 25 by Captain Blood, Licensed under the Creative Commons Attribution-Share Alike 3.0 Unported license. (https://creativecommons.org/licenses/by-sa/3.0/deed.en)

Photo of Makoko slum on page 60 © Heinrich-Böll-Stiftung. Licensed under the Creative Commons Attribution-Share Alike 2.0 Generic license. (https://creativecommons.org/licenses/by-sa/2.0/deed.en)

GNI data on page 69: World Bank national accounts data, and OECD National Accounts data files.

Development statistics on page 69 from 2015 Human Development Report, United Nations Development Programme from hdr.undp.org. Licensed for re-use under the Creative Commons Attribution 3.0 IGO license (https://creativecommons.org/licenses/by/3.0/igo/)

Statistics on page 70 (malnutrition, education, child death rates, vaccinations, maternal death rates, access to clean water) from Millennium Development Goals Indicators, by Department of Economic and Social Affairs. © United Nations 2016. Accessed 07.06.2016. Reprinted with the permission of the United Nations.

Poverty statistics on page 70 © World Bank. License: Creative Commons Attribution license (CC BY 3.0 IGO) (https://creativecommons.org/licenses/by/3.0/igo/)

Import/Export data on page 71 and UK birth/death rates on page 75: The World Factbook. Washington, DC: Central Intelligence Agency, 2016.

Land use map on page 74 based on: Cole, B.; King, S.; Ogutu, B.; Palmer, D.; Smith, G.; Balzter, H. (2015). Corine land cover 2012 for the UK, Jersey and Guernsey. NERC Environmental Information Data Centre. (http://doi.org/10.5285/32533dd6-7c1b-43e1-b892-e80d61a5ea1d.) This resource is made available under the terms of the Open Government Licence.

Data used to compile the UK average rainfall map on page 74 from the Manchester Metropolitan University.

2015 population pyramid on page 75 constructed using data from Population Division, World Population Prospects, the 2015 revision, by Department of Economic and Social Affairs. © United Nations 2016. Accessed 23.06.2016. Reprinted with the permission of the United Nations.

Graph on page 78 contains data from Welsh Government — Statistics © Crown Copyright 2015

Calorie intake map on page 89 © FAO 2015 World food supply 2011-2013 (http://faostat3.fao.org/browse/FB/FBS/E 11.3.2016)

Map of Global Hunger Index on page 89: von Grebmer, K., A. Saltzman, E. Birol, D. Wiesmann, N. Prasai, S. Yin, Y. Yohannes, P. Menon, J. Thompson, and A. Sonntag. 2014. 2014 Global Hunger Index: The Challenge of Hidden Hunger. Bonn, Germany; Washington, D.C.; Dublin, Ireland: Deutsche Welthungerhilfe; International Food Policy Research Institute; Concern Worldwide. Adapted and reproduced with permission from the International Food Policy Research Institute www.ifpri.org. The report from which this map comes can be found online at https://www.ifpri.org/ publication/2014-global-hunger-index.

Map extracts on pages 105 and 106 reproduced with permission by Ordnance Survey® © Crown copyright 2016 OS 100034841

Index

Index

Index